8 BILLION AND COUNTING

8 BILLION
AND COUNTING

How Sex, Death,
and Migration
Shape Our World

JENNIFER D. SCIUBBA

W. W. NORTON & COMPANY
Independent Publishers Since 1923

For information about permission to reproduce selections from this book, write to
Permissions, W. W. Norton & Company, Inc., 500 Fifth Avenue,
New York, NY 10110

For information about special discounts for bulk purchases, please contact
W. W. Norton Special Sales at specialsales@wwnorton.com or 800-233-4830

Manufacturing by Lake Book Manufacturing
Book design by Daniel Lagin
Production manager: Lauren Abbate

Library of Congress Cataloging-in-Publication Data

Names: Sciubba, Jennifer Dabbs, author.
Title: 8 billion and counting : how sex, death, and migration shape
our world / Jennifer D. Sciubba.
Other titles: Eight billion and counting
Description: First edition. | New York, NY : W. W. Norton & Company, [2022]
| Includes bibliographical references and index.
Identifiers: LCCN 2021052497 | ISBN 9781324002703 (hardcover) |
ISBN 9781324002710 (epub)
Subjects: LCSH: Population—Economic aspects. | Population—Social aspects.
| Demographic transition.
Classification: LCC HB871 .S395 2022 | DDC 304.6—dc23/eng/20211028
LC record available at https://lccn.loc.gov/2021052497

W. W. Norton & Company, Inc., 500 Fifth Avenue, New York, N.Y. 10110
www.wwnorton.com

W. W. Norton & Company Ltd., 15 Carlisle Street, London W1D 3BS

1 2 3 4 5 6 7 8 9 0

To all of my teachers, especially my mom, my first teacher

CONTENTS

8 BILLION AND COUNTING

Introduction

At the dawn of the Current Era, in Year 1 of the Western calendar, there were about 300 million people on the planet, a tiny fraction of the 47 billion who had ever been born. For our early human ancestors, life was poor, nasty, brutish, and short. In their brief lives, women in these primitive societies probably had well over four children on average, but many of these women starved before they could complete their reproductive years; up to half of babies died in infancy, and life expectancy at birth was a measly 10 years. In this nascent stage of human history, our population growth was similar to that of other species, where nature—abysmal living conditions and rampant disease—checked population growth. But humans are unique among species, and as our societies evolved, we began to accumulate knowledge about how to conquer nature. Those alive in 1750 were less than 1 percent of humans ever born. The almost 8 billion of us alive today represent around 7 percent of the 108 billion who have ever taken a breath. Clearly, tremendous forces have been at work to reshape global population from cradle to grave. And these forces will be no less powerful in the future.

If this were a story about demographic change in the twentieth century, it would be a story about exponential population growth. It took from the beginning of our species until around 1804 for Earth to have its first 1 billion people, and in the nineteenth century we didn't add too many more. But in the span of just 100 years during the twentieth century, world population exploded from 1.6 billion to 6.1 billion people.

The story of the twenty-first century is less a story about exponential population growth than it is a story about *differential* growth—marked by a stark divide between the world's richest and poorest countries. We've come remarkably far, but in the twenty-first century the world's population is still changing in ways never before seen. Today, there are more people on the planet than ever, the most aged societies in human history, and the widest gulf in life expectancy between rich and poor countries.

These population trends aren't just interesting in their own right; they also provide insight into some of the world's most pressing problems. When we understand population trends, we better grasp how dynamics of violence and peace, of repression and democracy, and of poverty and prosperity are likely to play out on a global scale. As the pages of this book will show, *how many* people are on the planet is far less important for issues of development and conflict than *where* and *who* these people are. Meaning, where population growth and decline are concentrated—either at the country level or within countries—and the characteristics of those populations are the real links between demographics and political, social, or economic outcomes.

How wide are the gulfs in fertility and mortality between countries? On average, there are about 240 babies born per minute in the world's least developed countries but only 25 born per minute in developed countries.* If we were to go to the heart of the Japanese countryside, we

• • •

* Unless otherwise indicated, all of the population data presented in this book are taken directly from or calculated from the United Nations' *World Population Prospects: The 2019 Revision.*

would likely see a lot of gray hair—50 percent of Japan's population is over the age of 48, the world's oldest. Japan is aging so rapidly that if current trends continue, the nation could eventually disappear altogether. Officially, the Japanese government projects that Japan's population will shrink from 128 million in 2010 to 87 million by 2060. At that time, an astonishing 40 percent of Japanese will be 65 years or older. This is unprecedented in human history.

If we were to go to the crowded urban areas of Lagos, Nigeria, though, we would likely be inundated with the sounds of children playing. With a median age of 18 years, Nigeria is on the other end of the spectrum. Fully half of Nigeria's population is children and adolescents. These huge cohorts will soon be mothers and fathers themselves—the eldest of them already are. With its young population and high fertility, Nigeria, simultaneously an engine of African economic growth and operating grounds for the violent jihadist group Boko Haram, is set to eclipse US population by 2050, when it will reach more than 400 million people—double what it is today—even with one of the highest infant mortality rates in the world.

World population will keep growing in the twenty-first century, but an astounding 98 percent of that growth will be in less developed countries like Nigeria. Figure 1 shows the 10 most populous countries in the years 2000, 2020, and 2050. One obvious shift during this 50-year span is that the most developed countries fall off the list, with the exception of the United States, which had near-replacement fertility and robust immigration until recently. By 2020, Japan had already dropped to the 11th spot, while the Democratic Republic of the Congo and Ethiopia were set to take places vacated by Russia and Mexico—a clear geographic shift in global population centers. Tremendous population growth in less developed countries during this half century is also clear. Between now and 2050, India will add the near equivalent of the US population, even as fertility declines there.

FIGURE 1. Ten Most Populous Countries: 2000, 2020, and 2050

	2000		2020		2050	
Rank	Country	Population (millions)	Country	Population (millions)	Country	Population (millions)
1	China	1,283	China	1,439	India	1,659
2	India	1,053	India	1,380	China	1,364
3	United States	282	United States	331	Nigeria	411
4	Indonesia	212	Indonesia	274	United States	390
5	Brazil	175	Pakistan	220	Indonesia	322
6	Russia	146	Brazil	213	Pakistan	307
7	Pakistan	139	Nigeria	206	Brazil	233
8	Bangladesh	132	Bangladesh	165	Bangladesh	202
9	Japan	128	Russia	146	Democratic Republic of the Congo	198
10	Nigeria	122	Mexico	129	Ethiopia	191

• • •

The diversity of global population trends means there's a lot to wrap our heads around. In some regions, population pressures are blowing the top off of a pot already boiling with poor governance, civil war, and environmental devastation. At best, there's only dim hope for a peaceful future. When the pot boils over, countries across the globe feel the effects in the form of refugees and terrorist extremism.

The Democratic Republic of the Congo (DRC), whose population is growing at more than 3 percent a year, has a gross domestic product (GDP) per capita of only $580.* Corruption and human rights abuses are rampant, and rebel groups foment violence, especially in the eastern and southern provinces. Such conditions enable the use of child soldiers

• • •

* Unless otherwise specified, all dollar amounts in this book are US dollars.

and displace people both within the country and across borders. With a population of almost 90 million, the DRC saw 1.67 million of its people displaced in 2019 alone. With a similarly high population growth rate, Somalia's youth rarely find meaningful jobs. Terrorist groups in the country, such as al-Shabaab, are likely to see their ranks grow as desperate young people search for belonging.

Sub-Saharan Africa isn't the only region struggling in the midst of rapid population growth. In Central Asia, Afghanistan's population has grown from 21 million at the start of the 2001 US invasion to 38.9 million in 2020—an increase of 85 percent. Is it possible for Afghanistan to find peace among the strains of such rapid population growth? Population growth isn't inherently bad, but when institutions, even the education system, or the economy can't absorb more people, the whole society feels the strains. The Afghans suffer, and those countries with an interest in Afghanistan's peace and prosperity are set for disappointment. As hard as it is to believe, Afghan women born under US occupation are now having children of their own. These young mothers have known nothing other than war and foreign soldiers in uniform and would almost certainly associate that trauma with the West, something that will take generations to overcome. Western militaries celebrate drone strikes that kill handfuls of al-Qaida fighters in Yemen, while 3,000 children are born into poverty there every day. Yemenis must not only defend against guns but also germs, as cholera infects 5,000 of them a day. With such turmoil—both armed conflict and health crises—it is no wonder that Yemen, and dozens of high-fertility countries like it, seems doomed to succumb to a dark demographic destiny.

And yet, as we will see, as much as population trends can tell us about upheaval in our world, they also have much to show about prosperity and peace.

In East Asia, rapid fertility declines from the 1960s to the 1990s led to a bonus of workers relative to numbers of youth and raised incomes per person, as both families and governments could invest greater resources in fewer child dependents. Economists have estimated that Asia's demographic transition was responsible for somewhere between 33 and 44 percent of the East Asian economic miracle that catapulted the region to the powerhouse it is today.

Demographic change can also bring about democratic change. In the lead-up to the 2011 Arab Spring, Tunisia's age structure began to look similar to those of South Korea and Taiwan during the mid-1990s. The high proportion of young adults in Tunisia in 2010 relative to all adults was exactly the same as South Korea's in 1993, and their median ages were nearly identical, too. The revolution and democratization that transpired in Tunisia echoed the political changes in several Asian states when their age structures were similar. Today, South Korea is an anchor of democracy and prosperity. Likewise, Tunisia is considered a "free" society, but just barely. Political demographers are hopeful, though, that as Tunisia's age structure continues to mature because of low fertility, the country will move past the fits and starts that characterize new democracies and turn into a peaceful, flourishing, and democratic country in a region where those markers are largely absent.

While there are similarities between Tunisia and South Korea, Egypt and South Korea provide a stark, but apt, contrast in demographic fortune, as noted by Egypt's former president Hosni Mubarak. In a speech to Egypt's Second National Population Conference on June 9, 2008, Mubarak backed up his call for more attention to family planning by citing how much the fates of Egypt and South Korea had diverged since they both had populations of about 26 million in 1960. When he spoke in 2008, South Korea's population had grown to 48 million, but Egypt's had more than tripled to 80 million. While South Korea had developed and prospered, Mubarak said Egypt suffered an imbalance between population and resources and blamed population growth for preventing economic gains and causing social instability.

What explains the great divide in population trends between richer and poorer countries? One factor is that in the world's poorest countries, fertility is still high. These countries are in the early stages of what demographers call the demographic transition—the shift from high fertility and mortality to low fertility and mortality.

In the first stage of the demographic transition, both birth and death rates are high. Because they effectively cancel each other out, the overall population doesn't grow much. That's why there were only 1 billion people on the planet just two centuries ago. But in the second stage of the demographic transition, as health measures improve and death rates fall, population growth tends to be high. It slows a bit in the third stage as fertility falls, and by the fourth stage, overall population growth slows a lot as fertility and mortality rates settle at low levels. The most notable recent fertility decline has been in the Middle East, which saw its total fertility rate, or TFR (the average number of children a woman is likely to have in her lifetime given current trends), drop from 4.12 children per woman in 1995 to 2.93 by 2020. Replacement-level TFR is generally considered to be about 2.1 children per woman—one to replace each parent, with a margin for those who don't live to reproductive age—and in 2020, 87 countries were below that mark and had aging populations. TFR was below replacement level for Latin America and the Caribbean by the period 2015–2020, nearly half what it was 40 years ago. TFR is an estimate we'll use a lot in this book because it is a useful way to capture differences in childbearing patterns across countries that otherwise can be difficult to compare because they have little in common.*

For most of the twentieth century, it seemed that although different countries and regions took different amounts of time making the transition to lower fertility and mortality, all countries in the world were moving along the same path to eventual population aging.

Until they weren't.

• • •

* We use 2.1 as shorthand, but the "margin"—what comes after the decimal point—actually varies depending on how developed the country is. More females live to complete their reproductive years in developed countries, and so true replacement is likely less than 2.1; it can be more than 2.1 in less developed countries.

Today, the demographic transition seems to be stalled for some of the world's poorest countries. While most of Europe and Asia have completed the transition, as we can see from Figure 2, there are still a significant number of countries with very high total fertility rates. In particular, some countries in sub-Saharan Africa don't even seem to have begun the transition or at best are in the second stage, where death rates start to fall. In sub-Saharan Africa, the TFR dropped from 5.88 to 4.72 during the past 20 years, but that was much slower than many demographers had anticipated. That means when we look out over the next several decades, we still need to expect tremendous population growth and very youthful populations in most of that region. Even if fertility declines somewhat, sub-Saharan Africa's population is on track to increase sixfold this century, driven primarily by very high fertility in Central and West Africa. But fertility rates as high as Nigeria's, for example, aren't necessary for a population to rapidly grow. Actually, a total fertility rate of just three children per woman means that each generation will be 50 percent larger than the preceding one. If fertility falls somewhat, median ages in these countries will still be incredibly young, and if fertility stays at today's rates, median ages will be even lower. So, again, demographic change in the twenty-first century

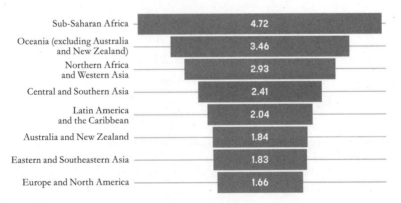

FIGURE 2. Total Fertility Rate for Sustainable Development Goal Regions, 2020

Region	TFR
Sub-Saharan Africa	4.72
Oceania (excluding Australia and New Zealand)	3.46
Northern Africa and Western Asia	2.93
Central and Southern Asia	2.41
Latin America and the Caribbean	2.04
Australia and New Zealand	1.84
Eastern and Southeastern Asia	1.83
Europe and North America	1.66

involves population aging and shrinking in some countries but still young and growing populations in others.

Here's why interpreting population trends correctly matters: A few years ago I was in Washington, DC, to give a talk on demographics and strategy and was performing my normal morning routine of scrolling through Twitter. I landed on a piece by someone in the US Army about China's demographics that argued population trends will constrain China's ability to challenge the United States as the world's number-one power. I sat straight up. That was a bold and risky leap. If policy makers are writing strategy on the basis of demographic assessments (and that's good, please do more of that), they should be thoughtful, nuanced assessments, not knee-jerk ones. The same goes for investors calculating risks or for advocates trying to make the most of limited resources as they work to help the world's forgotten. The links between demographics and economics or politics or culture deserve more than just cursory thought. As we'll walk through in Part II of the book, demographic trends don't occur in isolation, and as much as we can learn from studying them independently, as we do in Part I, we can gain new insights by studying their confluence and context.

• • •

Fertility is about the beginning of life, and another powerful force shaping the great divide in population is at the other end of the spectrum: death.

In 2010, a massive earthquake rocked Haiti. Poor to begin with, Haiti had little domestic capacity to deal with the property losses and population displacement, as somewhere between 1 million and 2 million Haitians lost their homes. United Nations forces were dispatched to help, bringing much-needed supplies and logistical know-how. And cholera. They brought cholera.

Owing to widespread poverty and poor sanitation, the cholera spread quickly. Now facing double the disaster, Haiti's infant mortality rate shot up from 81.5 per 1,000 in 2009 to 208.6 per 1,000, a commentary on just how poor a situation a new baby would have been born into. Infant mortality rate is a useful indicator of a society's quality of life, as is life expectancy at birth, defined as the average number of years a person born at that time could expect to live. It's important to interpret life expectancy as reflecting a range of mortality outcomes: If a society has a very low life expectancy, say age 55, it's not that no one in the society lives past age 55, but it's likely that the society has high infant and child mortality. Life expectancy at birth is best used as an estimation or an indicator, not as a prediction, and is a useful measure of societal well-being. That a child born in Haiti during this troubled time had an infant mortality rate as bad as that of sub-Saharan Africa in the 1960s reflected how fragile life was on that side of Hispaniola. Haiti is still dealing with the long-term consequences of that disaster, and the health problems of that time will reverberate in unknown ways as that cohort ages. And the hits keep coming, as they did with a magnitude 7.2 earthquake in August 2021.

FIGURE 3. Total Fertility Rate and Life Expectancy at Birth for Sustainable Development Goal Regions, 2020

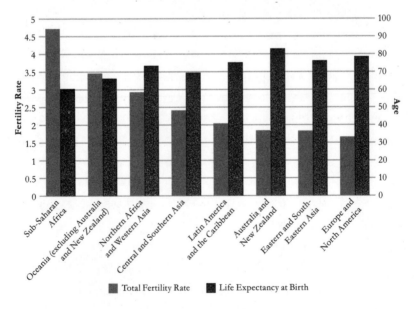

Total Fertility Rate   Life Expectancy at Birth

Worldwide, disparities in life expectancy say a lot about overall conditions: Sub-Saharan Africa's life expectancy is the world's lowest, a full 18 years less than that of Europe and North America, as Figure 3 shows, and is nearly the inverse of fertility trends.

Haiti's life expectancy at birth remains low—64 years—but not out of the ordinary for a less developed country. More remarkably, life expectancy declined around the year 2015 for several wealthy countries. Researchers attribute the shift to a spike in deaths from the influenza epidemic, particularly among older people. This was the first decline in longevity since the combination of World War I and the Spanish flu killed 675,000 in the United States. Then, because of excessive deaths from COVID-19, life expectancy declined in numerous wealthy countries between 2019 and 2020, according to preliminary research by José Manuel Aburto and colleagues. Of the 29 countries they studied (mostly in Europe, plus the United States and Chile), life expectancy at birth declined in 27, with the largest losses in life expectancy among males in the United States and in Bulgaria. COVID-19 aside, the life expectancy declines in the United States before the pandemic were an exception. On the whole, life expectancy only gets better with time.

That positive trend is what stood out to demographers Jim Oeppen and James Vaupel when they were crunching numbers about human life expectancy. They noticed that life expectancy for Japanese women—who are famous for their longevity—was increasing in a predictable upward pattern. And in fact, they noticed that record societal life expectancy for the past 160 years had risen steadily by 3 months a year, or 2.5 years per decade. Could this linear trend continue or is there a limit to societal life expectancy? A female born in Japan in 2020 is expected to live to age 87, the world's highest; is it reasonable to expect that Japanese women born mid-century will have a life expectancy of 94.5 years?

It's difficult to comprehend how the linear trend in record life expectancy could continue, but it was equally difficult for scholars less than a century ago to understand how societal life expectancy could ever reach the heights of any age over 65 years, which is what Louis Dublin in 1928 forecasted as the upper limit. As Japan's female life expectancy trend shows, today's developed countries have left that limit in the dust. Most notably, as Oeppen and Vaupel emphasize, the linear trend is not slowing. Global life expectancy was under 47 years in 1950; today, it's 70.81 for males and 75.59 for females.

Selfishly, we all care about how long we live, but forecasting life expectancy also helps governments and businesses plan long-term for large budgetary expenditures, such as pensions and health care. So far, maximum societal life expectancy has stayed well below 100 years; still, because fertility in most advanced industrial democracies has been dramatically declining for decades, these populations are growing older, shifting the proportions of young and old. What developments are responsible for such a revolution in life expectancy? When countries are in the early stages of the demographic transition, which tends to be when they are relatively less developed, improvements in infant and child health drive initial increases in estimated life expectancy. For example, China's increase in life expectancy during the second half of the twentieth century was among the fastest in human history, as infant mortality sharply declined due in large part to the rise in school enrollments (meaning more educated parents). As China developed, Chinese lived longer, from a life expectancy at birth of about 35 years in the 1940s, to 56 by 1957, 68 by 1981, and 77 by 2020.

Even pedestrian improvements such as hand-washing are incredibly important for increasing life expectancy and quality of life. Better sanitation, education, infrastructure, nutrition, and health services—markers of modernity—make a huge difference in initial gains. Improvements in medicine and public health are also helping people extend their lives in ways not captured by life expectancy at birth. If an infant makes it past her first birthday, her estimated life expectancy increases; the same for age 5, and so on. Life expectancy at age 5 is usually higher than at birth; likewise estimated life expectancy at age 65 is usually higher than estimated life expectancy at age 5 because if you make it to 65, it shows you have something good going for you. In theory, we are rewarded for making it another year (up to a point, of course). According to the US Social Security Administration life tables, at age 40, I'm estimated to live 45.8 more years, to age 85.3. If I make it to age 70, I'm estimated to live to age 89. Here's hoping.

Life *expectancy* reveals a lot about the conditions of a society—it's not the same as life *span*, which is more of a biological measure of the limits of the human body. The record was set in 1997 when Frenchwoman Jeanne Calment died at the unbeaten age of 122 years and 164 days.* Note the year again: 1997. We don't know for sure if there's a ceiling on life span, but some researchers believe that Calment hit it because she set the record more than two decades ago. Unlike societal life expectancy, there's no continuing linear trend upward. It seems there really are biological limits—the human body eventually breaks down. While it is possible that medicine and technology could extend human life span beyond today's limits, right now that's more science fiction than reality.

**FIGURE 4. Life Expectancy at Birth,
Ten Key States (in Years), Medium Variant**

Country	2015–2020	2030–2035
Japan	84	86
Germany	81	83
United States	79	81
China	76	79
Iran	76	79
Brazil	75	78
Russia	72	74
India	69	72
South Africa	63	67
Nigeria	54	58

• • •

* There's some controversy about whether or not Jeanne Calment actually holds the record, but if she was a fraud, my point here is underscored. See https://www.newyorker.com/magazine/2020/02/17/was-jeanne-calment-the-oldest-person-who-ever-lived-or-a-fraud.

As Figure 4 shows, there's just as much of a divide between poor and rich countries in life expectancy as in fertility. At the global level, life expectancy is still trending upward, though, even with the divide. During the nineteenth and twentieth centuries, world life expectancy more than doubled, from roughly 25 years to about 65 for men and 70 for women— that's a gain in life expectancy of about 2.5 years per decade for the past century and a half. Figure 4 shows how that trend is projected to continue, with a more accelerated pace expected for places where life expectancy is lower today. But such gains are not automatic, and it's important to constantly ask: What does it take to keep those gains on track?

• • •

Here's another way to visualize the population divide between rich and poor countries. Figure 5 is what demographers call a population pyramid (because they all used to be shaped like pyramids) or population tree (now that there's more diversity). Females are represented by bars on the right-hand side, and the bars on the left represent males. The vertical border in the middle, by 5-year increments, marks ages 0 to 100. As we

FIGURE 5. Japan's Population in 2021

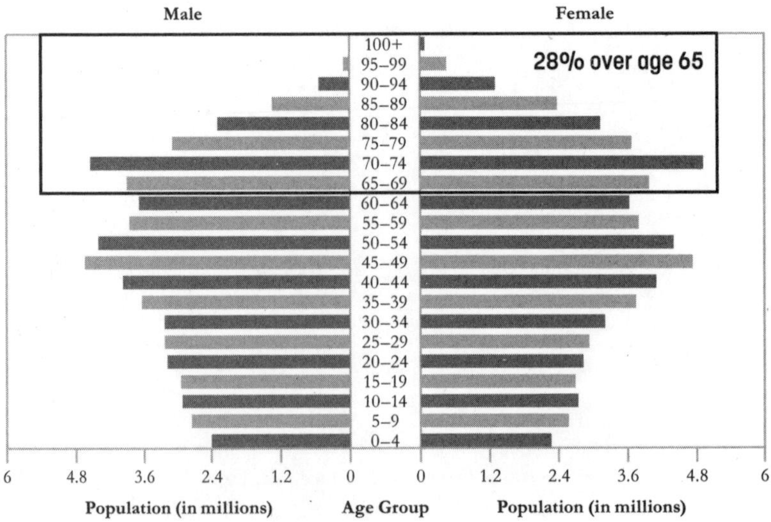

see from Figure 5, Japan in 2021 was already top-heavy; 28 percent of the population was age 65 or older.

When I first started studying population aging in the early 2000s, it was on relatively few scholars' radars because it was basically a new phenomenon. Positive population growth and relatively robust birth-rates were the norm—humanity had never before seen a population age structure like Japan's. But now it's not so new, and not so unique. Aging has intensified and diversified: No longer confined to Western Europe and Japan, the list of aged countries is varied in terms of geography, political systems and traditions, and economic strength and culture, as Figure 6 shows. And that's something for us to pay attention to over the next decades. How does this diversity in aging states challenge what we know about aging so far? Can we really use Japan and Western Europe as our models for understanding population aging in the twenty-first century? All of our modern economic theories were formed and debated and tried during a time when population growth seemed limitless, or at least when it was impossible to foresee a time when the workforce would permanently shrink because of population aging. New demographic realities mean we need a reassessment and recasting of how we think about what makes an economy strong.

Extreme aging is one side of the coin; extremely youthful populations is the other. Figure 7 is a snapshot of Nigeria's population in 2021. We can see why demographers used to call these population pyramids—it's obviously narrow at the top and wider at the bottom, like a pyramid,

FIGURE 6. Ten Oldest Countries by Median Age of Population in 2035

Country	Median Age (years)	Country	Median Age (years)
Japan	52.4	Slovenia	49.6
Italy	51.5	Germany	49.6
Spain	51.5	South Korea	49.4
Portugal	50.6	Bosnia & Herzegovina	49.2
Greece	50.6	Singapore	48.8

and pretty much inverse from Japan's. Birth patterns in each country show why their age structures are opposites. Women in Nigeria had, on average in their lifetimes, more than five children, whereas women in Japan had fewer than one and a half.

FIGURE 7. Nigeria's Population in 2021

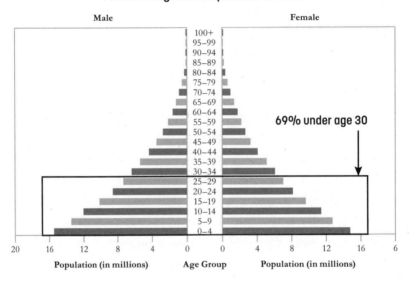

Because of this high fertility, more than two-thirds of Nigeria's population—69 percent—was under the age of 30 in 2021. Just glancing at this snapshot, it's probably no surprise that political demographers have observed that establishing effective political authority in such young societies is often difficult. And Nigeria is not even the world's youngest country. That title goes to Niger, where the median age in 2020 was only 15 years.

Japan and Nigeria are two extremes, but they don't tell the whole story of population trends in the twenty-first century. What about the countries in between?

A classic country to start with is China. As we can see from the left half of Figure 8, China's age structure in 2021 doesn't look like either

Japan's or Nigeria's; the bulk of the population is somewhere in the middle. Indeed, 64.5 percent of China's population in that year is considered to be of "working ages." Lots of workers and few dependents sounds positive, but doesn't that contradict what we commonly hear about China? In real time as I write this, I just Googled "China population" to take the temperature of the Web. The first results on the page? "China's Population Policy Now a Problem, Not a Solution" (*HuffPost*), "China's Newest Challenge Is Adapting to Its Aging Population" (*The Atlantic*), and "The Most Surprising Demographic Crisis" (*The Economist*, also about China's aging). It seems that you can't pick up a publication on national defense or economics without hearing how China will be the first country in the world to grow old before it grows rich. Is it that simple? Is population aging dooming China to fall from global prominence when it was just assuming the throne?

To answer these questions, let's think more about how we read snapshots in time. Any snapshot of a population tells not only the story of the present but also of the past and of the future. Today's 30-year-olds were children a couple of decades ago, and they will be 50 two decades from now. Demography sheds light on the past because, as we'll see throughout this book, when we understand how to interpret population trends, we unlock insight into political, economic, and social dynamics

FIGURE 8. China's Population in 2021 and in 2050

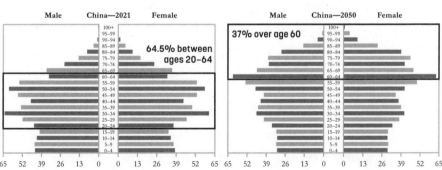

around the world. Demography gives us a long view on cycles of peace and conflict, economic boom and bust, and even cultural revolution.

But, again, there are a lot of things a snapshot of age structure doesn't show. Yes, China is aging. We can feel relatively confident that more than one-third of its population will be over age 60 by 2050, as Figure 8 shows. But what does that really mean? What if China's average age of exit from the workforce in 2050 is more like Japan's today (71) than France's (61)? If the box highlighting China's older population is meant to represent old-age dependents, we'd need to change the boundaries to show that only 21 percent (those age 70 and older)—not 37 percent (those age 60 and older)—of China's population would have aged out of the workforce, on average. We also can't tell from a snapshot of age structure that China only spends about 4.1 percent of its GDP on pensions for people of older ages, less than half the Organisation for Economic Co-operation and Development (OECD) average of 8.8 percent. Even the snapshot of aging Japan doesn't tell us anything about cultures of care for the elderly, laws governing older workers, or what level of support Japanese voters have for retirement reforms.

Russia is another country where it's well known that the population has a negative growth rate (that is, it's shrinking). Remember, this is in contrast to a country such as the Democratic Republic of the Congo that's growing at 3 percent a year. There's a similar trope among policy makers that Russia's aging is the death knell for its national security. When I worked in the Pentagon in the mid-2000s, people were eager to write off Russia because of its "dire demographics." Similar to China today, there were lots of publications with titles like "Russia's Depopulation Bomb" and "The Incredible Shrinking People." Of course, this was in the heyday of Russia's "major shrinkage," if you will. In the first 5 years of the new millennium, Russia's population shrank by 0.4 percent; that translated to a net loss of almost half a million people a year. And in fact, in 2009 then-secretary of defense Robert Gates even wrote that the United States didn't need to worry about Russia anymore because its demographics were going to be its destiny, reminiscent of the tweet about China's demographics that made me worry we were jumping to conclusions.

But if we fast-forward to today, we can see that Russia's leaders have decided to modernize the military and increase the money they're spending on defense, even as the country shrinks and ages. They're also unafraid to project power beyond Russia's borders, both in the region (Ukraine) and outside it (Syria, Yemen), which is something we wouldn't have predicted from an aging and shrinking population. Their moves into the cyber realm are an apt adaptation to population aging. Russia has even seen a modest turnaround in terms of its total fertility rate, which is slowing population contraction. Assessments of population trends need to account for that, too, as Chapter 2 will describe.

• • •

Pop quiz: What would you say is the proportion of the world's people that currently live outside the countries in which they were born? Is it: (a) 20 to 22 percent, (b) 11 to 12 percent, or (c) 2 to 4 percent?

If you answered (c), 2 to 4 percent, you are correct. If you chose one of the other two answers, though, it's not surprising. Each day, newspapers across the world announce another refugee crisis, publish vitriolic debates about immigrants taking jobs, and relate cultural clashes, making us think the real number is much higher. But that 2 to 4 percent has actually been pretty steady for the past 50 years. Outside of a handful of states, international migration contributes much less to national population change than does either births or deaths.

However, in certain regions and countries, migration changes the landscape dramatically. Certainly, no demographic trend can alter the fabric of a society faster than migration—fertility and mortality are sluggish in comparison. The exodus of Syrians after the start of the 2011 civil war is one striking example: In December 2011, 8,000 Syrian refugees were registered with the United Nations High Commissioner for

Refugees (UNHCR); 4 years later, 4.5 million out of a population of 18.5 million were.

Syria does not stand alone. Globally, there are more displaced people than ever before, nearly 80 million of them as of 2020. Sadly, prior experience hasn't forced a solution, and today's challenges have been intractable. The increase in civil conflict in the post–Cold War period has caused displaced people to remain so longer, from about 8 years on average in the 1980s to 20 years today. An additional challenge is that, globally, more than 50 percent of the world's refugees are children under age 18. Altogether, 1 in every 97 persons in the world is either a refugee, internally displaced, or seeking asylum—that's 1 percent of humanity.

War, persecution, disaster, and oppressive governments plague certain regions more than others, but any of these horrors can force people to abandon their homes. As of March 2017, 20 million people faced famine across Yemen, Somalia, South Sudan, and Nigeria—all countries with areas racked by conflict. The United Nations estimates that an astounding 80 percent of Yemenis (more than 24 million people) need aid. In just two months of 2017, 48,000 people there fled the devastation caused by Saudi Arabia and Iran's proxy war. In Nigeria, the fight against Boko Haram has killed 37,500 and driven 2.9 million from home. Venezuela's economic and political crisis, which unraveled over years but intensified after 2014, prompted the largest mass exodus in the region's history, an 8,000 percent increase in the number of Venezuelans seeking refugee status from 2014 to 2020.

A displaced global population of the size we face today is tremendous, but refugees are only a small proportion of the world's migrants. The majority of migrants move to be closer to family, to find better jobs or educational opportunities, to seek freedom, or even to shift to a warmer climate. Because global population is higher by the year, the absolute number of global migrants is higher than ever, about 272 million worldwide. Remember, in the majority of countries, international migration contributes far less to national population change than do either births or deaths, but in certain regions and countries, migration changes the landscape dramatically. That 272 million is concentrated in just a few places. In 2019, two-thirds of all migrants lived in just 20 countries, and more than half were in just 10 countries. The United States hosts the most, almost 45 million, followed by Germany, Saudi Arabia, and Russia, each with about 12 million to 13 million. Where things get interesting is with the Persian Gulf states, which have the world's highest share of foreign-born. Eighty-eight percent of the United Arab Emirates' population is foreign-born, 78 percent of Qatar's, 72 percent of Kuwait's, and 45 percent of Bahrain's. Most of these are temporary labor migrants from places such as the Indian subcontinent, not permanent settlers, and thus mostly affect the countries' economic dynamics, rather than broader political or social ones. Political ramifications are more obvious in Turkey, Jordan, Palestine, Lebanon, and Pakistan, who host some of the world's largest refugee populations and have been dealing with the economic and social strains of meeting the native population's needs along with those of their guests.

Europe has also struggled learning to deal with massive immigration after a long history as a continent of emigration. Just behind Asia at 83 million, Europe hosts the second largest number of migrants, 82 million, of any region in the world. On average during 2015, more than 2,300 migrants a day landed on Greece's shores, fleeing conflict and poverty in countries such as Syria. The population of the 27 countries that make up the European Union (excluding Great Britain) increased by 0.9 million overall in 2019. What's astounding is that net growth came from migration, and there were half a million more deaths than births— natural change in the European Union has been negative since 2012.

These demographic shifts are yielding dramatic political changes, including the resurgence of far-right parties in many European countries. British voters in 2016 overwhelmingly sent the message that Britain's sovereignty—particularly the ability to control its own borders against migrants—was paramount and withdrew from the European

Union despite nearly universal arguments that leaving the European Union would hurt Britain's economy.

Another shift is happening internally: exodus from the countryside in the form of massive urbanization. In the year 1800, only 3 percent of the world's population lived in cities, and in the nineteenth century, only 14 percent did. Even in 1950, just 30 percent of the world's population lived in urban areas, but now the world's population is 55 percent urban, having crossed the halfway mark in 2007, when just three countries accounted for 35 percent of the world's urban population: China, India, and the United States. Today, the most urbanized region is North America, with 82 percent of its population living in urban areas, followed by Latin America and the Caribbean with 81 percent, Europe with 74 percent, and Oceania with 68 percent. The majority of urban growth is natural (fertility over mortality), but in the least urbanized regions, rural-to-urban migration is significant. While Asia and Africa hold almost 90 percent of the world's total urbanites, that's because their total populations are large. Within those regions a significant proportion of the population is still rural: 50 percent in Asia and 57 percent in Africa.

But what it means to be "urban" differs greatly across the world, even within countries. There's no standard international definition of urban; in Botswana, an area qualifies if it has at least 5,000 inhabitants and 75 percent of the economic activity is nonagricultural. Canada counts urban areas as those with at least 1,000 inhabitants and a density of 400 or more people per square kilometer; Japan labels as urban those areas having at least 50,000 inhabitants. These differences are why assessments using urbanization data need some context and detail. Despite the imagery that surrounds urbanization, huge cities are not the norm. Almost half of the world's urban dwellers live in areas with a population of less than 500,000. One in eight live in megacities, urban areas with more than 10 million inhabitants. The absolute number of these cities is growing, though. In just over a decade, the world will have about 43 megacities, mostly in developing regions, 12 more than today. The number of metacities, those with a population of 20 million or more, is also growing. Tokyo is the world's largest city, with a population of 38 million, followed by New Delhi at 28 million—a major spread between the two.

The great divide in population between developed and less developed regions is clear with urbanization, too. Some cities in low-fertility countries are actually facing population decline. Tokyo is projected to lose about 1 million residents over the next decade or so. In contrast, Dhaka, Bangladesh, is one of the fastest growing megacities in the world and one of the most densely populated. In contrast to Tokyo's gleaming skyscrapers, a stark public-radio story on Dhaka in 2010 opened with the line, "The future is here, and it smells like burning trash." Between 1990 and 2005, almost half a million people a year flooded into Dhaka looking for economic opportunity, but if they didn't find it, they stayed anyway, leading to a "broken labyrinth of shacks," pollution, and disease. Although cities and their national economies grew in parallel for a long time, some researchers are arguing that there's been a shift and that since the 1960s we actually have urbanization without economic growth for the first time. Urbanization today is leading to a "planet of slums," according to some.

• ◉ •

As complex as demographics can seem, there are really only three forces that drive change: sex, death, and migration. More formally and accurately, FMM: fertility,* mortality, and migration.

I often think of fertility, mortality, and migration as dials that turn

• • •

* Because population trends are in large part about reproduction, the focus is on male and female couples, and for the most part about conception through intercourse. In vitro fertilization and other assisted reproductive technologies make up such a small percentage of successful pregnancies that I rarely mention them. Where such technologies are relevant is in somewhat extending the childbearing years for women wealthy enough to afford them. There are still biological limits, however. Abortion is relevant and significant, but you will not find any normative discussion in this book.

up or down in different combinations to produce infinite population dynamics. Throughout this book, we'll see what happens to overall population when these three factors are combined in different ways. As the fertility, mortality, and migration dials turn to different intensities, they produce changes in three main ways: population size, distribution, and composition. We've already talked about distribution, particularly where populations are concentrated within countries, with rural versus urban areas. How "important" a country is on the world stage generally correlates with population size. Big populations mean big potential labor forces and big consumer markets—with their near-universal literacy, it would be lovely if all 1.4 billion people in China bought this book. Size can boost military strength as well, as bigger populations have more potential soldiers to mobilize for conflict. There are plenty of exceptions, of course. Cuba, with a population of only 11 million, has occupied a disproportionate share of global political attention worldwide since World War II; the same goes for North Korea, with a population of only 26 million. Population is certainly not the only source of power a country has—Persian Gulf states have leveraged their oil-fueled economic power quite effectively to gain global influence—but the attitude of most leaders toward population has been "the bigger the better."

It's plausible that it's not the size of a population that matters, but how the leaders use it. Although there's an important psychological element to size, as we will see in Part II, Cuba and North Korea show population size isn't the only variable that shapes influence.

Whether, in what direction, and at what rate population size is changing are important aspects of this dynamic. Some countries' populations are growing, some are stagnant, and, increasingly, some are shrinking. A combination of fertility, mortality, and migration contributes to these changes. Canadian fertility has been below replacement level for decades, but the death rate is low and more people have been immigrating than leaving, so Canada's population is growing. Bosnia and Herzegovina, in contrast, is shrinking because deaths are outpacing births and because more people are leaving than coming in. In a lot of aging countries, the only reason there's even modest population growth is immigration.

Size is important, but the more interesting population dynamic coming from different levels of fertility, mortality, and migration is composition. Different societies have different proportions of young and old, male and female, ethnic groups, and so on, and these differences in composition are much of what make population trends matter for politics, economics, and social relations.

Identity is one type of composition: ethnic, racial, and religious. Fellow political demographer Monica Duffy Toft has pointed out that the world has fewer than 200 sovereign states but thousands of nations and ethnic groups. Some countries peacefully navigate their domestic differences; others suffer genocide or collapse into civil war.

A second type of composition is sex. In most societies, women outlive men, so at the oldest ages there are typically far more women than men. In the Persian Gulf states, men migrate in droves from the Indian subcontinent to work the oil fields, leading to tremendous imbalances in sex ratio at working ages. And in some societies, most famously China and India, preference for males has led to high abortion rates of female fetuses and skewed sex ratios at birth.

A third area of composition is age. The demographic transition described earlier happens as the fertility and mortality dials turn down. While countries start out with very youthful populations, as they go through and eventually complete the demographic transition they also go through what's called the age-structural transition. The age-structural transition is the shift from a youthful age structure to an older one, the difference described between Nigeria and Japan. Quite far along the age-structural transition, populations of prime working age (those 20 to 64 years of age) have already peaked in China, Germany, Japan, Italy, Russia, South Korea, and the United States.

In contrast, the age-structural transition in Afghanistan has only begun. The median age in Afghanistan is only 18.4 years, and each woman on average has about 4.5 children in her lifetime. While fertility has dropped rapidly over the last two decades, these numbers mean that almost 50 percent of Afghanistan's population is under the age of 17. As the United States considers how to address the destabilization of Afghanistan, it must also consider the role of population growth there and the strains that growth will continue to place on infrastructure, education, health care, and even governance for decades to come. Countries with a young age structure such as Afghanistan's are on average about two and a half times more likely to experience the onset of civil conflict than are older countries. And even if fertility in Afghanistan falls in the future, the large group of ages 0 to 5 will require a lot of jobs one day. Experiences in Tunisia, Egypt, and other countries since 2011 show us what happens when expectations about employment, political voice, or even marriage go unmet.

Age structure isn't the only issue with composition and age. Societies are also shaped by generations. A generation, or cohort, is a group of people sharing a common demographic experience. Generations are "made-up" designations, often based on historical circumstances that affect those living during that time, especially when big historical events happen at key life stages. Youth in Japan, for example, are shaped by pervasive technology throughout their lives; US baby boomers are influenced by the upheaval of the civil rights movement and the Vietnam War during their adolescence and young adulthood—a key time for forming opinions and beliefs. A focus on generations lets us look at how different age groups may have different experiences or opinions on the basis of their unique traits. But a generation is just one way to group age cohorts—populations can also be shaped by certain periods in time. Some historical events or broad social forces have lasting effects on the entire population, such as 9/11, the end of Apartheid in South Africa, or the breakup of the Soviet Union. Finally, we have to consider the influence of particular life stages, independent of generation or period.

These are called life-cycle effects. As a mother of young children, I have a lot in common with other mothers of young children, regardless of our educational or socioeconomic backgrounds. A deficit of sleep and a surfeit of diapers are great unifiers.

We see these life-cycle effects in political behavior. Across democracies, young people are almost always far less likely to vote than are older people. In the United States today, millennials are less politically engaged than are baby boomers, but when baby boomers were young, many were uninvolved in politics as well.

• • •

If we want to talk about military strategy, economic growth, foreign policy, public health, and a host of other key issues, we need to start with population. People are the foundation of every polity, economy, and society, and so understanding demographic trends and their political, economic, and social implications is important to get a full picture of our world. What is the effect of demographics on social cohesion, value systems, or social contracts? In so many ways, world population today looks nothing like it did 50 or even 20 years ago. Despite all of our technological progress, so much of what shapes our world comes down to one fundamental element: population. As this book will show, revolutions in fertility and mortality have profoundly altered the course of humanity. Migration and urbanization continue to remake how humans organize themselves in relation to others and to their environments. A variety of changes are on the horizon, and policy makers, businesses, and advocates can use the lessons of this book to prepare for the future.

As the world nears 8 billion, demography is having a moment. All across the world, headlines are dominated by debates about disease, immigration, race, gender, and retirement. A global pandemic has upended the lives of billions. Britain has voted to leave the European Union, partly over immigration. The world's first demographic billionaire—China—is now one of the fastest aging countries on the planet. Japan's population is shrinking, even as the country faces existential threats from North Korea. Now, more than ever, we need to understand how population trends shape our world. The countries that have led the global order since World War II are facing unprecedented population changes and challenges at the same time that the world's poorest and least powerful countries are suffocating under the imbalance of population and resources—too many people and not enough money. Ninety-eight percent of the world's future population growth will take place in developing countries, yet these are the countries least equipped to handle such growth.

These population dynamics shape our world. Whether a society has far more children than elderly, whether it has an abundance of healthy workers or an influx of immigrants, even whether it has more men than women all factor into that society's political, economic, and social relations—the way people vote, work, and play. *People* are consumers, producers, polluters. They are soldiers, smugglers, saviors. To understand the physical environment, the economy, the security environment, or cultural shifts, we need to understand who these consumers, producers, polluters, soldiers, smugglers, and saviors are. Demography is not destiny. But, it's a big part of destiny.

How can we use demographics to gain insight into questions about climate change, economic growth, and pandemic preparedness? How can we rethink metrics such as global power? How does demographic analysis help us prepare for the next military threat or anticipate social strains from future migration? As we will see, with the right tools you can train yourself to think like a political demographer and be ready for whatever the future brings.

PART 1

- • ● • -

COITUS, QUIETUS, EXODUS

CHAPTER 1

From the Cradle

When Romania's last Communist ruler, Nicolae Ceauşescu, took power in 1965, the wolves were at the door. Romania was falling behind the demands of the communist economic model and was in dire need of more workers. With a population that was 86 percent Romanian, Ceauşescu was hesitant to import labor and potentially upset the ethnic balance. What was needed, he thought, were more Romanian babies, but Romanians weren't having them—the fertility rate of 1.8 was below replacement, which meant that labor shortages would only intensify. And so, Ceauşescu decreed abortion illegal, stationed police at obstetric and gynecology offices, and subjected women under 45 years to monthly gynecological exams in their workplaces. His harsh measures worked—at least in the short term. Romania's fertility spiked 100 percent in just one year, to 3.66 children per woman on average. While labor shortages might persist in the short term, before long these children would ideally be able-bodied enough to staff Romania's fields and factories.

Romania's invasive policies are far from the only example of public involvement in family lives. Even well before modern methods gave us greater control over reproduction, leaders tried to influence—or more accurately, engineer—fertility to suit national goals. More babies for soldiers or workers. Fewer babies for faster economic growth and stability. Studying fertility and responses to it can seem a lot like reading the children's fairy tale Goldilocks: States generally think their fertility is "too high" or "too low"—it's rarely "just right" in their eyes. With such divergent patterns and responses, many of us in the business of foresight for economic growth or national security can have a hard time drawing conclusions about the role of high fertility or youthful populations.

Case in point: On the opposite end of the natalist policy spectrum from Romania are the world's demographic giants, India and China. At different points in time, British colonizers, American Cold Warriors, and various Indian elites were concerned about high population growth in India. A national family-planning program was put in place in 1952, but the state didn't launch serious action until after Indira Gandhi was elected to lead in 1966. Gandhi, who faced foreign pressure from America, was intent upon limiting Indians' family size and set family-planning targets at 6 million intrauterine device (IUD) insertions and 1.23 million sterilizations for her first year. Between 1974 and 1977, there were some 12 million sterilizations in India, the majority for men because vasectomy was quick and cheap. As in Romania, measures in India were coercive: Teachers who declined sterilization could lose pay, and villages receiving irrigation risked having their water supply cut if they failed to meet local sterilization targets. Although democratically elected, Prime Minister Gandhi was able to use forcible methods even with popular resistance—in June 1975, she proclaimed a state of emergency and ruled with a heavy hand until she was ousted along with her Congress Party in 1977.

Arguably, the real problem in India was poverty, not overpopulation. Although Indira Gandhi and the leaders from international agencies who offered loans to her administration assumed that population control was a prerequisite to economic development, as we've seen elsewhere around the world, with rising incomes it's likely Indians would have started to prefer smaller families on their own, and access to education and voluntary family planning would have helped them realize those preferences. Coercive policies were unnecessary at best, immoral at worst. One leader skeptical of the role of population control in economic development was China's Mao Tse-tung.

Mao, following Communist philosophers Marx and Engels, interpreted the rhetoric around overpopulation as the bourgeoisie shifting blame onto the poor for their own woes, when really capitalist exploitation made countries and people poor—not overpopulation. In fact, Mao initially saw tremendous benefit to a large population. One advantage was that he could mobilize citizens in massive, labor-intensive campaigns, such as widespread irrigation, dam construction, and even ridding China of the "four pests": rats, flies, mosquitoes, and sparrows.

Mao's opinion was a minority one among his fellow Chinese elites, however, and most readers know that as new leadership emerged, China would embark on the world's most famous family-planning campaign: the One-Child Policy.

The One-Child Policy, which took effect in 1979, 3 years after Mao's death, was actually the latter in a series of campaigns to lower fertility. Once other Chinese elites convinced Mao that at least some family planning would be beneficial, the state focused its early campaigns on urban areas in the 1960s, but the real commitment came in the early 1970s when Premier Chou En-lai tried to make population planning part of the overall national economic plans. The government moved from a slogan of "One child will do, two are good enough, and three are one too many" to "Later, Longer, Fewer." These campaigns and changing norms about ideal family size halved the birthrate. The One-Child Policy, which followed, had significant implications, including compulsory abortion, and likely accelerated China's already declining fertility rate.

Why are there such disparate and dramatic responses to what are sometimes similar fertility levels? No demographic trend is inherently good or bad, but it is true that population creates pressures on housing, job markets, schools, health care, and even family structures, and states often see fertility as a means to a more positive end. Research shows that empowering women to have the number of births they desire benefits the entire population by making a country stronger and more secure in the long run. The demographic divide of the twenty-first century is clear: In the 1990s, Europe and Africa had about the same size population; by the end of the twenty-first century, one-third of the people on Earth are expected to live in Africa. Much of that growth will be driven by sub-Saharan Africa, and even if fertility in that region falls from its current rate of 4.7 children per woman, the region's population will continue to grow rapidly because of the large cohorts entering childbearing ages over the next two decades. Population growth isn't automatically a recipe for disaster, but in many cases it's one of the long-term trends that undermines peace and stability. However, it takes longer than an election cycle to see results from policies that empower women to determine their own reproduction, and, unfortunately, such policies are almost always highly politicized. Coercive measures such as Romania's or India's or China's aren't necessary to achieve ideal fertility, but before we even get to the nitty-gritty of politics, it's worth questioning whether there's objectively such a thing as "ideal fertility" anyway.

• • •

Women's reproductive ages are generally considered to be ages 15 to 45 or 49 years—that's a long span within which to have children, and it's becoming less common for women to continually bear children throughout that time. As intended by China's "Later, Longer, Fewer" campaign to lower fertility, postponing the age at which a woman starts her childbearing, increasing the time between births, and helping women limit their fertile periods, if they desire to do so, are all effective ways of lowering fertility rates. A woman's average age at first birth differs widely around the world. In many developed countries, women don't start their childbearing until well into their thirties, meaning that the time in which they might conceivably have children is truncated to between 10 and 15 years. By contrast, in many developing states, childbearing starts early. On average, women in Chad have their first birth at age 18 (let me underscore: that means many women have their first birth before that age); in Sri Lanka, the average is over 25 years. Having children at such young ages can limit individual opportunities outside the home and strain household resources. One way to postpone the age at first birth is to discourage (or legally restrict) early marriage. Another is to keep girls in school longer so they wait to start their families. One of the more common strategies for lowering fertility, particularly targeted at lower-income groups, is birth spacing. Encouraging women to breast-feed their infants until age 2 is supposed to delay the onset of menses after giving birth and thus help with birth spacing (it sometimes works). Other methods of family planning, including contraception, can lengthen the interval between births as well.

Of course, "later" and "longer" contribute to "fewer," but there's much more to lowering fertility, and from a policy perspective "fewer" is perhaps the most challenging of the three. After all, even if a woman waits until age 24 to start having children and then spaces her pregnancies by 2 years, she could still feasibly have at least seven children well before she reaches the end of her reproductive years. In Somalia, women aged 40 to 44 have an average of 82.4 births per 1,000 women, whereas in Argentina they have 18.8 and in South Korea only 4.7. Later starts don't universally translate to earlier "stops."

In some regions, the transition to "fewer" was relatively smooth. Fertility declines were earliest in Europe, but the second half of the twentieth century saw tremendous declines in East Asia and Latin America, too, from 5.69 to 1.82 children on average per woman for the former and from 5.83 to 2.49 for the latter. Since that time, fertility has continued to decline in Latin America and the Caribbean to just below replacement level. The shift to preferring fewer children and then actually having fewer children has proven tough in many countries in sub-Saharan Africa, though, where fertility has dropped only modestly, from 6.57 children per woman on average in 1950 to 5.08 by 2000 and 4.16 by 2020. Why the difference? The most basic factor is that in the aggregate, people living in some sub-Saharan African countries simply prefer larger families than do people living in Latin America or Asia. We know this from a series of Demographic and Health Surveys (DHS) and similar surveys, which ask about ideal family size, how many children were wanted, how wanted recent births were, and desire for more children. These are imperfect surveys, as respondents sometimes tailor their answers to what they think the surveyor wants to hear, but the data are widely used.

What underlying factors shape such preferences, and how do they change? How do you enable people to have the number of children they prefer? In general, a higher standard of living and improving mortality, along with rising education, lead people to prefer fewer children. The more education, the fewer desired children. In Zimbabwe, for example, women with some secondary education or more report the ideal number of children as 3.6 on average, whereas those women with no secondary education report the ideal as 4.8. Zimbabwean men with no secondary education prefer even larger numbers of children—5.3. Although we know that secondary education, in particular, helps delay marriage and childbearing and is equitable in most areas of the world, in some states of the Middle East–North African region and sub-Saharan Africa, girls' enrollment rates are lower than those of boys. Gender is also a factor: As is the case in Zimbabwe, surveys show that men generally want more children than women do (although once the overall number of desired children is low, the differences narrow or disappear).

Sub-Saharan Africa lags far behind other regions in progress on standard of living, mortality decline, and education, and desired family size there is a full child higher than anywhere else in the developing world. As discussed in the introductory chapter, we know that nearly all of the world's future population growth will take place in less developed countries; much of that is in sub-Saharan Africa. Regional-level data obscure important national differences, however. South Africa, Botswana, Djibouti, and Eswatini have fertility at or below three children per woman. In these countries, fertility actually fell faster than what we might expect given current levels of economic development and child mortality. At the same time, the 10 fastest growing countries in the world from excess births over deaths (meaning natural increase, without immigration) are all in sub-Saharan Africa: Niger, Angola, Mali, Uganda, the Democratic Republic of the Congo, Burundi, Somalia, Gambia, Tanzania, and Chad. Not even on that list is Nigeria, whose population is on track to more than double by mid-century, knocking the United States from its long-held position as the world's third-largest country. The Democratic Republic of the Congo had the world's third-highest fertility rate in 2020, at 5.96 children per woman. Its population will increase by 74 percent, about 65 million people, between 2020 and 2040. Uganda's population will increase from 45.7 million in 2020 to 59.4 million in 2030, and to 74.5 million by 2040. And even once high-fertility countries achieve replacement-level fertility, they still face two to three decades of crowded youth cohorts, which have lower opportunity costs for expressing their discontent, whether through peaceful protest or armed rebellion. Such youthful populations have slim chance of becoming democratic.

Most demographers expected Africa to follow in the footsteps of other major world regions; that is, as it urbanized and developed, fertility there would fall. In 2004, the United Nations projected that world population would reach only 9.1 billion by 2050—by 2019 it had revised its estimate to 9.7 billion and foresaw a world of nearly 11 billion by the end of the twenty-first century, much of that driven by continued high fertility in sub-Saharan Africa. The 2019 version of the United Nations' population data (medium variant) projects that Africa's population will reach 2.5 billion by mid-century and 4.3 billion by century's end.

Because the third stage of the demographic transition has been slow in coming to several countries in sub-Saharan Africa, some demographers label their demographic transition as "stalled." How did earlier projections miss the mark?

First, projections were overly optimistic about the ability of some sub-Saharan African countries to overcome underlying socioeconomic and governance issues that would have driven greater economic development, and then lower fertility. Legacies of colonialism have led to poor governance and exploitative economic relationships. Despotic leaders have clung to power in many countries; the shift away from economies dependent upon natural resource extraction to diversified ones with manufacturing or service sectors has been rare. Second, even if Africa's economic development had been stronger, research has found that Africa still would have had relatively higher fertility. Demographer John Bongaarts found that "At a given level of development Africa's fertility is higher, contraceptive use is lower, and desired family size is higher than in non-African LDCs [less developed countries]." Pronatalist tendencies among the general population and many elites make up the difference. Uganda's long-time leader, Yoweri Kaguta Museveni, regularly shifts between pro-natalism and anti-natalism and in 2018 said, "The problem of Africa has been, actually, under-population and not over population. Africa is 12 times the size of India in land area." This, while Uganda's TFR is 5.01. With a similarly high TFR, Tanzania's then-president John Magufuli said in 2018 that Tanzanians should stop using birth control because the country needs more people. He feared that greater use of birth control would lead the country to have a problem with population aging and insinuated that contraception campaigns by foreigners had sinister motives. While he is correct that eventually Tanzania could face population aging, they are so early in the demographic transition, with a TFR of 4.92, that any population aging is decades and decades away. Finally, some African leaders resist family planning because of pervasive polygyny and a culture of male dominance.

While not all African leaders espouse such pronatalism and many have taken active roles in promoting rights-based family planning, such attititudes among important African leaders impede progress along the demographic transition and depress quality of life for millions. Leadership is crucial to fertility transitions because preferences only change in response to structural conditions such as quality of life. Educational and job opportunities don't appear without commitment from the top—neither do family-planning clinics.

• • •

"Later, Longer, Fewer" is a formula meant to alter societal expectations of childbearing. Changing women's and men's childbearing preferences is one part of the equation; empowering them to act on those preferences is another. Trying to reduce poverty, improve education, combat infant and child mortality, and create societal conditions that permit women to control their childbearing in order to change high preferred family size is daunting, to say the least, but family-planning programs can have a significant impact even without those structural changes.

One way to empower people to act on their preferences is through contraception. A bit of this is technology. Even in antiquity, people hoping to enjoy sex without adding to their families used vaginal suppositories, some of which may have acted as spermicides, and other resin-like substances, which would have blocked the entrance to the cervix. Vulcanization of rubber in 1844 led to more widespread use of condoms as birth control. Even the famous eighteenth century lover Casanova allegedly used condoms, what he called "English riding coats," quite extensively. And of course abortions and natural family planning, such as avoiding sex during a woman's most fertile periods in the month, have always been used.

The other bit of this is making the technology available and affordable. That's part of the reason for such minuscule gains in the past two decades. According to the World Health Organization, people face a "limited choice of methods; limited access to services, particularly among young, poorer and unmarried people; fear or experience of side-effects; cultural or religious opposition; poor quality of available services; users' and providers' bias against some methods; and gender-based barriers to accessing services." There are ways to overcome these barriers, though, even in places we might not expect, such as Iran.

Surrounded by states with high fertility, Iran stands out for early family-planning efforts that rapidly ushered the country through the demographic transition, despite the resistance of some elites. Starting in the late 1980s, Iran's leaders began establishing an effective network of free contraceptive and counseling services that ended up inducing a drop in fertility from 5.5 children on average per woman to just 2 in only two decades. Even rural Iranian women, who had the country's highest fertility, went from having an average of eight children to around two children in just one generation. Access to family planning was key. Richard Cincotta and Karim Sadjadpour note that "By 2000, about 90 percent of Iran's population lived within two kilometers of a family planning service-delivery point, and mobile public-sector providers periodically serviced remote areas." As we know, education also plays a role in preferences for smaller families—that was true in Iran, as the government encouraged education to the point where women outnumbered men in Iranian universities.

Within the Sahel, Botswana similarly stands out for its strides in lowering fertility rates. Free family-planning services began there in the 1970s and have strengthened over time. Girls' secondary school enrollment is more than 90 percent, and more than half of women in Botswana use modern methods of contraception. Today, while Botswana's TFR is around 2.5, one of the lowest in sub-Saharan Africa, the region's total TFR (including Botswana's) is nearly twice that at 4.8.

Once demographers identify preferred family size (as through the Demographic and Health Surveys), they can measure that against the actual number of children people have and see if there is a gap that policy can help fill. Demographers measure "unmet need for family planning" as when women are of reproductive age and say they want to stop having children or want to wait two or more years to have them but are not using contraception; women who are pregnant or immediately postpartum but who did not intend their last pregnancy also count in this category. Contraception use among women of reproductive ages has increased greatly during the past decades, from only 10 percent using any method in 1960, to 55 percent using modern methods—sterilization, the pill, injectables, condoms, and so on—by 2000. More recent gains have been slower, however. In 2019 there were 1.9 billion women of reproductive age worldwide, among whom 1.1 billion had a need for family planning. More than 76 percent of them were using contraceptive methods, while the remainder had an unmet need for contraception. Ten percent of women have an unmet need for family planning, and that number has been stable since 2000. As usual, global numbers are useful indicators but mask important national distinctions. Fewer than 15 percent of married women ages 15 to 49 in the world's poorest countries use any modern method of contraception, in contrast to developed countries where more than 60 percent of women do. In Libya, only 24 percent of married women have their demand for modern methods of family planning met. Globally, the unintended pregnancy rate is trending downward but is still high overall—44 percent of all pregnancies were unintended between 2010 and 2014. More than half of those pregnancies (56 percent) ended in abortion between 2010 and 2014, slightly more in developed regions (59 percent) than in developing regions (55 percent). Policies to address disparities in family-planning access should be a key part of broader policy packages meant to improve economic development.

• • •

Certainly, technology can be empowering, but it also has a dark side. The issue of Asia's "missing girls" shows what happens when preferences and technology collide. When nature has total control, there are slightly more male babies than female babies: about 103 to 106 boys ages 0 to 4 for every 100 girls. But when humans interfere, that sex ratio can get out of whack. Historically, when societies preferred males over females and acted on that preference, they committed infanticide or neglected girl babies to the point of death. Today, abnormal sex ratio at birth (SRB) comes from a combination of fertility decline and norms of son preference and daughter aversion—if families are going to have only one or two children and prefer males (as in cultures where sons have primary responsibility for caring for elderly parents), then they will do their best to ensure that their children are male. Technology makes that easier. The advent of ultrasound technology has allowed us to see a baby's sex in utero, and improvements in genetic testing can reveal a baby's sex through the mother's blood at just a few weeks' gestation. In both of these cases, girl fetuses can be aborted while boy fetuses are carried to term.

China's skewed SRB is the most well-known, in large part because it is discussed in the context of the One-Child Policy, which made son preference more transparent. And it is a real problem: China's SRB was 107.2 in the 1982 census, 116.9 in the 2000 census, and 117.9 in the 2010 census. But China is far from the only country with a skewed sex ratio at birth. Rather than being isolated in Asia, the problem also exists in southeastern Europe, the Middle East, and Africa. In 2020, the list of states with SRBs of 107 or higher included Serbia, Estonia, Suriname, Papua New Guinea, Cyprus, Samoa, and Kazakhstan. On the national level, SRBs appear to be improving toward the norm: While at the start of this century Armenia and Azerbaijan had the world's highest SRB at 117 boys born for every 100 girls, by 2020 the highest SRB was in China, down to 113.

Still, let me emphasize that most of the numbers we see are aggregated and national-level data; ratios disaggregated by birth order and by sub-national geography can be even more extreme. In South Korea, for

FIGURE 9. Numbers of Male and Female Children Aged 0 to 4 in China and India

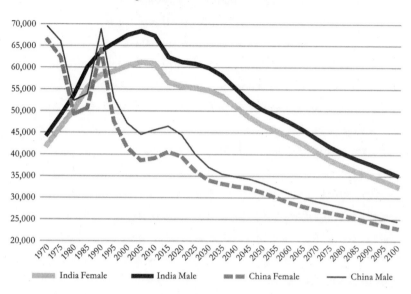

example, in 1990 the SRB for first births was skewed at 113.44, but for third births and above it was an astounding 192.22. In China, 2010 data on total SRB showed a notable difference between cities and villages—a total SRB of 118.33 for the former and 122.76 for the latter. Birth order was relevant there, too: In urban areas of China, first births had an SRB of 113.44, second births an SRB of 132.18, and third births or higher (which were rare) an SRB of 175.35.

These imbalances at birth translate to significant differences in the population size of men and women: As Figure 9 shows, there have been far more male children aged 0 to 4 than female children aged 0 to 4 in China and in India since the 1990s. In total, males outnumber females by 70 million (both countries combined). But as of now the effects remain confined to mostly younger ages; of those 70 million excess males, 50 million are under the age of 20.

To see why a skewed sex ratio matters, we can approach the issue from several angles. Some scholars frame the issue as "too many men."

Eventually, those currently 0 to 4 years of age will be of marriageable age, and the gap between young men and women hasn't yet peaked. In the most sanguine of interpretations, an excess supply of males leads to "an epidemic of loneliness" as heterosexual men are unable to find partners with whom to share their lives. There is much handwringing in the media about the social consequences of skewed sex ratios once they affect those of marriageable age, particularly in contexts where marriage is a nearly universal marker of adulthood, as in China. Relationships aside, there are even gloomier interpretations of the consequences of skewed sex ratios, as scholars surmise they could affect violent crime, human trafficking, or prostitution, or even lead to civil conflict.

But it's important to turn a critical eye to any interpretation of demographic trends, this one included. One critique is grounded in feminism. Concern about how men will possibly cope without wives validates the view of women as sexual objects whose purpose is to provide pacifying services for males. This critique, articulated by scholar Nancy Riley, offers that "even if a sizeable proportion of Chinese men are unable to find wives, that does not necessarily spell social disaster, but is likely to force a reconstruction of norms and institutions to accommodate such a change; perhaps being single will lose some of its stigma in Chinese society."

In answer to a feminist critique, we could focus instead on the missing girls. In this interpretation, skewed sex ratios are the embodiment of systematically devaluing women. Experts on the issue, Valerie Hudson and Andrea den Boer, go even further, arguing that sex-selective abortion is akin to violence against women, and the increase in the practice of sex-selective abortion is evidence that violence against women is acceptable. Certainly, some societies are organized patrilineally, with an emphasis on transferring property and power through the male line. Through their study of South Korea, Hudson and den Boer find that restrictive, anti-natalist policies (like a one- or two-child policy) make sex ratios worse, often taking what was just a cultural preference and turning it into action. They say, "In South Korea, although its two-child and later one-child policies were not enforced, these norms were quickly accepted in urban and then rural areas within this homogenous nation." Neither a strong state nor gender-equitable laws are enough to trump the cultural preference for sons. While Vietnam has tried to legally shed its patrilineality, in practice women still own little land, spousal rape goes unprosecuted, and women are still expected to assimilate into their husbands' families upon marriage, with few rights of their own. India also remains a highly patriarchal society with high rates of violence against women. In both, the 2020 SRB was 110 to 112.

Certainly, there are significant pressures on both genders: Men in such societies aren't considered fully adult until they have married; women are often seen as objects of exchange between men, sometimes used to create alliances with kin groups. Marriage markets can be obstructed through an alteration in the sex ratio, polygyny, and brideprice unaffordability. When marriage is that highly valued in society, men may go to extremes to get married. There is evidence that ISIS and the Syrian government have provided brideprice for soldiers, as has Boko Haram in Nigeria. Brideprice—money transfer from the groom's family to the bride's family—is customary law in many societies. Dowry, in contrast, is an exchange of funds from the bride to the groom, an important distinction.

The argument that skewed sex ratios have significant political and social consequences has grown in sophistication during the past two decades, from one that was accused of being reliant on "crude evolutionary theories and animal studies" to one that examines the character of male–female relations and how the underlying structure of those relations affects birth and death rates, as Hudson's latest work does. But some are still highly critical of the entire line of research, in particular for elevating the issue of skewed sex ratio and gender relations to a national security issue for the West. One scholar claims that "the re-surfacing of fear about China's male population continues a tradition of Orientalist stereotypes." The narrative is also caught up in larger fears about China's population as an economic and military threat to the West. As with any population trend, I urge caution in interpretation and encourage further study. We have competing theories about why and in what ways skewed SRB matters. Now, we need more empirical evidence and analysis.

• ● •

With a better understanding of the conditions that create high fertility and measures known to lower it, we can explore the societal-level consequences of high fertility. As we saw briefly in the introductory chapter, high-fertility societies have what's called youthful age structures and often very high proportions of the population under age 20. There are many benefits to a youthful society, but often those countries with large youth cohorts struggle to achieve economic growth, and they're prone to civil unrest.

There's no direct link between youthful age structures and instability, and mediating factors, such as government capacity, make a difference. In particular, governments that focus on providing education, jobs, and avenues for political participation benefit from helping youth achieve their potential and establish the conditions for greater economic dividends as the population transitions to an older age structure.

I always try to refrain from alarmism when interpreting population trends, but it's hard to ignore the track records of the world's youngest or fastest growing populations. Just look at the annual Fragile States Index produced by the Fund for Peace, as shown in Figure 10. This list shows countries most at risk for collapsing into violence or disarray, unable to provide even basic services to their citizens. Most of the countries we've named so far make the top 10. The world's most fragile countries—those in danger of collapse, or already there—all have youthful age structures. This set includes Afghanistan, the Democratic Republic of the Congo, Sudan, and Yemen. In fact, the average median age of the 20 most fragile countries in 2019 was 18.95 years, and that's including outlier Syria, with a median age of 25.6.

**FIGURE 10. Most Fragile States in 2020,
According to the Fragile States Index**

Rank	Country	Proportion of population ages 0–19 years
1	Yemen	49.6
2	Somalia	57.6
3	South Sudan	52.1
4	Syria	39.8
5	Democratic Republic of the Congo	56.4
6	Central African Republic	55.9
7	Chad	57.8
8	Sudan	50.7
9	Afghanistan	53.7
10	Zimbabwe	52.9

How do you govern a country where half of the population is children and adolescents? How do you grow the economy to put food in the mouths of these millions of young children? Turns out, in many cases you don't. Let's look at the relationship between age structure and civil unrest in more detail.

• ● •

On December 17, 2010, 26-year-old Mohamed Bouazizi marched to a gas station in the city of Sidi Bouzid, in central Tunisia. He filled a can and lugged it to the street in front of a government building. There, he crossed to the middle of traffic and doused himself with the gasoline. As he lit a match and set his body on fire he shouted, "How do you expect me to make a living!?"

Presumably, his question was directed at the municipal officials inside the building, who, earlier that day, had confiscated the scales Bouazizi used to peddle fruits and vegetables from his cart. He complained and in return was slapped across the face by a female officer, adding insult to injury. But that day's troubles were merely the latest in a string of similar affronts. He figured he'd have to bribe the officials to get his scales back, yet again, and he didn't have the money. As the eldest son, Bouazizi needed to help support his large family, and because there were no steady jobs, the produce cart was his only option. Now, he was out of business.

With burns that covered 90 percent of his body, Bouazizi lingered in the hospital until he died on January 4, 2011. His act of self-immolation inspired an uprising that just 10 days later forced Tunisian president Zine el-Abedine Ben Ali to step down and flee the country, ending his 23-year authoritarian reign. Some argue that Bouazizi's death was the spark that ignited the wave of revolution that swept across the Middle East and became known as the Arab Spring. But if his death was the spark, the region's population trends were fodder for the flame.

Bouazizi was part of one of the largest age cohorts in Tunisia— those aged 26 to 30 years (as shown in Figure 11). While his dramatic suicide has become historic, his situation was not unique. Because of Tunisia's youth bulge, competition for scarce jobs among that age group was fiercer than for any other recent generation. In sharp contrast to their fathers, it's unlikely that many of Bouazizi's friends had steady jobs, were married, or had been able to start families of their own. They were tired of being harassed daily by the police and other officials and resentful that corrupt politicians didn't listen to their concerns.

At the time, there were about 64 million other young men just like Bouazizi in the region, and it was no surprise to political demographers that protests and violence spread across borders and engulfed their homelands. In one study, Henrik Urdal found that in countries where youth are 35 percent or more of the total population, the risk of armed conflict was 150 percent higher than in countries with age structures more like those of developed states. Alone, population trends don't start a revolution, but in the case of the Arab Spring, the region's population

FIGURE 11. Tunisia's Population in 2011

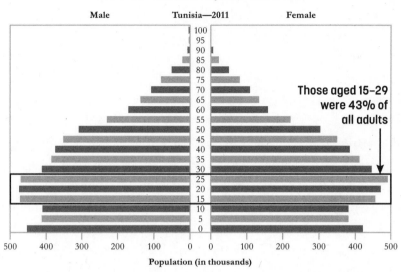

dynamics multiplied underlying social, economic, and political issues and set the stage for conflict.

Youthful age structures—those with classic "pyramid" shapes and large cohorts of children and adolescents—bring their own set of challenges, as we have seen, but children rarely take to the streets in protest. It's those who are emerging into adulthood and find their prospects for success limited or expectations unmet who speak out. That's why youth *bulge* age structures draw so much attention from researchers. In a country with a true youth bulge, such as Tunisia in 2011, the cohorts younger and older than the youth are smaller, as we see in Figure 11. The bars to focus on are those young adults aged 15 to 29, who are becoming politically, economically, and socially active. That age group remains interesting for our analysis even when there's no actual youth bulge, as in a *youthful* age structure. When the cohort of youth is large, especially when it is larger than the preceding cohort, we are more likely to find both motive and opportunity for civil unrest. Think about it this way: If every year the number of new entrants to the workforce grows, creation of new jobs will have to keep pace or unemployment will sky-rocket. And if youth cannot find jobs and aren't in education, what is there to occupy their time?

Two concepts emerge as important from Tunisia's experience: relative deprivation and opportunity cost. Tunisia's youth were doing relatively worse than the generation prior, meaning their expectations for how life should go were unmet—they had motive to rebel. But we know from television crime dramas that motive is only half the story, opportunity is the other. In Tunisia, labor was abundant, but jobs were scarce, so the opportunity cost of taking up arms in revolution was low. We can see how the combination of motive and opportunity interacts with demographic age structure across time and place. In fact, three-quarters of a century earlier, similar dynamics played out in dramatic fashion, albeit in a very different setting.

• ● •

After World War I, young adults were the largest proportion of Germany's population, with increasing numbers looking to enter the labor force each year, as the bulge in Figure 12 clearly shows. Without jobs or hope for the future, those young adults searched for any radical promise to deliver them. The demographic age structure for political violence was in place, and they had both motive and opportunity. In 1930, in the midst of this depression, more than 18 percent of voters cast a ballot for the Nazi Party, which celebrated victory with 107 seats in the German Reichstag, making it the second largest party in the country. Hitler had promised to restore the glory of Germany, a message that resonated across the population but was particularly appealing to youth with few prospects for the future. It was a perfect demographic storm: peak workers and a depressed economy. In this case, youth didn't need to work against the state to achieve change like they did in Tunisia—the state itself promised change. There was low opportunity cost of working against the status quo, so they cast their lot with Hitler and his promises to bring about a better future.

FIGURE 12. German Reich Population in 1925

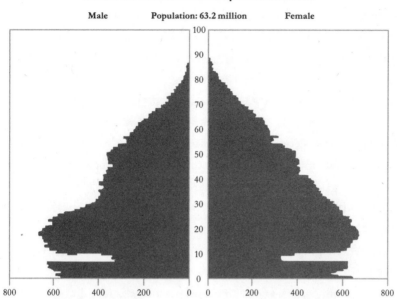

Male   Population: 63.2 million   Female

Population (in thousands)   Age Group   Population (in thousands)

There are other historical examples where youth played a pivotal role in regime change. We'll return to the case of Iran one last time in this chapter, as we can even view the famous 1979 Iranian Revolution through a demographic lens. You see, in 1975, just 4 years before the revolution, youth aged 15 to 24 numbered 6.6 million and were 37.7 percent of the adult population aged 15 to 64 (for comparison, that same age group was 16 percent of Taiwan's adult population in 2020). Although there were massive numbers of new entrants to the labor force every year, Shah Mohammad Reza Pahlavi was failing to invest in labor-intensive industries that would employ all of those young people and was focusing instead on capital-intensive industries, leaving millions unemployed. The shah redistributed land to peasants, but the plots were too small to be useful, and as rural fertility was high, individuals had less and less of an opportunity to make a living. It was simple math and a classic problem: The size of the land was staying the same, but the number of people who wanted a piece of it was growing. Researcher Eric Hooglund's 1977 fieldwork showed 65 to 90 percent of rural young men left for urban areas, except those resident in villages close enough to commute to the city. Most migrated by the age of 15 or 16. With new entrants to the labor market increasing annually, by 1979 those aged 15 to 19 were growing by 3 percent a year. At the same time, under the shah, 25 percent of Iran's income was being spent on arms, rather than on building the economy. The demographic pressures of a large, urban youth population, combined with an inability to employ them, led to mounting grievances. By 1979, protests had turned to violence, and violence had turned to revolution. The shah was out, and Grand Ayatollah Ruhollah Khomeini officially became supreme leader that December. Again, demographic structure, plus motive, plus opportunity equaled political violence.

Economic motivations aren't always the driver behind youth protest or rebellion. Quite often, feelings of political exclusion, of being ignored by older generations in power and wanting to change the status quo, prompt massive youth movements. Indeed, World War I was started by an assassin who had just finished high school. Gavrilo Princip, part of the revolutionary Young Bosnians, wanted to force a distant Serbian bourgeoisie to take action against the Austrians and win independence.

These are all examples involving violence, but violent revolt isn't the only possible outcome when youth feel excluded. Sometimes they're able to work through existing structures and push for change without taking up arms. For example, many times and places in history, youth have successfully pressured the government to lower the voting age. In the 1960s United States, young men ages 18 to 21 were being drafted into the Vietnam War and dying by the thousands—old enough to fight, but not old enough to vote, they argued. That, plus general feelings of alienation and rage against the status quo with regard to gender, race, and ideology, led activists to demand Congress lower the voting age from 21 to 18, which they did in

1971. In May 2018, Nigerian youth succeeded in getting their president to lower the minimum age for the presidency from 40 to 35 years and the age to serve in the Nigerian House of Representatives from 30 to 25. Given that the country's median age is a mere 18 years old, these changes enfranchised a significant proportion of the Nigerian population. The campaign's slogan was "Not Too Young to Run!" Youth also played an important role in the peaceful revolutions of Ukraine, Georgia, and Serbia in the early 2000s.

We're already thinking like social scientists here with the idea of motive and opportunity. In none of these cases did demographic age structure alone lead to protest or revolution. To deepen our understanding of the role of context, we can add in another social science concept: political institutions, or those organizations and structures that mediate and articulate the interests of a population. These include voting rules or access to decision makers. The same demographic structure can have very different effects depending on a setting's political institutions. As political scientist Graeme B. Robertson describes, even if a population is aggrieved, if its members have access to institutions there's little incentive to protest. If you can get your concerns heard by decision makers, you don't have to take to the streets. In authoritarian states, where leaders have less direct accountability, protest tends to be isolated, direct action; in democracies, it takes on a more symbolic form. As Robertson argues, "In the middle, however, where there is some access, there are substantial incentives to invest in protest both to influence specific decisions and to expand access. Hence middle levels of openness are associated with the highest levels of protest. The analogy to regime types goes as follows: We might expect low levels of protest in authoritarian regimes and higher levels in democracies, but we should see the highest levels in hybrids, where there is some access to political institutions but much remaining frustration with institutionalized politics." To add in the demographic element, we should see the highest level of protest in middle-open regimes with youth-bulge populations. If you're looking for a signpost for coming conflicts, that's a great place to start.

• ⦿ •

Although some youth grow up in a context of privilege and others in poverty, some experiences of youth are universal, and it's useful to take a moment and consider youth issues from a life-cycle perspective. Markers of adulthood are relatively similar across countries: people look to find meaningful jobs, establish their own households and families independent of their parents, and have some say in how they are governed. When youth find their opportunities in any of these three areas narrowed or even closed off, it comes to light in political, economic, or social changes. Singapore, for example, although one of the wealthiest countries on the planet, has tight restrictions on housing, and youth I spoke to there during fieldwork several years ago lamented time and again how they were unable to afford to move out of their parents' homes. Dating, they said, was awkward in such a context. No wonder Singapore's median age at first marriage for males is 30.2 and for females is 28.5. And no wonder its fertility rate is just 1.21.

A generational view is useful, too. That change in voting age in the United States grew out of the anti-war and civil rights demonstrations of youth throughout the 1960s, but America was far from the only country that experienced such change at the same time. In 1968, French university students famously protested and demonstrated for changes to the university system, which they felt was rigid and inadequate and unable to meet the increased demand from successively larger university-aged cohorts. In the 10 years prior, France's university student population grew from 170,000 to more than half a million; Paris alone contained 130,000 students. Young workers, unemployed workers, workers from coal mines, public transport systems, gas and electrical plants, ship-yards, the postal service, and even civil servants from several ministries, such as the ministry of finance, joined the cause. More than 2 million workers were on strike during the weekend of May 18 and 19; within 4 days, this number increased to 9 million. That same year, Soviet tanks rolled into Prague and crushed the student resistance, which started as protest against poor heat and lighting in the dormitories but turned into an indictment against the political status quo. The year 1968 shows the importance of both stage of life and time in history for producing massive political effects. There were a lot of youth from those post-war baby booms, but there was a lot more happening, too. As author Mark Kurlansky describes, "What was unique about 1968 was that people were rebelling over disparate issues and had in common only that desire to rebel, ideas about how to do it, a sense of alienation from the established order, and a profound distaste for authoritarianism in any form." He goes on to name four factors that worked together to create a perfect storm for the global unrest of 1968: the diffusion of the civil rights movement, the universally despised Vietnam War, and the advent of television. The fourth factor was more demographic: "a generation that felt so different and so alienated that it rejected all forms of authority." In some countries it was also larger. As Figure 13 shows, the US baby boomers were entering adulthood in greater numbers every year.

As we consider the role of youth and youthful age structures today, we can employ some of our political science theories about political insti-

FIGURE 13. US Population in 1968

Male	Age Group	Female
	100+	
	95–99	
0.1%	90–94	0.1%
0.2%	85–89	0.3%
0.4%	80–84	0.7%
0.8%	75–79	1.1%
1.1%	70–74	1.5%
1.6%	65–69	1.9%
2.0%	60–64	2.3%
2.4%	55–59	2.6%
2.7%	50–54	2.8%
3.0%	45–49	3.0%
3.0%	40–44	3.1%
2.9%	35–39	2.8%
2.9%	30–34	2.8%
3.2%	25–29	3.1%
3.8%	20–24	3.9%
4.6%	15–19	4.5%
5.1%	10–14	4.9%
5.2%	5–9	4.9%
4.6%	0–4	4.4%

Percentage — Age Group — Percentage

tutions. Although protest and political involvement are part of the democratic process, countries with high proportions of youth relative to other age groups have a slim chance of being democratic. Measuring youth risk factor (YRF) as the proportion of 17- to 26-year-olds in the total labor force, Noah Bricker and Mark Foley found that Syria, Egypt, and Tunisia all had a high YRF at the time of the Arab Spring, with Syria's the highest. Tunisia's risk of conflict has declined, as the cohorts entering working ages since the Arab Spring are actually smaller than the preceding ones; Syria's risk of conflict, on the other hand, increases because each successive cohort to enter working ages is larger than the preceding one.

As states age out of youthful age structures, their chances of being democratic grows. According to research by Richard Cincotta, a country with a young age structure has half a chance (literally, 50 percent) of being rated a liberal democracy after its young-adult proportion drops to about 0.40—that's roughly equivalent to a median age of 29.5 years. According to Cincotta's research, at or below a median age of 25 years, few of the states that are rated as free by Freedom House retain that status for more than a decade. At a median age of 15 years, only about 8 percent of states have a chance of being rated free; those with a median age of more than 25 years have just over a 30 percent chance; by a median age of 35 years, the chance rises to 75 percent; and those few countries that have achieved a median age of 45 years have a 90 percent chance.

As you may have realized, there are exceptions—a rising median age doesn't mean a natural transition to democracy. Some exceptions are to very young countries that have maintained a rating of free even beyond a decade: these include Mali (12 years), Benin (27), and Ghana—which is still going after 20 years. Exceptions also include those states that retain elements of autocracy even as their populations age. Cincotta and his colleague John Doces have found that "a dissipating youth bulge appears to strengthen the hand of democrats only in states ruled by military 'caretaker' regimes, weak personal dictatorships, or partial democracies. The most noncompetitive autocracies—single-party autocracies (for example, China and North Korea) and strong personal dictatorships (Russia, Singapore, Cuba)—seem, so far, to be virtually impervious to the effect." Although more research on the relationship between age structure and regime type is necessary, we can conclude with moderate confidence that we will see a greater variety of regime types in states with middle-aged and older age structures over the next several decades.

Yet, the number of countries with median ages of 25 years or younger in this category is shrinking, from 78 in 2015 to 50 by 2035. Notably, Pakistan, Egypt, Jordan, Syria, Haiti, and South Africa will age out of this category in the next 15 years, if the fertility of their populations continues to decline. Despite these declines, Pakistan's population will increase 39 percent by 2035, Egypt's by 37 percent, and Haiti's by 27 percent—these states are experiencing something called population momentum, or growth that continues because childbearing cohorts are large, even if overall fertility is declining. Although some of these states could begin to secure peace and achieve governance gains as Tunisia has (which has an intermediate age structure), democratic transitions, even in states with declining youth ratios, are rarely peaceful or rapid.

• • •

Viewed through one lens, youth are troublemakers, instigators of conflict who push for radical change that obliterates the status quo. Viewed through another, youth are liberators, the driving force behind civil rights and democratization. Where you stand depends on where you sit. If you're part of the establishment that sets the status quo, the youth are like an army of ants that need to be squashed. But, if you are part of the oppressed or disenfranchised of society, youth are more like saviors, sent to lead society to a better future. Reading the literature, one could conclude that youth, especially young men, are a danger to society. But framing one entire demographic segment as problematic seems misguided because it closes out conversation on the positive contribution a plethora of young men can make in a society. The logical policy goal, then, would be to focus on opportunities for young men—jobs, mainly. Sometimes, demography can be used as an excuse when inaction is really to blame. Leaders such as France's Emmanuel Macron and former Microsoft CEO Bill Gates have noted the link between Africa's high population growth and the continent's poverty and emigration rates. Yet critiques of this view offer that "the youth bulge theory is a convenient explanation for high unemployment or social conflict for Western actors and their authoritarian partner regimes as it puts the blame for these problems on demographics rather than decades of failing economic policies." Instead of blaming youth, the focus should be on factors such as corruption, inefficient institutions, and weak rule of law. Those issues, hallmarks of poor governance, mean that many countries in Africa have an unfavorable climate for business investment and are not moving forward in that regard. Reframing the youth bulge in overly rosy terms is also problematic. In Africa, there has been a continent-wide effort to reframe the youth bulge as the demographic dividend, as we will see in Chapter 6, and focus on the positive contributions youth can make to building Africa's economy. The impetus has been: Work with what you've got. Some scholars have argued that this reframing can lead to an unrealistic view of the youth bulge, distracting from a focus on much-needed family-planning efforts, as we will discuss later.

The transition to adulthood can be rough no matter the context because youth, even in states with older age structures, are generally seeking independence but don't have the opportunity to achieve it, and therefore experience and express more discontent than other age groups in society. Thus, even the lives of youth in wealthy countries are shaped by economic and political opportunities—or lack thereof. What happens after countries pass through the demographic transition and youth are far outnumbered by older persons? How different are the political, economic, and social dynamics? To see the future youthful countries are headed toward as their fertility declines, we now turn to the other end of the spectrum: low fertility, older populations, and older persons.

CHAPTER 2

Gray Dawn

In his sci-fi short story "Tomorrow and Tomorrow and Tomorrow," Kurt Vonnegut describes a world in which life expectancy has been extended to the point that six generations of a family live together under one roof. At a youthful 93 years, Em constantly complains that her 172-year-old father-in-law still rules the roost. He takes the only private room in the house, the best chair and food, and—the foulest injustice—he even controls the television remote.

Published in 1953, Vonnegut's story articulates his generation's fears of the political power that might accompany increased life expectancy alongside a post-war baby boom. It's the ultimate tale of generational warfare, with the young resentful that older generations are hoarding all the money, jobs, and votes. In the decades since Vonnegut wrote, such angst about demographic change translating into political power has only intensified, as we always fear what we do not understand. And humanity's newest and least understood population trend is most definitely population aging.

But from the perspective of a political demographer, population aging is cause for celebration. Japan's record-setting median age today—48.4 years—is higher than *life expectancy* was in much of the world just a century ago. According to the United Nations, in 2020 13.5 percent of the world's population, more than 1 billion people, was aged 60 and over—that group is growing at about 3 percent a year. Advances in medicine have all but guaranteed those in the post-industrial world will reach an age marked by silver hair and wrinkles (and likely hip replacements and adult diapers). Low fertility—although it follows from progress in combating infant mortality—has reshaped social structures and shifted the center of gravity of populations across the developed world to older ages. This "center of gravity" phrasing is important. When we talk about population aging, we mean just that: the aging of the population as a whole. Of course, individual aging is relevant in a discussion of why population aging matters, but through-out history at least some individuals have always made it to old age. And technically, as soon as a society starts going through the demographic transition, the population is "aging." That type of aging is common, but the truly new dynamic is the sharp increase in the median age of the entire population such that now there are fewer kids and many more seniors.

The phenomenon has spread rapidly. In 1950 the median age of developed countries was 29 years, and only three countries with popula-tions over 1 million had median ages that reached 35. Across the world, populations were young and growing, and it wasn't until the 1990s that median ages over 35 became more common, but even then, aging states were geographically limited to Europe and Japan. By the turn of the twenty-first century, North America had joined this first wave, bring-ing the total number of maturing countries to 32, and Germany, Italy, and Japan became the first countries ever to achieve a median age of 40 years. That's right around the time I started studying population aging, and it was tough to draw reliable conclusions from such a small sample size, as any social scientist will know. Yet, many did. According to most researchers and journalists tracking the developing trend, population aging was going to halt economic growth, make innovation impossible, and lead to a political takeover by old people—exactly what Vonnegut had imagined.

Those early predictions still form the basis of reporting on population aging today, but mature age structures are no longer new and no longer confined to the first wave. During the past several years, such age structures have become the norm for post-industrial countries. In 2020, the median age of developed countries was 42 years, and by 2035 it will have reached 45. In 2020, 38 countries had a median age of at least 40 years. Aging has intensified across Europe, North America, and Asia. Japan is no longer the only Asian country in this set; China, South Korea, and Singapore have all followed suit in a second wave. Not only is the club growing older and growing in number, it is also growing more diverse. More regions will soon join the ranks of the second wave. By 2035, the countries that will cross the threshold to median ages above 35 years include Iran, Tunisia, and North Korea. Brazil has just recently joined the club. By 2035, most states in Eastern and Western Europe and East Asia will have median ages above *45 years*, a group that includes China, Thailand, and even Cuba. This new wave introduces a host of new variables and will likely throw into question anything we think we know so far about the implications of population aging.

States in the first wave had a slow demographic transition, with gradual declines in both fertility and mortality. The pace of aging is much faster among the second wave, partly because the mortality transition has been much faster. In some cases that's because the West exported public-health knowledge and funding that accelerated aging. Others in the second wave had effective homegrown public-health campaigns, such as China and Iran, that led to rapid aging. In the period 1965–1970, China's TFR was 6.3; China reached replacement-level fertility in the period 1990–1995, and by 2015 its working-age population had already peaked.

In South Korea, aging has been fast and intense, with noticeable strains on social systems. South Korean pensions are just 6 percent of the average wage, one of the weakest pension systems in Asia. The population is demanding that the state support seniors, but thus far this movement hasn't garnered enough political clout to change things. And seniors are suffering for it. According to the OECD, the poverty rate of South Koreans over age 65 in 2015 was 45.7 percent—the highest in the OECD and far higher than Japan's, which was only 19.6 percent. The oldest South Koreans have suicide rates more than three times as high as the national average. As an article in the *Nikkei Asian Review* reports, "The generation of South Koreans now between the ages of 60 and 80 is the last one that supported parents financially and, broadly speaking, it is the first to go without such support."

Remember, population aging is driven by a combination of low fertility and long life expectancy. Before we go further, it's useful to dig into what we really mean when we say "low fertility."

Demographers coined the term *second demographic transition* to describe super-low fertility (below replacement level) and the postponement of marriage that seems to go along with it in an increasing number of countries around the world. What the theory is trying to describe is what happens when women decide to wait to have kids? Decide to have only one or two? Or maybe decide against having children altogether? Postponing having kids can have huge consequences, not only for individuals but also on a grander scale, which is why many governments around the world offer incentives such as tax breaks for parents or paid maternity leave.

This is not the same as the "later" part of the later, longer, fewer campaign discussed in Chapter 1. That was about postponing a woman's first birth until she's past her teenage years. With the second demographic transition, we're talking first births *way* later than that. The celebrity news (which I admittedly read during frequent periods of procrastination) is filled with stories of celebrities who give birth for the first time after age 40, such as Mariah Carey, Janet Jackson, and Nicole

Kidman. A much greater number give birth for the first time after age 35, including Jennifer Lopez and Gwen Stefani. Are these celebrities outliers or are other women really waiting that long to start having kids?

Turns out that yes, they're waiting. Let's take the United Kingdom as an example. In the late 1960s, the average British woman had her first baby at about 23 years old, but her contemporary waits until 29. That increase is typical. Women in all wealthy countries are having their first babies later and later, with South Korea highest at over 31 years. Among the developed countries of the OECD, the youngest average-age women have their first babies at 26 years—that's in the United States, Romania, Latvia, and Bulgaria.

Why does this matter? Remember, most demographers would argue that the older women are when they start having kids, the fewer they're likely to have during their lifetimes. It's an issue of opportunity—biologically, the longer a woman waits to get started, the shorter her childbearing years are, so she literally can't have as many as she could if she started very young. As we saw in Chapter 1, that's why some family-planning programs in poor countries, where women have five or six kids on average, will focus on keeping women in school and encouraging them to get married later, hoping to delay when women start having kids and reduce those "active" reproductive years.

The situation is different in wealthy countries. These women are starting later and having fewer kids overall, but they don't really want many to begin with, and there are actually national-level effects.

As we've seen, couples in wealthy countries are not having enough babies to even replace generations that are dying off. We don't actually know how many children women my age—40—will end up having in their lifetimes, because technically we're not done with our reproductive years; anything for my cohort is just a projection. But we can get actual numbers for women slightly older. So, how many babies did women born in 1974 have, on average? In Italy, Spain, and Japan they had just 1.4 children each. In Germany and Russia they had only 1.6, but in Australia, France, the United Kingdom, and the United States they had close to replacement level. Recently, though, even the United States seems to have joined the sub-replacement fertility club. Births in the United States are now at their lowest since 1979, and with a TFR of 1.63, the United States has its lowest fertility rate ever.

Looking only at TFR can mask differences among generations because it includes women of a 30-year age span who are likely to have different reproductive patterns, shaped by their time in history. That's what demographers have found in many Western European countries. TFR can also mask differences when fertility is low because a few women are having many children while others remain childless, bringing the average to somewhere in the middle. But an average doesn't tell us much about the range of choices women are making. In Italy, England, and the Netherlands, childlessness is fairly common, but in Russia, only 6 percent of women in the 2010 census who had completed their child-bearing years had no biological children.

Postponement and childlessness are not the cause of low fertility across the board. In Russia, the average age at first birth is lower than in much of Europe, but fewer women are having second, third, or higher-order births—a one-child family is the norm, with almost 68 percent of families falling into this category in 2010. What's interesting is that when surveyed, most Russians claim that a two-child family is ideal. The Russian government has taken this claim as a call to action and has tried policies such as financial incentives to narrow the gap between the number of children Russian women say is ideal and the number they actually have.

That women in wealthier countries have been going to college in ever greater numbers and finding success in careers outside the home is one reason we see a societal-level shift to postponing childbearing. I've seen this (and resemble this) firsthand. At my 15th college reunion there were pregnant women, nursing women, and women who were just starting to consider having babies (I went to a women's college). After graduation, these women were busy finishing graduate degrees, starting careers, traveling, and just living their lives. Not many had children right away.

But education and career aren't the only reasons women wait to start having kids. There've been changes in other rites of passage as well; namely, marriage. My college classmates and I waited to have kids, but we didn't necessarily wait to get married. I was just one month past my 23rd birthday when I tied the knot, and I was the last of our roommate foursome to get married. We are outliers: The average age of first marriage in the United States is 28 for women and 30.5 for men—that's 8 and 7 years higher, respectively, than it was in 1960. As author Rebecca Traister reports in her book *All the Single Ladies*, in 2009 there were more single women than married women in the United States for the first time.

These things are related, of course. Some women—and men—are more focused on education and early career building than on marrying. Some women don't want to wait to have kids until they find a partner, and finding one is not always easy. And some women are shunning marriage altogether.

• • •

One of my prized possessions is a 1967 *Teen Guide to Homemaking* textbook, found years ago in a successful dig through the thrift store shelves. On the cover is the side profile of a sweet strawberry blonde with a pink bow in her bobbed hair. Inside, girls and boys learn the basics of ironing and good nutrition—including plenty of then-in-vogue canned food. In the section on career advice, the authors explain that boys and girls might have different goals when it comes to a career. They say that a girl "can be pretty sure that she will have to know how to be a homemaker and mother," and so her career outside the home likely won't be as important as it would be to a boy.

The world teens live in today is radically different from the world in 1967 when the Susans and Tommys of America were reading the *Teen Guide to Homemaking*, but has the gender revolution completely freed women from those societal constraints? Is the struggle over?

Sociologist Arlie Hochschild tried to answer those very questions. She studied married women working full-time, with husbands who were also working full-time and who had kids ages 6 and under; in other words, me when I was writing the first draft of this book.* She watched them come home from work, fold laundry while on the phone, give the kids baths, and so on. She chronicled her observations in her book *The Second Shift*, in which she argued that although there had been a lot of changes in gender roles across the decades, there were still larger societal issues making some women question whether getting married and having kids was worth it. Working both a first shift outside the home and a second shift inside it was exhausting.

Multiple pressures on women is a global issue. Researchers Mary Brinton and Dong-Ju Lee find that post-industrial societies that encourage women to work outside the home while also painting them as natural caregivers have lower fertility because they impose conflicting narratives on women. We can see this difficult dynamic in East Asia. In much of East Asia, it's the norm that men are breadwinners and women are responsible for household and child-rearing duties, but women are also welcome to work. With this gender-role ideology, women struggle to reconcile work outside the home and family responsibilities. As a result, they often have only one or two children or forgo childbearing altogether. In low-fertility Japan, a 2009 survey by the East-West Center showed that Japanese wives of reproductive age did 27 hours a week of household duties while their husbands only did 3—and most of those wives worked a paid job, too. Having a family continues to be incompatible with work for Japanese women. An OECD study of 18 member countries ranked Japan second from last "in terms of coverage and

• • •

* The second draft was during the pandemic quarantine with said kids home. Fun!

strength of policies for work-family reconciliation and family-friendly work arrangements, pointing out that Japan's childcare coverage and parental leave offered by employers are both especially weak." Similarly, many South Koreans cannot afford to get married, and reticence about having children is in large part driven by high educational costs.

In contrast, when women are discouraged from working, their role as homemakers and mothers is clearer, and fertility is higher. But there are still insecurities that affect fertility: In traditional societies where men are expected to be the breadwinners and have secure employment before starting a family, fertility is lower when jobs are scarce. We've observed this in recent decades in Italy, Poland, and Slovakia. As we see, it's the interaction between gender norms and labor-market conditions that affects fertility, not just one or the other. Fertility is actually lower in countries where men and women have equal roles, because these norms lock women into a particular lifestyle rather than give them a range of socially acceptable choices about how to combine work and family. Countries that have more flexible arrangements, rather than strict equality, have higher fertility, as we see in Finland, the Netherlands, New Zealand, the United Kingdom, and the United States. The conclusion should not be that we need to restrict women from working in order to raise fertility. Rather, that finding ways to reduce the pressures on women and share household tasks can be an effective way to support women who do want children. In contrast to Finland and other states with flexible arrangements, we see astoundingly low fertility, below 1 child per woman on average, in South Korea, which has the highest gender pay gap among its OECD peers. Another reason for postponing may be worries about financial stability. Economic fortunes for today's reproductive-age women aren't always great. In South Korea, the unemployment rate for 15- to 29-year-olds was 9.5 percent in 2018, the same year that TFR hit a record low of 0.98.

This pattern could happen elsewhere. In the United States, women held more payroll jobs than men in early 2020 for the first time ever, but the quality and wages of those jobs were low, too low to support a family, particularly for the working class. And the record employment didn't last long. COVID-19 lockdowns, beginning in February 2020 and intensifying in March, had a dramatic impact on women in the US workforce. With children home from school and childcare centers closed, some women felt they had little choice but to step away from the workforce. Women disproportionately held jobs in the leisure and hospitality sectors before COVID-19 started, and those industries were hit hardest during quarantine. As a result, from February 2020 to January 2021, almost 2.1 million US women left the labor force, defined as no longer looking for employment and thus outside of official unemployment statistics. Women of color were hit particularly hard. The National Women's Law Center reports that 9.1 percent of Latinas aged 20 and older were unemployed in December 2020, almost 1 percent higher than the previous month and 1.7 times higher than their unemployment rate before quarantine, 4.9 percent in February 2020. This gap could end up further depressing fertility in the United States.

If gender roles at home are part of the problem, why don't women just bypass marriage and have babies anyway? In some countries, they do. Among OECD countries, the percentage of births that take place outside of marriage increased from 7.2 percent in 1970 to just under 40 percent by 2016.* That average conceals that in some wealthy countries there's a huge stigma against out-of-wedlock births, so women aren't having them—in Japan and Korea, only 2 to 3 percent of births happen outside of marriage. This stigma also explains why fertility is so low in predominantly Catholic or Orthodox countries, such as Italy, Poland, and Greece. In places where there is a stigma, if women don't want to get married, they're also not going to have kids.

Of course, this stigma isn't present everywhere. In many countries, couples live together without formally marrying, particularly in Central

• • •

* Among the 30 OECD countries for which data were available.

and South America. In Chile and Iceland, around two-thirds of children are born outside marriage. In many other countries, such as Belgium, Denmark, France, Mexico, and Sweden, more than half of all births are to mothers not legally married. Births out of wedlock are on the rise globally. In the United States, only 10 percent of births were outside of wedlock in 1970, but today 40 percent of all births are. In Europe the proportion is even higher—60 percent in France alone.

Postponement of marriage, stigmas against births out of wedlock, and postponing getting pregnant in general clearly affect individual lives. And when we aggregate these individual decisions, they add up to changes at the societal level in the form of decreasing fertility rates.

There's an elephant in the room with all this talk of having babies at older ages: infertility. Is it that women in wealthy countries don't want to have at least two kids or is that they can't? According to Elizabeth Katkin, author of the book *Conceivability: What I Learned Exploring the Frontiers of Fertility*, the "plan" part of family planning can fall apart when women postpone their childbearing. In her book she describes going through seven miscarriages, eight fresh in vitro cycles, two frozen IVF attempts, five natural pregnancies, and four IVF pregnancies across 9 years and to the tune of $200,000. Her personal journey led her to become an expert on infertility causes in general. As Katkin found through her research and experience, age isn't the end-all-be-all, but it does affect women's chances of having the number of children they desire, if for no other reason than that those who are destined to struggle conceiving run out of time to figure out what the problem is.

Demographers think we've seen a permanent shift in marriage and fertility patterns. Intense events such as the economic recession of 2008–2013 and the COVID-19 pandemic starting in 2020 strongly affect fertility patterns. The effect is not unidirectional. As with other times of crisis, COVID-19 is most likely to affect the timing of births for most women rather than the total number they have in their lifetimes— that's the postponement of fertility part. But while some women who delay childbearing because of COVID-19 but still end up having the same number of babies overall, other women will end up with fewer children overall.

One immediate consequence of the shift to super-low fertility: In some countries, the population is not only growing older, it's shrinking. Germany's population began to decline in 2005 and Japan's in 2010—these countries are trendsetters. According to United Nations data, between 2015 and 2020, Japan's overall population shrank by 1.5 million people—by 2035 it will have shrunk by a further 9.3 million. Japan's National Institute of Population and Social Security Research projects the country will shrink to 88 million by 2065—a drop of 39 million from 2015—that's the equivalent of the populations of Chile and Mali combined. At that time, elders aged 65 years and over will compose a record-breaking 40 percent of the overall population. It's a small world after all.

While globally, total population is still on the rise because so many countries still have young and rapidly growing populations, the United Nations projects that by the end of this century, 70 percent of developed countries and 65 percent of less developed countries will have shrinking populations. If we take a long look at history, we can see that populations have declined before. For example, from the 1840s to the 1950s, Ireland's population declined as a result of the Great Famine, which killed 1 million and forced many more to move abroad in search of a better life. But Ireland's case, and those like it from infectious diseases or emigration, tells us little about what we're seeing today, which are the first population declines resulting from a fundamental shift in age structure driven by low fertility and mortality. And they seem irreversible. Past population declines caused by diseases, wars, and famines were remedied by improved public health and technology (war being the exception), but today's decline is *caused* in part by improved public health, thanks to longer lives and smaller families. Because women are better able to control their childbearing, both men and women are choosing to have fewer children.

While a shrinking population is not inherently bad, none of our economic theories were developed under such conditions, and we are intellectually unprepared to understand this shift. For example, two key markers of economic health are high consumption and positive GDP growth, but do we need GDP growth rates of 2 to 3 percent when the overall population is declining by that percentage? This population shift should be forcing economists and policy makers into that conversation, but on the whole such fundamental questions are absent from public and academic discourse.

We saw in Chapter 1 how societies with very young populations often face tremendous instability and significant challenges creating jobs, governing, and fostering social harmony. But aged populations aren't problem-free. Kurt Vonnegut's predictions were extreme, but we can't deny that political power is in the grasp of the oldest generations, who vote and serve in political office around the world at rates that far outpace youth. The average age of French senators is a hoary 64 years old, and only 7 percent of them are under the age of 50; the 2020 US presidential election was a contest between a 74-year old and a 77-year old. Even if they aren't shrinking yet, wealthy countries are worrying about how to preserve economic growth in the face of declining work-forces. And aging isn't the only demographic shift for most developed countries: The arrival of immigrants has changed the ethnic (and religious and political) composition, particularly of younger generations, as historically majority groups decline. Societies across the West, in particular, are struggling to adjust to these relatively rapid demographic changes, and identity politics has seized the agenda.

But for all the challenges population aging brings, remember the positive side of this human evolution. Unsustainable consumption and population growth are choking the seas with plastic, clogging our rivers with chemicals, and filling the planet's atmosphere with greenhouse gases. In the long run, fewer wealthy consumers will likely be a net positive for Earth. Our reproductive patterns are evolving to reflect valuing quality of life over quantity of family members. If aging and shrinking populations are the inevitable result of humans finally feeling secure and satisfied with smaller families, then it seems imprudent to label that a tragedy, especially if we're simultaneously buying into a doomsday read on high population growth in poorer countries. It will take our world's best thinkers to grasp what this new reality means, but starting with the assumption that aging is fundamentally bad is misguided.

• ● •

Before we dig into the implications of aging, we first need a note on measurements. Technically, any country where fertility is falling and median age is rising is aging, but our focus in this chapter is on populations where those dynamics have been rolling for at least a few decades and which have already achieved higher median ages and shifting proportions of old and young.

The indicator often used for these shifting proportions is dependency ratio, particularly old-age dependency ratio, which measures the proportion of those age 65 and over to those of working ages, typically 15 to 64. These ratios are meant to capture the effect of population aging, implying that the proportions of those who "put in" to the economy (prime-age workers) are shrinking at the same time that the proportions of those who "take out" (seniors) are growing. For example, Europe reached a record-high old-age dependency ratio in 2018—now, 1 in 5 people are over age 65. In most interpretations, that means there are only 3 people working for every 1 person over 65. The ratio has been shrinking rapidly, as dozens upon dozens of stories in *The Economist* or *Financial Times* report. Twenty years ago there were 5 workers for every person over 65, and 10 years ago there were 4. As we often read, in most countries the ratios are moving toward only two workers per old-age dependent. But are they really?

Conceptually, dependency ratios are fraught with unsubstantiated assumptions. One problem is with the label "dependent"—in reality, not all persons over 65 are economically dependent, nor do they require care for their daily living, such as meal preparation, toileting, or even driving. In fact, some seniors actually provide services for younger generations, such as caring for grandchildren. What we call "dependency" ratio tells us about the various age proportions of a society, but not about their dependent status. For that, we have to look at the economic and cultural practices of individual societies.

A second issue is with the label "old." At what age is someone "old" anyway? It's impossible to pick an age and apply it around the world to meaningfully compare dependency ratios. In some societies, life expectancy is only 40 years old—an age I would enthusiastically argue is quite young. Like youth, old age is a cultural construction, and like all cultural constructions, its meaning can be and often is rebuilt.

There's probably no better example of reframing old age than the evolution of the powerful political lobbying group AARP, based in the United States. In 1998, the group made a radical shift, going from the full name American Association of Retired Persons to acronym only. As AARP realized more than 20 years ago, working lives are getting longer and more complicated in general, and the group would be better served by switching to a familiar acronym that now is divorced from any specific meaning. The group's influence partly comes from including anyone aged 50 and over as its constituents, and because so many of its members were still working, it needed to drop the word "retired" from its name.

As we see, we need more nuance to get an accurate picture of population aging, maybe even a new vocabulary to understand the revolutionary trend.

• • •

There's no clearer example of how unprecedented and unanticipated population aging has been than the mismatch between retirement age, often set decades ago, and life expectancy today.

FIGURE 14. Average Effective Retirement Age
Versus Normal Retirement Age, 2013–2018

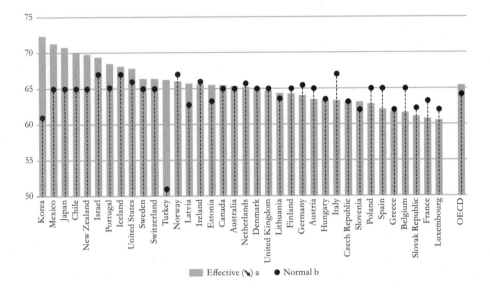

Effective (◣) a   ● Normal b

According to the actuarial tables used by the US Social Security Administration to calculate the probability that individuals at a certain age will die before their next birthday, I can expect to live 47 more years. If I make it to age 62, when I'm currently able to take partial social security benefits, I can expect to live an additional 26 years, and if I make it to age 67, when I'm eligible for full benefits, I'm expected to have more than 21 years of life left. That's quite a long gap between retirement and death, which is personally fine with me but in the aggregate spells trouble for the solvency of the US Social Security Administration.

The United States is far from the only country with this issue. German men today spend about 18 years in retirement.* In France, Belgium, Spain, and a host of other countries, the effective retirement age—the

• • •

* The effective retirement age for German men is 64 years, and the life expectancy at age 65 is just over 18 years.

age the average person actually retires—is several years lower than the normal age for receiving a full old-age pension, as Figure 14 shows.

But in South Korea, Mexico, Japan, Chile, and Israel, especially, men and women (although this chart shows only the men because they participate in the labor force in greater numbers) work well beyond pensionable age. That work culture encourages longer working lives (or that circumstances necessitate longer working lives) means these countries are better positioned to deal with the economic challenges of aging than are countries where pensionable age and effective retirement age are low, such as Germany. Timing of retirement is incredibly important, because in some countries people can claim partial retirement benefits at younger ages than they can full retirement benefits, and there are alternative ways to exit the labor force, such as through taking disability or unemployment. In Germany, about 56 percent of those retiring in 2014 did so early. Italian men can receive a full pension (what the OECD calls "normal" retirement age) at 67 years, but the average Italian man retires 5 years earlier. And in general, women retire 1 or 2 years earlier than men, even though women typically live longer. Across the OECD, effective retirement age was higher in the 1960s and 1970s when life expectancy was shorter than it is today, with the exception of only two countries: Japan and South Korea.

When Germany adopted a compulsory, work-related contributory scheme for old age in 1889, there's no way Germany's chancellor at the time, Otto von Bismarck, could have foreseen that in just 100 years his country's demographics would have flipped and the state's burden would be almost too heavy a load to bear. On the whole, these systems have done what they were intended to do: raise the living standards of the poorest elderly. In the United States, in the year prior to the passage of the Social Security Act, more than half of elderly Americans were unable to support themselves. Even the fiscally conservative Peter G. Peterson Foundation in the United States acknowledges that two-thirds of elderly Americans would be poor today without social security benefits. This point is important to remember when we discuss the global

spread of population aging—seniors in regions without dedicated benefits may not be so fortunate.

• • •

The tectonic shift in proportion of older versus younger caused by
population aging means that the cohorts exiting the labor force are
larger than the cohorts beginning their working lives—that's the case
for about half of the OECD countries. To soften the economic blow of
aging, then, what options do countries have?

Currently, there are just four options on the menu: increase immigration, raise retirement ages, cut benefits, or get more people already
in the country to work. To boost its workforce, some have estimated
that the European Union would need to either add 100 million immigrants (which is not going to happen) or raise retirement ages 10 years
by mid-century *and* increase labor-force participation. Raising retirement ages has been slow-going. In many cases, retirement ages were
set low at their inception, so efforts to increase them have been politically tough and only incremental. If set into law for the first time today,
they might be much higher, just like life expectancy is. Now, though,
it's considered a victory when the retirement age is raised by a measly
1 or 2 years. And there's always a fight. In France, where the official
retirement age is 62 years, a 2019 proposal by President Emmanuel
Macron to make 64 the age for full pension eligibility led to protests
throughout December that shut down transportation during the busy
holiday season. Out of the 34 OECD countries, between September
2015 and September 2017, only six countries changed their statu-
tory retirement ages, a third changed contribution levels, and a third
changed benefits for some or all retirees. On average, these reforms
will bring retirement to an OECD average of just under 66 years by
2060. It's a step, but the economic problem remains: On average across
the OECD, if someone makes it to age 65 today, they're expected to
live another 21 years. Cutting benefits, a proposal often packaged with

raising retirement age, is just as politically unpalatable. In 2017, 6,000 Brazilians took to the streets of Rio to protest then-president Michel Temer's proposal to overhaul pensions, including both a raise in retirement age and a cut to pension amounts.

The final option on the menu is getting people to work longer, or (re)incorporating people who are out of the workforce for various reasons: women, those underemployed due to mismatch between their skill sets and market needs, older persons. Different societies have different cultures of work, as the gap between when people are eligible to retire and when they actually retire shows. There's no one model for retirement in aging countries. Although in some countries people try to leave the workforce even before official retirement ages, the opposite has been true in Japan. For example, Japanese have fought for the right to continue working in old age, asking for—and receiving—removal of mandatory retirement and age discrimination. Japanese women and older Japanese have historically had low rates of labor-force participation, but Japanese women and men hold the world record for longest healthy lives: 75 and 72 years, respectively. As in many European states, Japan has worked to reduce barriers to older persons' participation in the workforce—and it has worked. This prime-age—a more accurate term—population (those aged 20 to 65) will shrink by 15 percent by 2035, but work practices are shifting, too. From 2000 to 2016, the employment rate of 55- to 64-year-olds increased by almost 10 percent, and almost 43 percent of those aged 65 to 69 were employed in 2016. "Flexible retirement," which might allow combining work with partial benefits or retiring early with reduced benefits, has thus far been unpopular among aging OECD states but holds promise for lessening entitlement payouts and boosting the economy through the workforce.

I'll underscore a previous point: The marker of success in our modern, global, capitalist economic system is growth. Is this still the right measure of success for a country with a shrinking population? All of our theories and calculations and indicators have been shaped around the goal of perpetual economic growth. As that's how we measure a country's economic health, no wonder we're collectively so scared of population aging. As someone who teaches environmental politics and has to daily tell young adults they're inheriting a world falling apart at the seams, I know it's worth considering alternative views of economic health and not simply unending growth.

And if you want to cling to the growth-at-all-costs framework, there may even be economic opportunities from population aging. Economists expect that consumption in these aged societies will increasingly shift toward services, especially health care, and away from consumer goods or capital-intensive goods such as homes. This shift means that economic growth in an aging state is still possible—pharmaceutical companies and others in the health industry will reap the benefits of increased spending. It also means that certain sectors of the economy may grow, while others will stagnate. The director of the Massachusetts Institute of Technology's Age Lab, Dr. Joseph Coughlin, argues that in developed countries, societies have come to see older people as seeking only leisure and needing only products that help them survive the decrepitude of old age, such as hearing and mobility aids. This homogeneous view has led to a vastly untapped segment of consumers, he argues, and is completely misguided, he says. Some industries, such as health care, can thrive from higher proportions of elderly in society. Where there are large numbers of children, there are opportunities to make cash from products aimed at children. The year Theodor Seuss Geisel—Dr. Seuss—published both *The Cat in the Hat* and *How the Grinch Stole Christmas* happened to be the peak of America's baby boom—amazing timing. Now that those boomers are older, there are opportunities to sell products and services to that large market. Given that the elderly tend to have some of the highest savings of any generation, products and services aimed at that group are potential areas for growth, too. Older people spend a lot of money: In the United States in 2015, people age 50 and above spent $5.6 trillion while those under age 50 spent $4.9 trillion.

As older people and their governments navigate how to meet the financial needs of both individuals and the state, something is bound to get caught in the crossfire. There's good reason to believe it will be the family. We know that politics is about who gets what, when, and where, and it's always about trade-offs. But what are the trade-offs in an aging society? Is education sacrificed for entitlements? Is military spending sacrificed for Medicare? In the face of fewer young workers to support growing numbers of elderly, who will bear the brunt of the sacrifice?

In part, the answer depends on the ways political systems amplify or dilute voices. If a society's "old" band together with one voice, leaders of democracies and authoritarian regimes alike may listen. But, are they really singing from the same sheet of music? While it's true that in democracies such as the United States and Japan, older voters show at the polls in far greater numbers than do younger voters, voter turnout gives an incomplete picture of the gray power. So far, age hasn't been a salient identity. I have yet to see a Gray Pride T-shirt (calling dibs on trademark), and there are at least three good reasons.

First, age is transitional, not permanent, meaning that each person passes through different ages; other divisions, such as social class or cultural identity, cut across age divisions. In one of my first political demography studies, I found that in the world's three oldest countries, Japan, Germany, and Italy, age had not emerged as a cohesive political identity as of 2008—it had been unable to supplant regional identity, for instance. A 16-year-old Bavarian had more in common, politically, with a 60-year-old Bavarian than with someone her own age living in northeastern Germany. We see plenty of diversity in political party preferences within age groups: Race, class, and even gender often matter much more than age. Second, issues of old age are important to all, as everyone anticipates being aged one day. Third, older people are not purely self-interested but also care about the support of other age groups, as the $179 billion that American grandparents spend annually on their grandchildren attests.

While the evidence that a politics of aging is arising at the polls is mixed, this is a rich area for future researchers to explore and one to keep an eye on.

• • •

Younger generations in developed countries worry that they will share less in the prosperity of their countries as increasing numbers of elderly demand more of the state's resources—and more from younger workers to pay for those entitlements. But on the flip side, many elderly worry that as family size shrinks, there will be too few young to care for them and society will cast them aside. Japan's elderly have made headlines for increasingly committing petty crimes, often to garner a spot in jail, where they will be taken care of, as many can no longer rely on the care of their children. According to a story in *BusinessInsider,* one out of every five Japanese prison inmates is a senior citizen, which by itself doesn't mean much because they could have aged in place. But, 90 percent of elderly women in prison got there by shoplifting—a great way to land in the slammer without hurting anyone. Japan's elderly inmates not only get their three square meals a day and room to rest their heads, they also get care for their special medical needs. Effectively, the jail becomes the nursing home.

With stories like this and other popular images of the elderly, one might think that all elderly are desperate for social security supplements and handouts from family. In truth, many older people are just as likely to share their resources with family members of other generations as they are to receive from them, as anyone who has benefited from grand-parent babysitting services knows. Transfers between generations are not unidirectional, nor are they single-faceted. They may take the form of time (service), co-residence, or financial transfers, which could mean monetary or material support. Older people also provide important intangible exchanges, such as emotional support, to younger genera-tions. In many ways, the young and old in society are set up for a symbiotic relationship. In the Netherlands, there's housing that mixes college students and seniors—two groups with relatively less money than those in the middle ages. This system works because the younger Dutch have more time for volunteering and helping out their elderly neighbors. In Italy, Milan's "Take Home a Student" project matches elderly in the most expensive city in the most aged country in Europe (tied with Germany) with university students. It helps both groups combat loneliness and deal with economic challenges. The project, run by MeglioMilano (Better Milan), has matched 600 pairs since 2004. Social expectations about care relationships between young and old differ radically around the world and within societies, often depending on whether someone is rich or poor, male or female. The burden—or benefit—is not equally spread. Yet, when we discuss aging, we often leave out these distinctions.

The elderly may be choosing to go to jail in Japan, but in Singapore it's the adult children who face penalty if they neglect their elders. The Maintenance of Parents Act of 1995 (and 2010 amendment) mandated that adult children have a legal responsibility to take care of their aging parents. In an academic study of Singapore and Taiwan, my colleague and I found that Singapore's policy was an attempt to institutionalize a system that encourages individuals, rather than the state, to shoulder the expenses of population aging. This "Confucian welfare state" model emphasizes society's responsibility, while Taiwan has gone from a similar system to a social welfare state more reminiscent of European countries as it has become increasingly democratic.

Certainly, there is no one model of family support among the countries around the world or even among those with similar cultures. Among Asian states, for example, care patterns vary greatly. In China, sons are still expected to care for their elderly parents; this expectation has made sons more valuable than daughters and was one driver of the high abortion rates of female fetuses during the tenure of the One-Child Policy. If a couple could only have one child, they'd need to ensure it was a son who could take care of them in old age. Likewise, in Singapore the elderly rely much more on their sons than on their daughters, but in the Philippines and Thailand there's no clear pattern of elderly relying on sons or daughters more than the other. In some countries the elderly may be more likely to receive transfers from daughters and in others from sons. Thus, when we study population aging, we need to be aware that adaptations can't be one-size-fits-all.

I commonly hear two bold assertions about the implications of population aging. One concerns China: When I give talks in policy circles, the audience typically argues that China's government will *have to* start giving more generous support to older people because their numbers are growing. But as of now, the government, children, and parents in both China's rural and urban areas see the responsibility for elder care lying with the family—not with the state—and because political power is centralized there, public opinion has limited influence on policy making. China is not alone. Social security or pension coverage for the elderly is meager in several other countries facing population aging. While that's good news for the state, in the sense that the financial burden is relatively lower as the population ages, it's bad news for the elderly, who may suffer higher rates of poverty or neglect.

The second assertion is that aging and shrinking countries will *have to* start opening to immigration. Is there more truth to that assertion? When a country's population ages and its workforce shrinks, the immediate worry is that there won't be enough workers to support all the older people who benefit from generous entitlements such as social security and health care. Those worries are justified (although the calculus is not that simple, as we have seen), and many countries have chosen to supplement their workforces by bringing in outsiders: immigrants. But not every country. Although it lets in small numbers with specialized skills, Japan has chosen to shrink rather than to risk the upheaval of bringing in a mass of culturally different outsiders to supplement its labor force. In Japan, just 1.7 percent of the population (or roughly 2.2 million people) is foreign or foreign-born. Japan is on pace to have three workers for every two retirees by 2060, but Japan doesn't *have to* open its doors to immigrants even though it has a shrinking workforce. The country has choices, and one of them is to preserve ethnic homogeneity instead of accepting foreign workers—right now, that appears to be the top choice. In 2010, an *Asahi Shimbun* newspaper poll asked Japanese about accepting immigrants to "maintain economic vitality": 26 percent of respondents favored the idea, and 65 percent opposed it. But choices have consequences. Even with issuing visas for unskilled guest workers, there were 163 vacancies for every 100 job seekers as of November 2018. In Shinzo Abe's words, "We are not considering adopting a so-called immigration policy . . . [but] [t]o cope with the labor shortage, we will expand the current system to accept foreign workers in special fields. We will accept foreign human resources that are skilled and work-ready, but only for a limited time." Despite Japan's ethnic homogeneity, the population has mostly been supportive of the guestworker program, perhaps because leaders have insisted on the temporary nature of the program, but if temporary changes to permanent, there will be many political and social consequences.

Immigration can offset population aging, but it won't reverse it. And influxes of large numbers of immigrants bring their own social challenges (as Chapter 4 will discuss in more detail). Given the diverse models of the relationship between the family and the state worldwide, the social implications of population aging are varied. In every country and culture, the eldest in society need care in their last years, and someone has to provide it or the elderly will suffer neglect. Innovative solutions such as multigenerational housing or immigration of elder-care workers can fill in, but comprehensive and innovative policy solutions are needed, not stop-gap measures.

Case Study: A Geriatric Peace?

We close with trying to understand what aging means for national security and how it might affect potential global power shifts. Many prominent thinkers have identified a large, healthy population as a resource for state power, from Thucydides to Henry Kissinger. A large population of military-aged males, who are the majority of soldiers, can contribute to state power because they can be conscripted to provide boots on the ground. Because these young adults are also of prime working ages, they help fuel the economy so that more money can be spent on defense, and, through national economic success, the country gains global influence. Yet for those very reasons, many question whether states with aged populations can continue to staff or fund a military or compete on a global stage. For example, in part because of Russia's actions with Crimea in 2014 and in part because of US pressure to increase military spending as part of NATO, Germany since 2017 has desired to increase its ranks of active soldiers by about 20,000 by 2024. That's not easy with its aging population, so Germany has turned to recruiting underaged soldiers (age 17, with some restrictions on service) and immigrants from other European Union countries to fill its ranks.

Aging can affect a state's readiness to counter threats to national security, as we see with South Korea and North Korea, on the brink of conflict for decades. North Korea has been unpredictable, and South Korea is vulnerable: Its capital area, Seoul, holds about half of the country's total population, just 35 miles from the Demilitarized Zone and only 121 miles from North Korea's capital, Pyongyang. South Korea's government projects that the country is set to have its first population decline any day now, having revised a previous estimate that shrinking would begin after 2020. In the most pessimistic scenario, which is honestly likely, South Korea's population would shrink from the current 51 million to about 34 million in 2067. The rapidity with which South Korea is aging is staggering—its median age will be over 62 years by 2062. That means nearly half the population would be approaching retirement or already retired, even under a medium-growth scenario, making South Korea the oldest developed country in the world. North Korea has severe population issues of its own, but the United Nations estimates its TFR at 1.9, below replacement but nearly one child higher than South Korea's. South Korea has about 625,000 troops, compared with 1.2 million in North Korea.

An aging society forms the backdrop against which policy makers base their decisions by influencing both the willingness and ability of the state and people that compose its society to strengthen or maintain national defense. But aging is far from the only influence on defense decisions, as the tense Asia Pacific region shows. Japan is the vanguard of aging states but is investing more in its national defense than at any time since the end of World War II. It has changed laws to loosen restrictions on the country's military, increased the defense budget, built a network of alliances, and invested in adapting the economy to population aging. Likewise, China's defense spending has been rising steadily and consistently over the past two decades, at an inflation-adjusted average of 9.1 percent from 2011 to 2021. Despite aging, China is seeking greater autonomy in the Asia Pacific region, including in contested areas such as the South China Sea.

Russia, too, is flouting expectations. In the first decade of the twenty-first century, the country seemed on the brink of disaster. Oil prices were devastatingly low for a country that had put its eggs in the basket of fossil fuels. America was again asserting itself in the Middle East and had a presence in the former Soviet battlefield known as Afghanistan. NATO was enlarging uncomfortably close to Russia's borders, and Western media sources were regularly reporting on the country's demographic disaster—births and life expectancy were both in the tank, setting Russia on course for a population implosion.

Although it was only recently that Russia was one of the two major Cold War global powers, the country's overall population shrank after 1996 through 2009 (it has since climbed but was beginning a downward slope again in 2020). In 2006, President Vladimir Putin called population decline the biggest crisis facing Russia. But rather than slipping quietly into senescence, Putin's speech was preceded by a decision to cut gas supplies to Ukraine and Georgia. Russia repeated this move with Ukraine and parts of Europe in 2009 and has employed the threat of further cuts multiple times. Infamously, Russia invaded Georgia in August 2008 in retaliation for Georgia's actions against South Ossetia and announced that it recognized South Ossetia and Abkhazia as independent states. Russia rolled tanks into Crimea in 2014, began military intervention in Syria in 2015, and attempted to influence the US 2016 election. An aging and shrinking country was not supposed to act like this. So, I argue, if none of this behavior was expected by early theorists of population aging, perhaps we should recalibrate our expectation of the relationship between aging and national security. One relevant theory does come to mind: Power transition theory, which argues that a state with declining power will act aggressively while it still can, would explain Russia's actions as a last gasp and shed light on why rapidly aging China is doubling down on its military.

We should consider alternative interpretations of demographic changes on Russia's military strategy and capabilities. Shifting to a cyber strategy, as Russia did in using social media to spread disinformation during the 2016 US presidential election, is a brilliant strategy for an aging country because technology compensates for the limited manpower. Also, whereas youthful populations need labor-intensive industries to employ a growing number of entrants to the labor market, the importance of natural resources to Russia's economy is an asset for the shrinking population because such industries are not labor-intensive.

What we see from Japan, China, and Russia is that policy makers will choose guns over butter if the threat level is sufficiently high. A country with an aging population can still be a strong military power. Militaries are increasing their reliance on technologies that do not require soldiers to put themselves in harm's way or do not require soldiers period. Aging states can also find strength in numbers, as through alliances. In Europe, European Union member states have been working to increase the efficiency of their militaries. Each state uses its comparative advantage in different sectors such as air, naval, or ground, so that the militaries of member states complement one another to produce an effective European force, rather than be redundant or compete.

It's true that aging will somewhat decrease the ability of states to project political, economic, and military power, and thus will have implications for global security. Some states will be worse off than others. But we should not expect that aged states will be unable to have militaries. There are military-aged men and women in each of these states, even if their numbers are dwindling. In other words, there's little reason to believe a geriatric peace is on the horizon and enough reason to consider that these countries could go down fighting.

• • •

What are we to conclude about the effects of population aging? First, multiple factors can change the trajectory of aging states headed down an economically unsustainable path. For a country with a shrinking labor force, increasing automation can create useful substitutes for labor. The problem, though, is that while the net societal or economic benefit may be positive, somebody always loses. Those who staff manual-labor jobs risk being displaced if the whole industry shifts. Besides automation, labor-force participation rates can change as older groups extend their working lives and family-friendly policies make it easier for women to reconcile work and child-rearing.

Second, the increasing diversity of aging states means that countries with nondemocratic institutions, such as Cuba, China, and others in the second wave, are newly facing aging and are likely to respond to aging in different ways than did the first wave of aging states. In particular, countries where decision making is concentrated in the hands of a few powerful figures are freer to put policies in place that require tough choices, such as higher retirement ages or more austere social benefits for the elderly. In these cases, the state passes along the strains of aging to the family or the individual. Meaningful increases in pensionable age have been nearly politically impossible in aging democracies—in non-democracies, can we assume that governments will yield to pressures to expand entitlement coverage for growing numbers of seniors? From what we see so far, it's misguided to assume governments in this next wave of aging states will be expected to provide health benefits for seniors the way they have been in aging OECD states. In truth, population aging may not bankrupt newly aging, second-wave states, but it will increase pressures on women and other family members with aging parents. There were many states in the first wave that were old before they were rich, but for the most part they had capitalist, democratic institutions. The tie between regime type and economic system is close, and I argue that we should be paying less attention to "old before rich" as a general problem and more attention to how a poor country is likely to allocate economic resources when it is not democratic. Entitlements and retirement policies in the first wave of aging countries were institutionalized before aging was a problem, now they're hard to change. At least in the second wave, some of those institutions don't exist prior to aging. By 2035, at least 20 additional states are likely to join the existing 54 that have median ages over 35 years, depending on how fertility changes in the interim. The states on deck to join the club will bring even more political, geographic, and cultural diversity, including Iran, Tunisia, Vietnam, Turkey, Saudi Arabia, and Mexico. Soon, aging will have truly touched every continent, although the majority of sub-Saharan Africa is still in early stages of the demographic transition, if they're on the path at all.

Third, citizens around the world have different expectations of their governments, and vice versa. This so-called social contract between young and old or state and individual can lead to vastly different policy outcomes in aging countries. One policy choice is immigration. As we saw with Japan, it is not a given that an aging country will open to immigration to fill spots in the labor force vacated by those aging out. But some countries, such as Germany, are choosing that path, and their ethnic composition is shifting as a result. There can also be social shifts that affect the impact of aging. Age groups, such as "the young" or "the old," aren't static. As countries redefine what it means to be old, particularly if that redefinition includes longer working lives (even part-time) and time transfers to younger generations, such as community volunteering or babysitting grandchildren, the impact of aging can be diluted. Finally, reduced environmental pressures could be an upside as populations shrink and there are fewer consumers putting pressure on resources. We've seen in this chapter and the preceding one how low fertility, in particular, is shaping age composition across societies, but that's only part of the picture. To deepen our understanding, we need to explore that second fundamental force behind population change: mortality.

CHAPTER 3

A Billion Ways to Die

One of the world's most prestigious medical journals, the *Lancet*, published its first issue in 1823. Today, it prints articles on uses of artificial intelligence and bioengineering in medicine, but the journal is named for the instrument physicians used to bleed their patients in a primitive effort to rid them of illness. Bleeding through cuts or leeches and planting fragrant bushes as a defense against miasma (bad air thought to cause diseases) are examples of the misguided medical practices of the past that did little to heal the ailing human body. As bizarre as such medical treatments sound to our modern ears, in the nineteenth century, "The idea of microscopic germs spreading disease would have been about as plausible as the existence of fairies to most practicing doctors," as Steven Johnson, author of *The Ghost Map*, has said. For a minority of scientists and physicians, though, such ideas didn't sound so crazy, and a great many of us owe our lives to them. One was Jacob Henle. In his 1840 essay, "On Miasmata and Contagia," he pitted the popular theory about toxic smells against his early formulation of modern germ theory. Two decades later, French scientist Louis Pasteur proved the role of two deadly microorganisms in causing France's silkworm blight, which had devastated the lucrative industry. In 1882, German doctor Robert Koch built on Pasteur's early anthrax vaccines and proved that bacteria could be transmitted when a mouse he injected with cultured anthrax from a sheep died of the disease. Koch's assistant was Julius Richard Petri, known to us as the inventor of the petri dish, which he used to help culture Koch's bacteria.

Scientists such as Pasteur and Koch were the first to scientifically prove the merit of inoculation, but they weren't the first to discover its power. In Europe, the practice was documented as early as the 1500s, but it looked little like the sterile vaccinations of today. Until vaccines became widely available in the twentieth century, inoculators would generally take scrapings from a pustule and scratch them into the skin of an uninfected person to create a mild reaction with resulting immunity. This practice, called variolation, was global, present in China, India, Persia, Europe, and the American colonies, among other places. In the latter, Cotton Mather, the scientist, minister, and author who wrote about the Salem witch trials, prevented what could have become a lethal smallpox epidemic when he tried variolation on the advice of an African slave. Today, pharmaceutical giant Merck's measles vaccine alone saves about 1.5 million lives a year. But before it was widely used, 90 percent of American children contracted the measles virus by the time they were aged 15; the disease killed or impaired thousands every year. And vaccines have come a long way since variolation. The COVID-19 vaccines didn't involve injecting the virus—even a dead or weakened version—at all. Instead, scientists used a tiny bit of the protein from the virus in the form of mRNA (messenger RNA; a relative of DNA), to get an immune response in patients.

Despite their merit, vaccines remain controversial in multiple respects. Early on, many people were hesitant to receive the COVID-19 vaccines, citing mistrust of the approval process, and preferring to wait until they could observe longer-term effects on those vaccinated. A study of 428 parents whose children were patients in the Children's

Hospital of Ankara City Hospital, Turkey, showed significant hesitation toward foreign COVID-19 vaccines, as opposed to domestically produced ones, with 66 percent of parents reluctant to receive the former while only 37.4 percent felt the same about the latter. While polio has been almost completely eradicated, the global health community can't quite cross the finish line because pockets of people in Afghanistan and Pakistan, primarily, remain less than fully vaccinated. One reason is vaccine refusals "due to misinformation, mistrust, cultural beliefs, fatigue or other priorities," according to the Global Polio Eradication Initiative.

The unusually rushed circumstances of COVID-19 vaccines aside, some are refusing well-established, routine vaccines on the basis of unscientific fears that they cause autism or mistrust about their safety in general, while many who would be glad to use them can't get them. The world learned the term "vaccine nationalism" when the richest nations came under fire in 2020 and early 2021 during the COVID-19 pandemic. UN secretary-general António Guterres pointed out in February 2021 that although vaccination rollout was proceeding, at that time only 10 nations had administered 75 percent of the world's vaccines. According to Guterres, 130 countries had not yet received a single dose of COVID-19 vaccine. Then, as vaccination rates in countries such as the United States improved, so did sharing of doses. While vaccine "hoarding" deepens the health inequality between rich and poor countries, it is far from the only problem poor countries face in inoculating their populations, and providing doses wouldn't have been enough to halt the global spread of the pandemic. The poorest countries with the most vulnerable populations couldn't easily distribute the vaccine even if they got it, for reasons including conflict, weak health systems, and inaccessible geography, among others.

The divide in health access between rich and poor countries is truly astounding. When I traveled to Rwanda for the first time, I was able to park at a strip mall 5 minutes from my house, walk into the Memphis Pizza Company and order dinner, go next door to a private business called The Shot Nurse, get my typhoid and hepatitis A vaccines and a malaria pill prescription, then pick up my pizza, all in under 30 minutes and with no appointment. In Yemen, cholera vaccines sat on United Nations–chartered planes for 16 months because of the country's violent civil war. That ongoing cholera epidemic is the largest in world history, with more than 2.5 million cases between October 2016 and December 2020.

• • •

A great part of human history is the story of humankind's battle with nature. For most of human history, nature won—remember that we didn't reach a global population of 1 billion until after 1800. But over the past several centuries the battle became more evenly matched, and in most parts of the world humans have the edge over nature, as evidenced by an excess of births over deaths, which has resulted in a rapidly growing global population.

Our control—or lack thereof—over sickness and death is one of the strongest forces that has remade global population. Today, most of the people in high-income countries who die are old; in the world's poorest countries, almost one in three deaths are of children younger than 5 years, and more than a third of children have stunted growth because of poor nutrition. In many of those countries, diseases such as malaria, absent in rich countries, are still rampant—it alone kills one child every 2 minutes, almost exclusively in low-income countries. In 2016, the gap in life expectancy between low- and high-income countries was 18.1 years. In low-income countries, less than 60 percent of newborns will reach age 70, but more than 80 percent of newborns in high-income countries are expected to live beyond that age. Differences in political capacity, political will, infrastructure, institutions, and funding are some of the factors responsible for health disparities both between and within countries. These factors are important whether we are talking about pandemics or pregnancy.

Although humans have made tremendous strides against mortality, there are always new challenges, such as new strains of COVID-19 appearing just as vaccines for the original strain were finally being distributed in early 2021. Many of these challenges we can't control, but some are of our own making. Climate change, for example, has the potential to unleash novel diseases; our "evolution" toward processed foods and sedentary lifestyles has increased rates of cancer, heart disease, and stroke. Good health is key to prosperity, but we aren't investing in it enough. Health is too often politicized, whether health-care systems and the government's role in those services or the politicization of scientific knowledge in general.

While the world was rocked by the spread of COVID-19 in 2020, new diseases that infect humans actually emerge all the time—we've seen more than 30 in the past 30 years. Zoonoses, or diseases that originate in animals, were about 75 percent of those 30 new diseases. Most readers are familiar with plague, a disease carried by rodents, and rabies, which is carried by animals such as dogs and raccoons. Ebola, too, emerged from rain-forest animals (likely bats and chimpanzees) and made its way to humans with horrific consequences. Knowledge of the origins of COVID-19 is evolving, but that disease also appears to have zoonotic origins, possibly from bats. Demographic factors, namely expansion of urban areas, population growth, and mobility, play a major role in the creation and spread of these new diseases. Agricultural practices, too, facilitate new diseases, particularly as they disturb habitats, such as rain forests, or bring humans into close contact with animals.

Social and political factors are also relevant. For example, disease outbreaks are more likely in conflict-ridden countries. In August of 2018, the Democratic Republic of the Congo (DRC) faced its 10th outbreak of the deadly Ebola virus, this time in North Kivu, a region close to Uganda where rebel groups fight over strategic minerals such as gold, diamonds, and coltan. DRC is poor, which compounds public-health issues because the country lacks sanitation systems and infrastructure to treat diseases. Armed conflict adds additional challenges. For one, large swaths of the population have been uprooted and displaced, leading to poor nutrition and broken social ties. Conflict often makes a bad situation worse: During the recent war, Yemen's already poor infrastructure was wiped out by bombings and blocked by rebels, making health access even more of a problem.

At least a modicum of infrastructure, such as waste management, and of governance can improve health outcomes. Yet, infrastructure and institutions are nearly absent in poor countries. Much of the world still lacks access to health-care services, and when they are available, the costs are often staggering. In 2017, only one-third to one-half of the world's population had coverage for essential health services. Shortages of personnel—doctors, nurses, and dentists—is a significant issue, too. At the start of Liberia's 2014 Ebola outbreak, the World Health Organization (WHO) reported that the country had only one doctor available to treat every 100,000 people.

Access to advanced medical care isn't a prerequisite for significant health gains in countries with high mortality. Even simple measures such as hand-washing make a tremendous difference in curbing disease spread. It's unfathomable in rich countries, but in poor countries the equivalent of 32 school buses of children die from diarrhea every day. Between 2000 and 2017, yearly deaths from diarrhea among children under 5 decreased by 60 percent, but it's clearly still a significant, and preventable, issue. Oral rehydration solution, which is just a simple combination of salt, sugar, and water, not too different from the Pedialyte I give my feverish sons, has saved 50 million people worldwide, the majority of them children in less developed countries. Up to 80 percent of cholera cases could be effectively treated by such solutions—if they were available.

Even when health challenges aren't as easily preventable, better planning can help lessen their impact. Health infrastructure, such as availability of hospital beds, transportation networks that make medical facilities accessible to all, and well-trained medical professionals, can be the difference between life and death.

• • •

Gains in addressing communicable diseases have extended life around the globe, but the longer you live, the more likely you are to die from a noncommunicable disease (NCD), such as heart disease or cancer. Scholars have developed the epidemiologic transition model to describe this societal-level shift from high infant and child mortality and mortality due to famine and epidemics to one where death occurs primarily from NCDs—in other words, a shift in the leading causes of death from infectious to chronic disease. According to the Institute for Health Metrics and Evaluation (IMHE) of the University of Washington, in 2017 the top causes of death in Japan, one of the world's healthiest countries, were Alzheimer's disease (up 57.7 percent since 2007), ischemic (meaning constricting the blood vessels) heart disease (up 16.4 percent), stroke (up 13.17 percent), lower respiratory infection (up 30 percent), and various cancers of the lung, colon, stomach, pancreas, and liver. Among the peer group of countries IMHE identifies for Japan, those diseases are typical. That percentages are rising isn't itself cause for alarm, as countries that have completed the demographic and epidemiologic transitions will by definition see rises in NCDs compared to levels of infectious diseases—their populations have to die of *something*. When we see rises in NCDs outside of this situation or at earlier ages, there's more cause for alarm.

In general, these so-called lifestyle diseases are responsible for mortality in wealthier countries, but the more surprising—and arguably more challenging—issue is when such diseases become more prevalent in countries that haven't yet reached high levels of development.

Thomas Bollyky, of the US-based Council on Foreign Relations, points out that, for the first time ever, viruses, bacteria, and other infectious diseases are no longer the top cause of death and disability anywhere in the world. According to the WHO, 71 percent of all global deaths in 2016 were from NCDs. In fact, in only two regions of the world do infectious diseases account for more than 8 percent of death and disability: South Asia (one-fifth) and sub-Saharan Africa (just less than 44 percent)—that's down from the majority of death and disability in both in 2011. This is great news on the surface, but Bollyky sees a deeper problem: Poorer states have made these strides through outside intervention, without developing the capacity and institutions to deal with them internally. As NCDs, such as heart disease, diabetes, and cancer, become the main health problems even in poorer countries, these countries don't have the infrastructure to treat them, and the population suffers in ways—or at ages—that people in developed countries don't. Dying of NCDs is common, but what's problematic is premature deaths, generally defined as before age 70. Of the 15 million deaths between ages 30 and 70 in 2016, 85 percent were in low- and middle-income countries. In essence, poor countries have leapfrogged diseases, and that jump is affecting people in their prime of life.

This lack of infrastructure isn't just a problem for NCDs—the 2014 Ebola outbreak was quickly curtailed, but it exposed severe issues with infrastructure in less developed countries and an overreliance on foreign aid coming from developed states. Liberia, plagued by corruption and government distrust, saw between 300 and 400 new Ebola cases a week during the peak of the 2014 outbreak there. At the same time, Nigeria saw only 19 people infected, and only 7 died thanks to a widely praised government response to identify and track exposure. The same has happened with other diseases. Because of a lack of health infrastructure and scarcity of care, Kenyan member of Parliament Justus Murunga died prematurely from COVID-19 in November 2020. In Kenya's rural areas, as where Murunga was, emergency services are scarce—three-quarters of the country's intensive care units are concentrated between Nairobi and Mombasa, and the country of 51 million has only 527 ICU beds. When Murunga was taken to the nearest hospital, the public facility had no oxygen with which to treat him. Once transported to a private hospital 20 minutes away, it was too late to save him. Even Western countries with sophisticated systems saw their capacity overwhelmed during COVID-19, so it is easy to imagine how dire the situation is when few hospital resources exist in the first place.

The issue of leapfrogging spills over into other demographic areas as well. In eighteenth and nineteenth century Europe, mortality declined through accumulation of knowledge about infectious disease and the development of public-health laws, medical and sanitation infrastructure, and responsive government. Fertility declines followed as families grew more confident that children would live to adulthood. Europe's demographic transition was gradual, taking place over about 150 years. In today's less developed countries, mortality is declining, but quickly—in mere decades—and without those internal developments. As a result, fertility is not necessarily declining in the same way—the "stalled" fertility transition in parts of Africa mentioned in Chapter 1 is one consequence. And, declining mortality no longer goes hand-in-hand with other markers of development, such as economic growth and governance. As one example, Niger has seen significant health improvements: Life expectancy is up, the infant mortality rate is down, the HIV/AIDS death rate dropped almost two-thirds in a decade, and so on for malaria, malnutrition, and diarrheal disease. But we know that without underlying domestic reasons for mortality drop, such as educational gains, fertility isn't likely to drop apace—Niger is a case in point, with the world's highest fertility and a population that has been growing at 3.8 percent.

It's also hard to rally global attention and funding for NCDs in less developed countries. Chronic diseases, such as cancer, heart disease, diabetes, and respiratory diseases such as asthma, kill more people worldwide than all other causes combined. But which international donors want to mobilize to deal with these diseases in poor countries when risks are increased with tobacco use, physical inactivity, alcohol abuse, and poor diet; in other words, poor choices?

Case Study: Maternal Mortality

Globally, 808 women die every day from pregnancy and childbirth complications. The main measure of this is the maternal mortality ratio, which indicates the number of maternal deaths for every 100,000 births, and is generally measured out to a year after birth (counted if the death is as a result of the childbirth itself). In 2017, the global average was 211 deaths per 100,000 births, a number that masks tremendous differences across countries depending on their level of economic development. Sub-Saharan Africa has the highest maternal mortality ratio at 542, and low-income countries in general clock in at 462. A 15-year-old girl in Chad has a 1 in 15 lifetime risk of dying from childbirth. High-income countries, however, have only 11 maternal deaths on average per 100,000 births, 9 in Europe and 16 in North America. Altogether, maternal mortality ratios in low-income countries are 42 times higher than in high-income countries.

That some countries are doing so much better than others shows that the majority of maternal deaths today could be prevented if women could visit a health-care provider or have an assisted delivery. According to Sarah Barnes, program director of the Maternal Health Initiative at the Wilson Center in Washington, DC, women often die when there are no skilled birth attendants available, which could be midwives or doctors. Women also die for lack of family planning; a woman's risk of dying in childbirth rises when her births are close together or when she gives birth at too young an age. Some scholars have calculated that greater access to family planning could reduce maternal mortality by up to a third. HIV-positive women are also at greater risk from secondary infection, sepsis, or the more rapid progression of AIDS in the period after birth. Three-fourths of all maternal deaths are caused by either postpartum hemorrhage, hypertensive disorder such as preeclampsia or eclampsia, infections that tend to happen during delivery or shortly after, unsafe abortion, or other delivery-related complications. According to Barnes, we're also starting to see noncommunicable diseases—such as heart disease or cancer—play a growing role in underlying causes of maternal deaths.

Of those 808 women who die from childbirth every day, almost all of them are in poor countries, and two-thirds of those are in sub-Saharan Africa alone, but maternal mortality remains a global issue. In fact, tennis superstar Serena Williams's harrowing birth story in the January 2018 issue of *Vogue* magazine described how she nearly died from post–cesarean section complications after giving birth to daughter Olympia. Williams's story was amazing in its own right, but it also brought to light significant racial disparities in maternal and child health in the United States. A Black woman in the United States is 243 percent more likely to die from pregnancy- or childbirth-related complications than is a White woman. The data show that it's race, not class, that drives higher maternal and infant mortality rates for Black people in the United States. As Linda Villarosa put it, writing for the *New York Times Magazine*, "a black woman with an advanced degree is more likely to lose her baby than a white woman with less than an eighth-grade education." The politics of race, class, and gender run throughout discussions of maternal mortality in developed countries.

The same is true in less developed countries. Although we might attribute high maternal mortality to poverty, broadly, health is a reflection of societal values. As described by Jeremy Youde, a colleague of mine who is an expert on global health, major political actors give and take funding and attention for the issue of women's health depending on the political weather. To understand why women are still dying, he directed my attention to the role of women within a society—he argues that maternal mortality numbers can indicate how much the government and society value women. The political dynamics in a country also matter for success or failure of efforts to make motherhood safer. While there have been global strides in reducing maternal mortality, Youde says it's not as easy as getting everyone behind the idea that we don't want mothers dying in childbirth. Maternal mortality initiatives become political because they intersect with so many social, economic, and cultural issues within societies. There may be discrimination among various groups within society that exacerbate maternal mortality for some—the same dynamic we see in the United States—or cultural norms around early marriage, so policies to remedy this need to take the larger context into account.

Ethiopia, one of the countries that gets the most attention by international donors for its success in improving maternal mortality, set a goal of ending child marriage by 2025, and while it still has one of the highest rates of child marriage in the world, it has accelerated declines in child marriage rates over the past 10 years. According to UNICEF, of the 15 million Ethiopian women married before age 18, 6 million were child brides, married before age 15. The majority of those gave birth as adolescents and were less likely to have receive skilled care during their last pregnancy and delivery. Rwanda was one of the few countries to meet the Millennium Development Goal around maternal mortality by 2015, which was to decrease the maternal mortality ratio by 75 percent. Rwanda decreased its maternal mortality by 78 percent between 1990 and 2015, lowering its maternal mortality ratio to 290 deaths per 100,000 live births. That number is still above the Sustainable Development Goal of no more than 140 maternal deaths per 100,000 live births, but it is a huge improvement.

We're still behind in terms of valuing women at the global level. To tackle all of these challenges, we need attention and funding, but we also need data: One of the major hindrances to progress in the health sector is lack of useful data, which can help to measure problems and evaluate the success of programs to target health outcomes. Although we've seen that sex and gender are highly relevant to health issues, the WHO has reported that in 2019, fewer than half of the Sustainable Development Goal indicators had sex-disaggregated data. If we can't statistically show the problem exists, it's especially hard to fix it.

• ● •

Socioeconomic conditions are important for health outcomes everywhere. Although Russia and the United States were the two most powerful countries in the world during the decades of the Cold War, both have serious health challenges that put a ceiling on their potential success and power.

Russia suffered serious setbacks during times of economic and political crisis over the past several decades, and its improvements haven't been at a pace rapid enough to catch up to its peers. In Russia, after the fall of the Soviet Union and the turmoil and uncertainty that resulted, life expectancy decreased rapidly, by more than 6 years for men between 1990 and 1994 and reaching as low as 57 years. Although life expectancy estimates increased between 2006 and 2016 as socioeconomic conditions improved and new policies were implemented, a divide remains: A 1-year-old Russian boy today has about the same life expectancy as a Russian girl celebrating her first birthday under Nikita Khrushchev in the late 1950s. Russia actually has the third widest disparity in life expectancy between men and women of any country in the world, behind Syria and Bulgaria. The gap has narrowed to 10.6 years in 2016 from 11.6 years in 1980, but in 2016 life expectancy at birth was only 65.4 years for men, while it was a historic high of 76 years for women.

While we've discussed life expectancy quite a bit, it's important to add some differentiation and introduce a new term: HALE, or health-adjusted life expectancy, the number of years someone can expect to live in full health. Long life expectancy represents better mortality outcomes across the life course, which is great, but if a significant number of years are lived in debilitation, people will require expensive care and have little chance of contributing to the economy. Strains at the family and individual levels are terrible, too. When the gap between the number of years someone is expected to live and the number of years they're expected to be healthy is large—in other words, when there's the expectation that people will live a significant number of years in poor health—that's a problem. In 2016, the global gap was 9.5 years for women and 7.8 years for men. Because women generally have lower labor-force participation throughout their lives than men yet outlive men by so many years makes women especially vulnerable to poverty and its ills in old age. In Russia, poor HALE is an especially significant problem with severe economic and social consequences: it's 67.5 years for women, and only 60.7 years for men. This begs the question: Why are Russians so unhealthy?

Part of the reason is that Russian men are literally drinking themselves to death. The role of alcohol in Russia is a trope, but it's spot on. Russians over age 15 consume about 11 to 13 liters of pure ethanol on average per person, per year—that's like 30 bottles of Tito's vodka per year, *on average*, one of the highest rates of alcohol consumption in the world. Until 2013, Russia didn't even classify beer as an alcoholic beverage, according to the WHO. Although men have struggled, alcohol is an issue for both sexes. In a study of Russian disease and mortality that covered the period 1980–2016 and was published in the *Lancet*, researchers found that about half of mortality of those in the prime of life could be traced to behavioral choices, such as alcohol and drug use and smoking. Specifically, for those aged 15 to 49 years, such choices explained mortality for 59.2 percent of men and 46.8 percent of women. Ischemic heart disease and cerebrovascular disease—basically, stroke and heart disease—are the top two causes of years of life lost prematurely. Self-harm is the third, and that order has been pretty steady for decades. Even Russia's issues with HIV/AIDS can be traced to alcohol, the cultural environment of which contributes to unsafe sex.

But context matters: Social stress is a significant cause of high mortality in Russia. Some of that stress was caused by the abrupt political and economic transition as the Soviet Union collapsed. Researchers have linked this stress to "an increased risk of circulatory diseases, which are exacerbated by increased alcohol consumption as a behavioral response to stress." Evidence supporting this theory is clear when comparing

Russia to the Baltic states, which had similar stresses at first but recovered life expectancy losses during the late 1990s even as Russia faced further political and social issues, including its 1998 economic crisis. Social stress shows in another way, too. Scholars have referred to Russia's "abortion culture," which treats abortion as a "'normal way' of dealing with the medical and socioeconomic hardships in personal and family life." The Soviet Union was the first country in the world to legalize abortion, which it did in 1920, and at times abortion rates have met or exceeded birthrates—in 1965, abortions were three times the number of births. In 2009, Russia registered 1.7 million births and 1.2 million abortions, according to health minister Tatyana Golikova. Arguably, this is a public-health crisis, too, as unwanted pregnancies are preventable through contraception, and abortion carries risks to the mother generally greater than contraception would. Alcohol abuse can also contribute to unwanted pregnancy. Compared with the United States and Germany, Russia's abortion rate is far higher, around 480 abortions per 1,000 live births, compared with 200 for the United States and 135 for Germany.

Mortality, social stress, and alcohol are tightly interwoven in Russia, meaning that changes in these will work in tandem. Making sure alcohol isn't too cheap or easily available have been two of the most effective measures. Because of such policies, consumption of hard liquor and unregulated alcohol are way down, and, as a result, total per capita consumption dropped by 43 percent between 2003 and 2016. Highly dangerous binge drinking is way down as well, although it is still higher in Russia than anywhere else in Europe. These consumption changes have already translated into huge improvements in mortality for both men and women, including those causes of death directly related to alcohol and those secondarily related, such as violent deaths. High mortality and disability rates among Russia's working-age population are clearly a problem for the economy and military, moving health issues up the priority list for Russia's leaders.

Now, we turn to the other great Cold War power, which has its own unique health troubles. The United States was relatively better off than its peers but has slipped over time as socioeconomic and racial disparities persist. In 1960, the United States had the highest life expectancy among its peers, 2.4 years higher than the OECD average. But in the 1980s, the United States started losing ground, and by the 1990s, the US average was below the OECD's. The United States recovered slightly as death rates declined overall in the country between 1990 and 2016, while between 2006 and 2016, life expectancy at birth increased by 0.8 years for the population as a whole. This is a modest increase but far off the pace of the typical gain of 2 years of life expectancy per decade for most developed countries. More notably, toward the end of that time period, life expectancy at birth actually *decreased* by 0.2 years between 2014 and 2015 and by 0.1 years between 2015 and 2016. Developed countries aren't supposed to see losses in this area—life expectancy should only get better, and if it doesn't, something is horribly wrong. In the case of the United States, increases in drug overdose and suicide drove that life-expectancy reversal. Increases in childhood and adolescent obesity and the related health complications, such as diabetes and heart disease, contributed, too. Improvements in some factors, such as neonatal preterm complications and smoking—which was down by almost 43 percent from 1990 to 2016—have been offset by worsening outcomes in others, such as hypertensive heart disease and self-harm. High fasting plasma glucose, which indicates diabetes, and drug use are up in all but three US states. And the problems don't end there: Because of the severity of the COVID-19 pandemic in the United States, the Centers for Disease Control and Prevention (CDC) estimated that life expectancy dropped by a full year in the first half of 2020.

As bleak as the national picture is, the greatest disparities are at the state level. There is a 6.6 year gap in life expectancy at birth by US state, highest in Hawaii at 81.3 years and lowest in Mississippi at 74.7 years. The difference between highest and lowest health-adjusted life expectancy was similar, with Minnesota at 70.3 years and West Virginia—a state hit hard by the opioid epidemic—at 63.8 years. We can't remove these patterns from the socioeconomic and racial contexts. For example, in poor communities, which are sometimes majority non-White but not always, there are too few healthy food options or opportunities for outdoor recreation.

Other structural factors have been (perhaps less noticeably) contributing to worsening US health. While the 2016 Affordable Care Act increased insurance coverage for many Americans, there are still some without any coverage. Diabetes care is expensive, and its prevalence is projected to continue increasing. Access to and quality of health care is low in many areas, and costs are high. Although the United States spends more on health care than any other country in the OECD— nearly 17 percent of GDP, twice the average—a 2013 study found that in the United States, expensive medical technology and higher health care prices were the main drivers of that high spending, rather than more frequent doctor visits or hospital admissions. That health problems are rampant among younger Americans bodes poorly for the future because the ramifications will unfold in the coming decades, particularly with regard to rates of noncommunicable diseases such as cancer. Physical activity was up over the period 1990–2016, but not enough to compensate for poor dietary choices, and rates of overweight and obesity are high, even among children. The United States will need significant reforms in a wide variety of areas, from gun reform to reduce homicide and suicide deaths, to interventions to curb increasing alcohol consumption and binge drinking (up especially among women), to structural changes such as better educational outcomes and alleviating poverty. All this besides needed reforms in the health-care system, including better insurance coverage.

• ● •

Needless to say, the negative effects of poor health are felt most acutely at the individual and family levels. But at a more macro level, we can see significant political, economic, and social implications, too.

Epidemics cause tremendous economic devastation. In under a decade, one-third of Europeans died from the fourteenth century Plague—that translated to 25 million out of 75 million. Children and poor working-age cohorts in society were struck hardest. The devastated working-age population meant the Black Death led to serious problems for European economies, as there were too few workers to provide labor for agriculture or to provide services that people were demanding, such as priests, physicians, and even gravediggers. As economists would predict, this labor shortage drove wages up dramatically, both immediately and as the labor shortage reverberated over the next several generations (as the young cohorts were unnaturally small because of fewer parents).

Some financial losses are at the household level, whether from out-of-pocket costs or missed days of work. During 2006, the average household in Burkina Faso spent more than one-third of its annual economic output on meningitis. In the short term, at least, the 2020 COVID-19 pandemic exacerbated income and wealth disparities. In the early months of the pandemic, 39 percent of US workers in households with annual incomes below $40,000 reported having been laid off or furloughed. Aggregate losses are severe, too. In the midst of the West African Ebola outbreak in 2015, Guinea, Liberia, and Sierra Leone lost an estimated $2.2 billion in GDP. That breaks down to a 50 percent loss in tourism in Sierra Leone, an estimated 4.9 to 9.4 percent loss in government revenue across all three countries, and more than half of Liberian wage earners out of their previous jobs 9 months into the epidemic. The epidemic effectively wiped out 5 years of development in Sierra Leone, 20 percent of GDP. The 2003 severe acute respiratory syndrome (SARS) epidemic brought losses of more than $40 billion in productivity. The 2009 H1N1 influenza pandemic cost the global economy $45 billion to

$55 billion, the 2014–2016 West African Ebola outbreak $53 billion. You get the picture. COVID-19 estimates are still being calculated as of this writing but range from the World Bank's estimate of $10 trillion to the $28 trillion estimate of the International Monetary Fund (IMF). Developed countries feel these shocks, but unequally—the most vulnerable in those societies (typically ethnic minorities and women) are always hit the hardest. The same is true at the global level. While developed countries feel the shocks, they can absorb them; less developed countries can lose years of growth, something they absolutely cannot afford.

Some economic challenges are unique to our time. Although disparate parts of the world were connected through trade in the time of the Plague, today's world is far more globalized—and vulnerable. The 2020 COVID-19 pandemic highlighted how business closures in response to the pandemic could disrupt global supply chains. Overreliance on China, in particular, became clear to many companies. According to consulting group Deloitte Canada, "more than 200 of the Fortune Global 500 firms have a presence in Wuhan, the highly industrialized province where the outbreak originated, and which has been hardest hit." Because of this vulnerability, Deloitte calls for global manufacturing practices to change in a way that will make us more resilient to global shocks.

Epidemics can also depress fertility, as people refrain from or postpone having children in response to economic and social strains. Decisions to abstain from having children for economic reasons and general pessimism about the future are reminiscent of fertility patterns in Eastern Europe after the collapse of communism.

Epidemics can also bring social divisions to light. The rise of right-wing nationalism in Europe, for example, is in part a response to social changes brought about by population aging and immigration. Across the globe, discrimination and violence against those from an Asian background increased after COVID-19 spread from Wuhan, China.

It's useful to consider what's universal and what's different about the political, social, and economic backdrops of high-mortality events over time so we can better condition our collective responses in ways that make humanity more resilient. After all, the hits will keep on coming. We need to be ready.

• • •

There's nothing disease loves more than chaos. Political instability, natural disaster, and civil conflict prevent the effective distribution of health supplies and wipe out infrastructure. Bombings erase roads and health clinics overnight. Armed rebels can make leaving home so threatening that sick people are unable to seek care. Absent a strong, central government, aid agencies face few reliable partners on the ground to distribute health supplies. To adequately address today's health challenges we need global cooperation, public trust, and political will—the opposite of chaos. Here, we examine how shortcomings in each of these areas inhibit our ability to effectively respond to or proactively address health issues.

At the World Health Assembly in 1966, the body decided to double down on efforts to remove the scourge of smallpox and eradicate it once and for all. The following year there were more than 10 million cases of smallpox globally and 2 million deaths. But intense focus on vaccination, surveillance, and containment brought triumph in only one decade—one of the greatest health victories the world has ever seen. On May 17, 2010, a statue commemorating the 30th anniversary of the eradication of smallpox was unveiled outside the World Health Organization headquarters in Geneva. The bronze and stone statue depicts a young girl about to receive vaccination in her arm, and in the words of the WHO, "pays homage to all those who were involved in the eradication drive, including governments, health care workers, donor agencies, non-governmental organizations, commercial firms, and village leaders who supported the vaccination of their residents and provided food and shelter on many occasions to vaccination teams."

Global problems, such as communicable diseases, require global solutions. The volume of trade and travel mean that infected animal, insect, or human hosts are just one flight away from anywhere in the world. Diseases can spread in a matter of hours. The WHO's description of how the SARS pandemic unfolded sums it nicely:

> On 21 February 2003, a 64-year-old medical doctor from China's Guangdong Province, flew to the Hong Kong Special Administrative Region (Hong Kong SAR) of China, and booked into a hotel room in the city. That night would change the world as he unwittingly transmitted a new, mysterious respiratory disease to at least 16 other guests. Those people travelled on to Canada and Viet Nam. . . . By July 2003, when the outbreak had been contained, there had been 8422 cases of people with SARS in more than 30 countries and areas, of which 916 had died.

Global connectivity also means a deeper well of resources to draw from in addressing diseases. Russia—as the Soviet Union—played a key role in the development of effective vaccines from the 1950s through the 1970s, first with polio and then with smallpox. In fact, Russia donated more smallpox vaccine to the WHO than any other country and pioneered a freeze-drying technique to make the vaccine more stable and usable in tropical climates. As with smallpox eradication, there are some global efforts to address today's diseases. For example, the Coalition for Epidemic Preparedness was founded in 2017 by Germany, India, Japan, Norway, the Bill & Melinda Gates Foundation, the Wellcome Trust, and the World Economic Forum. But there are as many examples of uncooperative behavior as of cooperation. On May 29, 2020, US president Donald Trump announced his intention to pull the United States out of the WHO, what would have been a devastating loss, as WHO's biggest funder. The United Kingdom has been the largest funder of the United Nations Population Fund (UNFPA), which is the UN's sexual and reproductive health agency, but, because of COVID-related budget crunches, decided in 2021 to cut 85 percent of its funds to the UNFPA flagship program for family planning.

Cooperation isn't always easy. While Russia tried to emerge as an early leader in a COVID-19 vaccine, some argued its "Sputnik V" vaccine was rushed to market, and it failed to meet quality standards to gain approval in Western markets. Part of the issue is lack of public trust in Russia's vaccines. Grandiose claims by Putin in the past about developing an AIDS vaccine, which failed to materialize, and global distrust of Russia generally meant that all but the most desperate countries were initially hesitant to accept Russia's COVID-19 vaccine. International acceptance isn't Russia's only problem; polls showed that even Russians had lower trust in government in mid-2020 than at any other time during Putin's administration, and that only 16 percent of Russians had plans to be vaccinated immediately, while 4 percent were awaiting a foreign vaccine and 38 percent said they would never get vaccinated against COVID-19.

Yet, public trust is necessary to effectively tackle health challenges. For centuries, fears that ships might be quarantined and money lost if disease was present aboard have discouraged honest reporting. Later, as the WHO says, "what was true of ships was true of 'ships of state'. Over-strict quarantine, the closing of borders—all such actions had the potential to discourage the disclosure of outbreaks, thereby encouraging the spread of disease." Given the widespread business and border closures during the COVID-19 pandemic, it is justifiable to worry that economic actors will feel incentivized to delay reporting outbreaks out of fear of financial losses. At the same time, it was a delay in reporting, then delayed trust in what was reported, that made the COVID-19 pandemic so severe. China's argued suppression of early disease reports and the US president's dismissal of warnings may have exacerbated the disease spread. Transparency is key when managing public health—the Spanish flu is so named, not because it originated in Spain (it likely originated in the United States), but because Spain was the first country not to censor reports of the virus.

Conflict further breaks down public trust. In Afghanistan and Pakistan, for example, conflict hindered polio-eradication efforts, and national and international health-care workers suffered attacks. Lack of trust in authorities is also made worse in the chaos of conflict, as we saw with failed efforts to stem the spread of Ebola in the DRC's 10th outbreak and in Liberia's 2014 outbreak as well. Some Liberians were skeptical of outbreak reports, believing it was a "scam crafted by the government to attract funds from international donors," and many failed to heed warnings and precautions.

Public trust is an issue even in contexts absent conflict, as we see with vaccine campaigns. Vaccinations are important to preserve herd immunity, an indirect way of protecting against disease spread once a significant portion of the population is immune. Herd immunity gives a measure of protection to babies not old enough to be vaccinated and to those members of the population medically or religiously unable to be vaccinated. But, there are trends in the West to refuse routine vaccinations, and diseases briefly thought conquered, such as measles, are reappearing. Although measles had basically disappeared from the United States for a decade, there were 1,282 cases in 2020, while in the first year of that decade, there were only 63 cases. To prevent measles from spreading, 90 to 95 percent of the population must be vaccinated; for polio, herd immunity is achieved somewhere between 60 to 97 percent. Thus, as proportions of the population unwilling to trust vaccines grows, herd immunity is compromised, and public health takes a step backwards. Many people I know are unwilling to get the seasonal flu vaccine, which in most years isn't a huge problem. But a 2010 study in the *New England Journal of Medicine* of the novel H1N1 flu outbreak in the United States in 2009 showed that more than half of parents polled by the Harvard School of Public Health who said they were not getting or might not get the H1N1 vaccine cited concerns over its safety. Thirty-one percent of parents "indicated that they did not trust public health officials to provide correct information about the vaccine's safety"—

that's versus 19 percent of all adults. Similar findings with regard to historic influenza outbreaks underscore the importance of public trust. Those cities that encouraged people to stay home and avoid public gatherings during the 1918 Spanish flu had far fewer deaths, but as Michael Osterholm and Mark Olshaker point out, "for this approach to work, they had to have reliable information from central authorities in public health and government, which requires honesty, responsiveness, and credibility from the beginning."

Even some public leaders, who are supposed to command trust, particularly in democracies, have at times been responsible for exacerbating disease trends. Thabo Mbeki, president of South Africa from 1999 to 2008, restricted nevirapine, a drug used to prevent mother-to-child transmission of HIV. He wrongly spread the message that HIV didn't cause AIDS, and so anti-retroviral therapy (ART) would not help. Even at the peak of South Africa's epidemic, Mbeki refused donations of nevirapine and grants from The Global Fund to Fight AIDS, Tuberculosis and Malaria. Through modeling, Pride Chigwedere and colleagues found that failure to implement an effective anti-retroviral program cost more than 330,000 lives in South Africa. Because South Africa did not use the nevirapine to prevent mother-to-child transmission, they estimate that 35,000 babies were born with HIV.

The final piece is political will. While those trying to eradicate smallpox faced nonexistent national health services, almost no funding, rampant conflict, and impassible roads, they were successful through "a triumph of management, not of medicine," in the worlds of Dr. Halfdan Mahler, WHO director-general at that time. In sharp contrast, COVID-19 showed a failure to lead in the short term and a failure to plan for the long term—officials knew the risks of a pandemic were high but failed to make significant changes after outbreaks of SARS and Middle East respiratory syndrome (MERS). Funding is a key part of political will. Of those paying large sums out-of-pocket for health, 87 percent are in middle-income countries. States aren't ponying up enough money to meet today's public health challenges, much less future ones. The World Bank and the WHO estimate that countries would need to spend $1 to $2 per person per year on average to "reach an acceptable level of pandemic preparedness," but they don't. Investments like that can pay big benefits, though. Eradicating smallpox meant savings of more than $1 billion a year, while the cost of eradicating the disease was less than a third of that, about $300 million from 1967 to 1980, and two-thirds of that paid by the endemic countries themselves, not wealthy developed ones.

While political capacity and political will are often lacking, there are some promising trends. One, we know how to defeat most of the diseases killing us today. Two, some health trends are on the upswing. Globally, the number of males using tobacco has declined for the first time, and the WHO projects that by 2025 there will be 5 million fewer tobacco users. Technology is promising, too. When I was in Rwanda, we saw how drones are being used to deliver blood in emergency situations, compensating for inadequate roads and mountainous terrain. This blood-delivery system, which can cut delivery times from 4 hours to 15 minutes, has helped Rwanda achieve its recent gains in child and maternal mortality.

● ● ●

We have seen how powerful a force mortality is for reshaping populations. The population divide is just as much of a divide in mortality as it is in fertility. This divide really started to solidify in the nineteenth century, when in the industrialized parts of the world knowledge about disease and infrastructure for sanitation grew and spread, drastically reducing death rates. As those societies adapted to the new reality, people could invest family resources in fewer children rather than spread time, attention, and money thin. While a rural, agrarian family whose children had a high chance of dying in infancy might have wanted six or seven children to help at home and to improve the odds that some would survive to adulthood, an urbanizing, industrial-oriented family needed far fewer children. But population growth in those settings didn't abruptly stop. One reason is population momentum, which is the tendency of a population to keep growing even after fertility falls because the women of childbearing age are part of larger cohorts from when fertility was higher—there are more women around to have kids, so the number of children is higher even if the average per woman is dropping. Another reason growth continued is that even though fertility fell, it was generally still above replacement rate.

Age structure and mortality trends are intertwined. Although some diseases are more deadly for younger people than older ones, with COVID-19 those in the youngest age groups were least likely to die. Death rates in 2020 for those 1 to 14 years were just 0.2 per 100,000, but the death rate among those over 85 years was 1,797.8. The 2009 H1N1 strain was novel in that it was more deadly for those of younger ages, unlike the seasonal flu, in which mortality is highest among older adults. The CDC estimates that 80 percent of H1N1 deaths were of those younger than 65 years—the most economically productive or potentially productive segments of the population.

Health and mortality also intersect with migration issues. Displaced populations—refugees, asylum seekers, and internally displaced persons—are especially vulnerable to disease outbreaks. One example is refugees from the fight for liberation in East Pakistan (now Bangladesh) in 1971. By that May, 9 million refugees had fled into India, and when the rains came in June, the population streaming into refugee camps swelled, as did cholera, which thrived in the wet, unsanitary environment. In fact, this is the first public-health situation in which the miraculous oral rehydration solution mentioned earlier in this chapter was first used. Social distancing—a catch phrase from COVID-19 but a common prevention strategy—and other preventative measures are difficult in crowded camps. When vulnerable populations already have a hard time getting basic needs such as clean water, it is unrealistic to expect delivery of personal protective equipment. Even migrants and refugees living in developed states are especially vulnerable, as they are overrepresented among the homeless population. We also see how public-health crises affect refugee operations. As COVID-19 became widespread in March 2020, the International Organization for Migration and the UNHCR announced a temporary suspension of resettlement travel for refugees. Seach and rescue operations were suspended in the dangerous transit corridor of the central Mediterranean.

Finally, health and mortality intersect with environmental issues. In our discussion of zoonoses, we saw how diseases jump from animals to humans. Ebola only spills over from animals to humans when tropical rain forests are clear-cut and roosting bats displaced or when people consume infected chimpanzees. Climate change also exacerbates disease, in ways we have just begun to understand. The geographic distribution of diseases carried by the *Aedes aegypti* mosquito, such as Zika, dengue, and chikungunya, are increasing because of climate instability. When winters are not cold enough to kill mosquitoes and when mosquito season grows longer because of shorter winters, then mosquitoes end up in new climates where the population may not have immunity to diseases they commonly carry. The same goes for ticks and other creatures that carry vector-borne diseases, such as Lyme disease. Changing rainfall patterns, high temperatures, and humidity are three factors that influence the distribution of vector-borne, disease-producing pathogens, and all of these are affected by climate change.

When we're using mortality and disease trends to inform forecasts about political, economic, and social trends, one of the flags should be cases that deviate from expected patterns. On the whole, life expectancy gets longer, rates of communicable diseases decrease with development, and technological progress gives us greater understanding into tackling early death from NCDs. So, when life expectancy declines, as it did in the United States over recent years, or when rates of diseases such as cholera spike, we have the opportunity to review how well we've invested in our health foundation and should heed the warning to do better now so we can be healthier in the future.

CHAPTER 4

People on the Move

If you could make it past her platinum hair, arched brows, dark lashes, and pouty lips, you might notice actress Tippi Hedren's perfect manicure. In the style of the time, Hedren and her glossy, elegantly rounded nails graced the big screen in Alfred Hitchcock's 1963 film *The Birds* and in dozens of other films.

It was those nails that drew the eyes of a group of refugee women Hedren was working with through her outreach as an international relief coordinator with Food for the Hungry. After the United States wound down its involvement in Vietnam and Saigon fell to the communist North Vietnamese, South Vietnamese refugees fled for the United States and elsewhere. As Hedren aided the so-called boat people from her station on a rented Australian battleship in the South China Sea, the actress and the refugees developed a deep connection. Once back in California, she continued working with the refugee camps there. When the women she encountered in Camp Hope complimented Hedren's nails, she had the idea to fly in her personal manicurist, Dusty Coots, every weekend to teach nail technology to 20 promising young women. One of those original 20, Thuan Le, recalls that Hedren encouraged them to learn the novel technique of silk nail wrapping because they could earn more money than traditional manicures paid. And earn they did. From its humble start in a Sacramento refugee camp in 1975, the Vietnamese-dominated nail industry today is worth $7.5 billion. As those first 20 women worked and grew their businesses, word spread to friends and family back in Vietnam and among those already in the United States. Today, about 80 percent of California's licensed manicurists are Vietnamese, as are 45 percent of all manicurists in the United States.

Like Chinese investors in Sydney, Pakistani construction workers in Abu Dhabi, or Korean greengrocers in New York, people who move to find opportunities play an important role in driving the train of migration worldwide. The remarkable story of Vietnamese nail salons in America not only illustrates the importance of networks in facilitating migration from one country to another but also shows how the line between political and economic migrants can blur. This situation is not unique and is often problematic.

Vietnamese migrants in the United States are a small fraction of the 272 million people today living outside their country of birth. Altogether, these migrants would be the fifth most populous country in the world. Of course, they're not all together, and it's their dispersal across the globe and their diversity that makes issues of migration so politically, economically, and socially interesting.

What drives people to leave home? Who moves? How does migration change both sending and receiving societies? Why do some countries have more open borders than others? And how should we expect migration—and reactions to it—to change in the future? Throughout this chapter, we'll explore each of these questions in depth and consider how issues of identity, law, and capitalism play a role in the movement of people across borders. While migration is the least predictable of the three population drivers (fertility, mortality, and migration), we can observe patterns that help us better project the impact of migration in a world of 8 billion people—and what it might mean for our understanding of the world more generally.

One way to think about why people move is to zoom out and consider the structures within which people live and work. One structure is the global economy, which operates as a series of transactions between countries and corporations of various sizes, places, and power. Industrialization drove the first era of mass global migration between 1850 and 1914, but between World War I and the end of World War II, global migration declined because of conflict, xenophobia, economic stagnation, and tighter national borders. After 1949 migration again picked up, due in large part to the new opportunities created by global economic growth.

As we know, such opportunities aren't evenly distributed around the globe—the great divide between wealthier and poorer countries is clearly reflected in migration patterns. Naturally, migrants are generally more attracted to places with higher earning potential.

Place matters in other ways as well. Geography, particularly proximity, is always a factor in shaping flows of people: It's the simple reason why more Mexicans go to the United States than to Europe and why sub-Saharan Africa hosts more than a quarter of the world's refugees.

Relative power is its own structure. As an example, many European countries have relationships with their former colonies and often receive migrants from them in a unidirectional flow, such as South Asians to the United Kingdom. Proximity aside, economic structure and the distribution of power help us understand why migration follows a clear pattern—individual choices about whether or not to move are constrained by place in society, access to means and information, and even the confines and expectations of cultures.

At this macro level are other theories about why people move. Some of these theories treat societies much like biological organisms, which they assume to have a natural tendency toward equilibrium. One such example is the classic push–pull model of migration, the theory that likely first comes to mind for most readers who try to understand why people move. This model assumes that lack of economic or political opportunity "pushes" people to emigrate, while at the same time a chance to work or gain freedom "pulls" migrants to particular destinations. Migration theoretically continues until there's no longer a strong push or a strong pull, when the system reaches equilibrium. For decades, lack of job opportunities in Mexico "pushed" emigrants while the promise of jobs "pulled" them to the United States. After the 2008 recession, there were fewer jobs in the United States, and because of population aging, Mexico's youngest working-age cohorts began to peak, meaning wages there started to rise. Fewer migrants left Mexico, and high numbers left the United States to return home. The system began to equalize.

What's nice about the push–pull framework is its simplicity; that's also what's problematic. If lack of opportunity or repression were alone enough to push people to leave, we would see far greater numbers of migrants around the world. With this framework, it's hard to see why anyone would stay in a poor, conflict-ridden country when they could move to a richer, stable one. We know there's more to migration than these macro-level theories illuminate, because although stories of migration pervade the media, global migration rates have stayed stable during the past 50 years, with only 2 to 4 percent of the world's people living outside of their countries of origin. Obviously, there's something missing from a purely structural account of migration flows.

We might buy that the global capitalist structure or the historical relationships between countries such as India and the United Kingdom drive the direction of migration flows, particularly from poor to rich settings, but it can be hard to see how those large-scale factors end up directly affecting the decisions of a particular person or family to move. Micro-level theories complement the macro by considering the influence of family ties, individual beliefs, or practices in shaping migration flows. Migration to reunify families is one example; a mother or father may leave their home country to find work elsewhere, save money, and then try to bring their family to the new country a few years later.

Between these broad and narrow theories is another set of theories that attribute migration patterns to factors such as the "migration industry," immigrant communities, or businesses that cater to migrants, all of which help facilitate and shape flows. The growth of the Vietnamese nail industry in America from the initial 20 women trained in the refugee camp is a perfect example of the importance of those network ties and helps explain how the robust Vietnamese American community of today came to be. The presence of some Vietnamese in the US nail industry and their ties back to Vietnam makes that line of work more accessible to those in Vietnam wishing to emigrate to the United States to work; thus, the pattern continues and deepens.

As we consider various historical, contemporary, and even future migration throughout this chapter, we can keep these macro-level, micro-level, and intermediate-level (also known as meso-level) theories in mind. No one theory is "right"—all have value in shedding light on particular cases and situations, which is the very purpose of theory. As we continue to deepen our understanding of global migration, our next big question is: Who moves?

* ⊛ *

It's a common myth that migrants are the world's poorest and least skilled, but it takes money and know-how to leave the country in which you were born and find a new home—think of the knowledge it takes just to get a passport in an industrialized country or a visa to visit a country that requires one, plus the need for a second language, time to fill out bureaucratic paperwork, and so on. The same is true of internal migration, even though the barriers are fewer. The poorest citizens in the world's poorest countries aren't able to afford to emigrate, and many wouldn't have a clue how to navigate the process. In 2013, less than 3 percent of impoverished Niger's population, for example, lived outside its borders. But India, Bangladesh, China, Pakistan, and Mexico—all rapidly developing countries—are major sources of international migrants, dispersed across the globe. According to the United Nations, the Indian diaspora counted 18 million Indians abroad in 2019—the top spot. Given that India has 1.3 billion people and an increasingly educated and skilled population, that's unsurprising. What's a bit more surprising is that Mexico, with one-tenth of India's population, had the second highest diaspora population in 2019, at 12 million. Geography clearly plays a role, as Mexico shares a long and somewhat porous border with one of the richest countries in the world. Other major diaspora countries in 2019 were China with 11 million, Russia with 10 million, and Syria with 8 million.

It's obvious from the makeup of that list that both conflict and economic factors play a role in which countries are the world's top senders; those same factors determine where they go as well; namely, places that are conflict-free and with economic opportunities. High-income countries are home to almost two-thirds of all international migrants; the lowest income countries have only 4 percent, and the rest reside in middle-income countries.* Between 2000 and 2010, the migration "corridor" from China to the United States was the third largest in the world, partly due to the large number of Chinese students at US universities. While migration to the Global North—advanced, industrialized countries—is still robust, migration within the Global South—less developed countries—has been increasing, particularly within Asia. In fact, by 2019 the China–US "corridor" had dropped to seventh largest in volume of migrants, below the 12 million who traversed from Mexico to the United States, the 3.7 million from Syria to Turkey, the 3.4 million from India to UAE, the 3.35 million

• • •

* Using the World Bank income classifications, high-income countries are those with an average per capita income of $12,616 or higher. Middle-income countries have an average per capita income between $1,036 and $12,615.

from Russia to Ukraine and another 3.3 million in the reverse flow, and finally the 3.1 million from Bangladesh to India.

In some countries, emigration is a pillar of the economy—it would collapse without the "export" of human capital. The Philippines is one example. The Philippines has been one of the world's most reliable providers of foreign labor during the past couple of decades, with 2.2 million overseas foreign workers (OFWs) in 2019 out of a population of just over 100 million. Some portray migration as a last resort, as a haphazard by-product of domestic and global dynamics. We can also see it as a deliberate strategy, as it is in the Philippines, where the government takes an active role in helping its citizens find jobs outside the country. With an underdeveloped economy at home, OFWs have become an integral part of the Filipino economy, sending back billions upon billions of dollars to support their families. In just 6 months of 2019, Filipino OFWs sent back 211.9 billion pesos, or $4.7 billion. In fact, many economists have criticized the country's leaders for depending on migration *instead* of developing.

But, not everyone moves by choice. That's true historically and today. The United Nations Office on Drugs and Crime defines human trafficking as "the acquisition of people by improper means such as force, fraud or deception, with the aim of exploiting them." Africa experienced negative population growth between 1600 and 1900 in the largest scale of human trafficking imaginable, with at least 12 million Africans loaded as human cargo onto ships bound for the Americas and other parts of the world. The exploitation of African slaves was a complex system perpetrated by the highest levels of government and the most powerful countries in the world, making complicit a host of actors along the way. Today's slavery is most often perpetrated by transnational networks of organized crime. Those African slaves were trafficked to toil in fields; today, about half of trafficked people are trafficked for sexual exploitation, sometimes forced into marriage. Among adult women, who compose just under half of trafficked persons, 77 percent are trafficked for sexual exploitation, 14 percent for forced labor, and 9 percent for other exploitation, such as forced involvement in criminal activity or begging. Two out of every 10 trafficked persons is an adult male, and the reasons for their trafficking are nearly reversed: 17 percent for sexual exploitation, 67 percent for forced labor in industries such as mining and fishing, 1 percent for organ removal, and 15 percent for other forms of exploitation. Scale is another difference between historical trafficking and today's. In 2018, the number of recorded human trafficking cases reached 49,000 (although that number is a fraction of the cases the United Nations estimates actually exist), whereas during slavery, flows out of Africa remade the demographics of entire countries. The slave trade was a massive transatlantic flow; today's trafficking victims are generally sent to the same subregion or region or frequently trafficked within their own national borders.

I mention trafficking because it is a form of migration, but historical slavery and contemporary trafficking introduce a host of complex factors that deserve extended treatment and are not the focus of this chapter nor of this book. Trafficking, by definition, lacks consent of the person being moved, and such persons are trafficked to labor in the world's most dangerous jobs, such as mining, deep-sea fishing, pornography, or child soldiering. Smuggling, however, is an important part of the migration story in this chapter. In contrast to trafficking, would-be migrants generally consent to being smuggled. Although the United Nations and many others conflate the two as equally negative, for many living in conflict-ridden countries, smugglers are the only way out, the only hope for a better future. Yet, there's some truth to this conflation: The displaced and desperate make ideal victims, especially when smugglers promise them deliverance to safety, only to trick them along the way and traffic them into a situation as dangerous as the one they fled. Human trafficking networks thrive on conflicts such as Syria's: as the UN Office of Drugs and Crime found in its 2016 report, Syria experienced a "rapid increase" in victims after the start of the civil war.

This brings us to our last major category of migrants, those forcibly displaced, including refugees, asylum seekers, and those internally displaced, which we examine in greater detail later in the chapter.

Legally, refugees are migrants who have crossed an international border and are seeking resettlement in a third country through legal pathways. Asylum seekers are migrants who do not have legal migration status and who have already crossed an international border or borders in order to apply for asylum; according to the United Nations High Commissioner for Refugees (UNHCR), they "have crossed an international border in search of protection but . . . have not yet had their claims decided." To illustrate, a Syrian refugee might cross into Turkey, register with the United Nations there, and eventually be resettled in Germany. A Syrian asylum-seeker might cross *through* Turkey, make his way across Eastern Europe, and apply for asylum *after* arriving in Germany. Refugees and asylum seekers are just a fraction of the world's forcibly displaced people, a category that includes those internally displaced, meaning forced to leave their homes but still within their home country's borders, and stateless persons, meaning those who can't get citizenship anywhere. The area of the world where statelessness has become an endemic problem is also an area of the world where population growth is the highest, and conflict is as well. It may be surprising to learn that the majority of those displaced today aren't refugees at all, they're internally displaced, more than 55 million at the end of 2020, 48 million of which were displaced by conflict and violence. An additional 26 million people are refugees, and another 4.2 million are asylum seekers. There also 4.2 million stateless people on record, but likely millions more uncounted. Altogether, the UNHCR estimates that conflict and persecution have forced 1 percent of the world's people to flee their homes.

As it did for nonemergency migration, the great divide in population trends of the twenty-first century shows up in refugee situations in both expected and unexpected ways. As we would expect, the 79.5 million forcibly displaced people (as of end-2019) across the globe hail from the poorest, least democratic, or most unstable countries in the world. In fact, 68 percent of the world's refugees come from only five countries: Syria, Venezuela, Afghanistan, South Sudan, and Myanmar. It may be more surprising to learn that the burden of displacement today doesn't fall on high-income countries, such as the United States or Australia. Instead, 79.5 percent of the people forcibly displaced today are being hosted by developing countries such as Lebanon, Jordan, Turkey, Pakistan, Iran, Ethiopia, and Kenya. Turkey, gateway to Europe from the conflict-ridden Middle East, had 3.6 million refugees at the end of 2019. Colombia and Pakistan hosted 1.8 million and 1.4 million, respectively, and Uganda had 1.4 million. The only high-income country in the top five refugee-hosting countries was Germany, with 1.1 million. The issue is even more complex when we consider that refugee crises almost exclusively occur in the poorest areas of the world, and, contrary to media images, most refugees are not in camps. Instead, they are dispersed among the local population, which creates its own set of issues as these displaced persons compete with locals for housing and jobs.

Although they shoulder far less of the burden, richer countries go to great lengths to keep refugees and asylum seekers out. "Fortress Europe"—with tight controls on who gets in—arose during the 1990s as asylum became increasingly politicized. In 1992, the European Union established the principle of "safe third-country" states as a buffer zone around Europe. This meant it could reject someone seeking asylum in Europe if that person transited to Europe via a "safe country" on the principal that the person could be safely returned to the safe country and avoid persecution. There are other laws and practices along these lines. According to the Dublin Regulation, asylum seekers arriving in Europe are not able to choose which country processes, and potentially grants or denies, their asylum application. In practice, that means a migrant transiting to Europe via the Mediterranean may land in Italy or Greece but try to make his or her way to Germany undetected before applying for asylum. Italy and Greece may turn a blind eye so that they do not have to deal with applications in an already overloaded asylum system. The designation of "refugee" was political from the start—Palestinians don't fall under the mandate of the United Nations refugee agency, but have their own agency, the United Nations Relief and Works Agency for Palestinian Refugees in the Middle East (UNRWA). The UNRWA manages refugee camps and provides aid for the original Palestinians who fled home as a result of the 1947–1948 war in Palestine and their descendants. Those who lived in Mandatory Palestine between June 1946 and May 1948 and who lost their homes and means of livelihood as a result of the 1948 Arab–Israeli conflict are considered refugees, as are their patrilineal descendants, no matter where those descendants have citizenship. In 1950, the number of Palestinians eligible for UNRWA services numbered 750,000. Four generations later the number has grown to 5.6 million.

From the poor Somali trafficked for forcible organ removal to the wealthy Singaporean businesswoman moving to a posh corner of London, there's no "typical" migrant today. All sorts of people move, and for all sorts of reasons, but it's how their arrival affects their new communities and how it affects the dynamics of the communities that they leave behind that we now turn to.

• • •

The United States is known as a "country of immigration," but its neighbor to the north models how immigration can change a country's composition and the very definition of nationhood more acutely. More than one in five Canadians is a first-generation migrant,* and Canada was one of the first countries in the world to adopt an explicit policy valuing multiculturalism, where citizens are encouraged to keep their identities and take pride in their ancestry. At the same time, even a diverse, liberal

• • •

* First-generation means foreign-born people that came through the Canadian immigration system.

country such as Canada is not immune to debates over immigration. Pockets of Canadians have vocally and vehemently resisted the changes immigration can bring, including French Canadians, who "were not interested in being demoted to one of many 'cultures'" and are concentrated in the province of Quebec, which uses an integration policy instead of multiculturalism to preserve its distinctiveness. Resistance to immigration happens across cultures, times, and polities because when people move, they move their skills, beliefs, values, and problems along with them—the good and the bad, the similar and the unique. Immigration can change receiving societies by giving them a huge economic boost. It can also cause tremendous backlash among the native-born population. The identity politics within Western democracies these days is clear evidence of the latter, and the combination of low fertility and high immigration in this set of countries means there's more to come.

Just as trends in fertility and mortality fundamentally alter a population's size and composition, so does migration. Demographer David Coleman has labeled the change in ethnic composition within societies as a result of long-term migration the *third demographic transition* to show how fundamental and permanent the shift is.* When studying immigration, there's a tendency to focus on new immigrants, but the big changes often come with subsequent generations. Although there's no set definition, in migration research we typically define people born outside the country in which they reside as first-generation immigrants, and second-generation immigrants are defined as native-born persons with both parents foreign-born. Adding those two categories together we get "persons with a migration background," which in Australia was already 45 percent of those ages 20 to 29 in 2005. Australia's 2016 census showed nearly half of Australians had at least one parent born abroad. Persons with a migration background numbered 37.5 percent in Swit-

• • •

* For reference, remember that the first transition was from high to low fertility and mortality, and the second transition was to super-low fertility.

zerland in 2018, 32.5 percent in Canada, and 20 to 30 percent in Sweden, the United States, the Netherlands, France, and the United Kingdom. In Germany, only one parent without German citizenship by birth qualifies someone as having a migration background in the state's eyes. In 2017, approximately 19.3 million people in Germany were in this category, 23.5 percent of Germany's population and 4.4 percent higher than in 2016. These percentages are only increasing over time with new immigration.

Looking more closely at Europe illustrates the significant changes in size and composition immigration brings. Cross-border movement within Europe has been going on for centuries, and the continent has seen periods of mass exodus, too—between 1850 and 1914, about 55 million people left Europe to settle elsewhere. But Europe is relatively new to the receiving end, a change fostered by decolonization, growth in non-European populations around the world, rapid economic growth, and the creation of the European Union as a free trade and migration zone. Given the newness of this status, it's not really surprising that immigration is hotly debated in the European political arena. Immigration changes the racial, cultural, and religious composition of a community, and such changes are not always welcome. Many of the immigrants to European states come from other European states; migration from east to west is still popular, even decades after the end of the Cold War shook up Soviet bloc countries and freed its people to move elsewhere. These changes matter, but it's the non-European immigrants that are making some of the most obvious changes in composition and fueling right-leaning political movements. In particular, religious changes are becoming an important part of the political narrative around migration.

Remember, when people move their identities come with them—differences in ethnicity or religion are thrown into stark relief. While still a small fraction, Muslims are increasing as a proportion of Europe's population, and that growth is creating angst among some non-Muslim Europeans, particularly those who adhere to a strong ideal of secularism, as in France, or Christianity, as in Poland. Muslims composed almost 5 percent of Europe's population in 2016, and even if there were no new immigration, with natural increase that proportion would grow to 7.4 percent by 2050, according to projections by the Pew Research Center. With regular migration (assuming the record-high refugee flows of the latter 2010s stops), the proportion of Muslims could reach 11.2 percent. This composition shift is magnified by the aging and shrinking of Europe's non-Muslim population. Excess of deaths over births meant the non-Muslim population decreased by 1.67 million between 2010 and 2016 while the Muslim population increased by 2.92 million from excess births over deaths. Net migration added even more to the latter. But a Muslim majority is not in Europe's near future: Even if the refugee flows of 2014–2016 continued, along with regular immigration, Muslims would only make up 14 percent of Europe's population by mid-century. In fact, almost half of the recent migrants to Europe were non-Muslim, and significant portions were Christian. The most likely scenario, a doubling of the proportion of Muslims, is notable, but not nearly as high as much of the political rhetoric in Europe leads us to believe. Still, change is hard on a society, particularly demographic change. More important from a political perspective, the demographic impact of immigration to Europe is uneven. Germany was one of the most desired destinations for asylum seekers who entered the European Union via the Mediterranean or Turkey during the 2015 refugee crisis. As of 2016 (which was before the influx of asylum seekers), Germany has a large number of Muslims—4.9 million—but they're only 6 percent of the population. Other countries have higher proportions: Bulgaria (11.1 percent), France (8.8 percent), and Sweden (8.1 percent).

In the Pew Research Center's projections to 2050, with high immigration of refugees and economic migrants, Germany's population would reach 20 percent Muslim, 11 percent in the medium scenario with consistent levels of immigration, and 9 percent in the zero-migration scenario. Whichever happens, when it comes to politics, the actual numbers of migrants rarely matters as much as does the perception of those numbers.

Although the sources of migrants and the numbers are different, the politics of immigration is just as heated in the United States, home to the world's highest number of international migrants—defined as the number of people living in a country in which they were not born—at 45 million. That's about one-fifth of the world's migrants just in the United States. Immigrants have been an increasing proportion of the US population since the passage of major immigration reform in 1965. That reform, known as the Hart–Celler Act, rolled back the nativist 1924 Johnson–Reed Act that established a national origins quota system to prevent immigration of Southern Europeans and Asians. The 1965 reform was passed smack in the middle of the US civil rights movement, just 1 year after Congress passed the Civil Rights Act that banned discrimination on the basis of race, religion, color, sex, or national origin. The removal of those national origins quotas quickly remade the US immigrant population, first increasing the proportion of Southern Europeans, and then non-Europeans in general. As of 2018, more than 13 percent of the US population was foreign-born. Three-quarters of US immigrants are legal, leaving 11 million unauthorized immigrants in the country, down from a record 12.3 million in 2007. The US migrant population is diverse, as the top global destination for migrants since 1970, even despite slower flows since the 2008 financial crisis. If trends in new arrivals and births to immigrant parents continue, immigrants and their descendants could account for 88 percent of US population growth through 2065.

• • •

Given all of the domestic changes immigration brings, how do governments and their people calculate the pros and cons? Why do some countries decide the benefits of allowing immigrants are worth the challenges?

Although the rhetoric is often magnanimous, only rarely do human-itarian considerations drive immigration policies. Even multicultural Canada's immigration policy is skills-based, not based on reunifying families—economic considerations predominate. The Persian Gulf states have the world's highest share of foreign-born people, mostly temporary labor migrants from the Indian subcontinent, and they are prohibited from permanently settling. Those countries that are cur-rently the world's top immigrant receivers, the United States, Canada, the United Kingdom, Australia, Germany, the Russian Federation, and Italy, have all benefited from an influx of high- and low-skilled workers to fill domestic labor shortages. As we know, population aging means shrinking workforces in all of these countries—should we expect more liberal immigration policies to compensate for rising median ages? To answer, let's first look at the economics. Without future immigration, Europe's population would shrink from about 521 million to about 482 million by mid-century, but with steady levels of regular immigration, the population size will remain fairly stable, according to Pew projec-tions. Immigrants have a relatively younger age profile: More than 75 percent of the people who applied for asylum in EU-27 countries in 2019 and 2020 were younger than 35 years, and just under half (47 per-cent) were between ages 18 and 34. But European economies have to be structurally equipped to receive extra labor, and with unemployment rates already high, particularly for youth, it's clear those structures are not in place. And not all "migrants" are the same; for example, accepting more refugees and asylees won't necessarily solve the labor shortages from population aging. The influx of refugees to Europe from Syria and other war-torn areas only offsets economic losses from population aging if migrants are allowed to obtain employment, if they are quickly economically integrated, and if their skill sets match Europe's labor mar-ket needs. Syrians of all skill sets have emigrated, but we know from research in other settings that for various reasons, including lack of established networks and a mismatch between skills and labor demands in the destination country, refugees often have lower employment rates than those of economic migrants. Even with immigration, Europe's age structure will grow older (not all immigrants are children who could bring the median age way down, and any immigrants who stay will age).

We also have to consider the political consequences of more liberal immigration. Immigration partly offsets population aging, but to replace retiring workers, European states would have to virtually swing their doors open to migrants—an untenable policy in an atmosphere of increasing resentment against Muslim immigrants and public concerns about native youth unemployment. In projections by the Pew Research Center, with regular immigration patterns, Sweden's Muslim population could rise to 21 percent by 2050 and because of past immigration would reach 11 percent even absent any future immigration. If the record-high immigration of 2014–2016 continued, almost one-third of Sweden's population would be Muslim. That's not likely to fly with some voters.

When countries open to immigration, it's often for economic reasons; when they close their doors, more often than not it's for nativist ones. There are many countries in the world with very low levels of immigration by design. Japan is a global innovator in figuring out ways to avoid increasing immigration by trying to bring more women and older persons into the workforce and using technology in place of eldercare workers. The same is true for South Korea, although it has been more open in the past few years. What we have to remember is that openness to immigration is a choice, not a necessity, even for the most aged countries on the planet. Much of that choice is driven by fear of change, a fear that is pervasive globally, historically, and culturally.

• • •

In the sixth book of L. Frank Baum's fictional Land of Oz series, *The Emerald City of Oz* (published in 1910), Princess Ozma, the rightful ruler of Oz, fights off invading gnomes while simultaneously welcoming Dorothy, Aunt Em, and Uncle Henry as permanent new residents of Oz. Toward the end of the book, Ozma says:

> It seems to me there are entirely too many ways for people to get to the Land of Oz. We used to think the deadly desert that surrounds us was enough protection; but that is no longer the case. . . . So I believe something must be done to cut us off from the rest of the world entirely, so that no one in the future will ever be able to intrude on us.

As author Bruce Handy notes, the New York–born Baum was finishing his Oz series during the peak of immigration from Europe to the United States and the growing anti-immigration sentiment. That sentiment manifested in the Immigration Act of 1907, one of several restrictive laws debated around that time in the wake of increasing angst about immigration to the United States. As a result of the 1907 law, a commission, named the Dillingham Commission, investigated immigration patterns and found that "new immigrants," those from Southern and Eastern Europe, were a threat to American society and culture. The Dillingham Commission report would eventually result in America's extremely exclusionary laws of the 1920s, including the aforementioned Johnson–Reed Act. Princess Ozma, then, captures well the pervasive sentiment toward immigrants in the United States at the time.

Other "countries of immigration" have similar histories. Australia's illustrates the tension between humanitarian, economic, and nativist concerns. Home first to native aboriginal peoples, then famously a settler colony for English prisoners, Australia has been responding to its popularity as a destination for those seeking a better life throughout its history as a nation-state. Despite the importance of migration for shaping Australia's population profile today, the country has one of the world's toughest border policies. It turns back boats filled with those seeking asylum, detains migrants in overcrowded centers, and refuses

resettlement—it has even excised several outlying islands from its juris-
diction in order to evade the laws requiring due process for asylum seekers if they reach the state via one of these excised territories.

The first modern wave of boats arriving to Australia for sanctuary
was in 1976, transporting Vietnamese fleeing the war. More recently,
boats carrying those fleeing conflicts in the Middle East and South
Asia have found an unsympathetic reception. In August 2001, when
a Norwegian freighter, the MV *Tampa*, rescued and then transported
438 Afghan asylum seekers to Christmas Island, an Australian territory,
Australia's Howard government refused the ship's entry. The event was
intensely publicized, and increasingly hostile public sentiment toward
the illegal arrivals characterized this period, giving the Howard government the mandate to act accordingly. Introduced a few weeks later in
September 2001, the "Pacific Solution," which allows Australia to house
asylum seekers in detention centers throughout Pacific Island nations,
rather than on the Australian mainland, enjoyed the bipartisan backing
of Howard's Liberal Party and the Labour opposition. One of these is
the poor island of Nauru, which agreed to house asylum seekers for
Australia in exchange for millions of dollars in aid and processing fees.
In 2013 Australia went even further, excising even the mainland from
the migration zone, meaning that someone arriving illegally, such as by
boat, and hoping to obtain a visa or apply for asylum may not do so. If it
sounds like fancy legal maneuvering to simply say that no one may show
up in Australia and apply for asylum, that's because it is.

Australia's harsh policies are out of sync with its relatively open
economic immigration policies and are partly driven by public disdain
for the perceived "queue jumping" of those trying to arrive illegally.
Despite social strains, because Australia has important relationships
with sending countries in the region, politicians will walk a fine line
between appeasing nativist interests and migrant communities. These
opposing pressures in democracies with immigration backgrounds are
ever present.

Case Study: Refugees, Asylum Seekers, and the Limits of International Law

In May of 2015, thousands of ethnic Rohingya from Myanmar crowded into rickety boats, their bodies so tightly packed they threatened to spill into the water at the slightest tip from a wave. And many did, swallowed by the ocean, succumbing to the very fate they had fled from in the first place: death. The people who filled these boats were part of the rare but sizeable number of around 4 million stateless persons across the globe.* They weren't citizens of any country, and no one would take them in. Country after country denied them landfall, shirking any obligation to help. So they drifted, stranded in the Andaman Sea, west of Thailand, in what the media termed "floating coffins." Many starved to death; others died of dehydration. Like an apocalyptic nightmare, the living were forced to toss the dead, including babies and children, overboard. This is the exact situation international refugee law was designed to prevent, but as with so many international laws, there are ways around it.

According to the 1951 United Nations Convention Relating to the Status of Refugees, a refugee is someone who, "owing to a well-founded fear of being persecuted for reasons of race, religion, nationality, membership of a particular social group or political opinion, is outside the country of his nationality, and is unable to, or owing to such fear, is unwilling to avail himself of the protection of that country." That treaty, and the 1967 Protocol that affirms it, is supposed to protect groups such as the Rohingya, but leaders from Thailand, Malaysia, Indonesia, and Australia claimed they couldn't be sure that the people on the boats were actually fleeing persecution; some of them were surely just economic migrants looking for a better life, and if so, there was no legal obligation to take them in. These people needed to go through the usual channels,

. . .

* As of the end of 2019. The United Nations estimates the actual number is higher but is unable to obtain a more accurate figure.

not crash-land. Or, as Australian prime minister Tony Abbott said of the Rohingya boat people: "I'm sorry. If you want to start a new life, you come through the front door, not through the back door." Similarly, the 2015 European migrant crisis demonstrated both the difficulty in disentangling economic and conflict migrants and the limits of international law. Sovereign states such as Hungary could and did close their borders to migrants, citing as justification the intermixing of economic migrants with asylum seekers who might qualify to receive refuge under international law.

Since inception, there have been significant problems with the governance—or lack thereof—of refugees and asylum seekers. Here are five reasons why.

First, refugees were not always an international political concern, nor were they always framed as a "problem." Caroline Moorehead, in her book *Human Cargo*, relates how political refugees Voltaire and Jean-Jacques Rousseau were considered assets, not liabilities. The international community became more concerned about refugees after the breakup of the Austro-Hungarian and Ottoman empires after World War I. Then, in the show of goodwill and cooperation that abounded in the aftermath of World War II, the international community formed an international refugee regime, or set of laws, to govern such displacement. Part of the impetus was the feeling that what happened to refugees who were turned away by countries like America as they fled Hitler[*] should never happen again. But another part was political. Western states designed the international refugee system at the beginning of the Cold War to send a message that people wanted to flee communism for the West, a victory in this burgeoning ideological war. Once the Cold War ended, though, and that sharp divide disappeared, the ideological message sent by refugees no longer resonated. Refugees had been flee-

• • •

[*] Such as those aboard the ill-fated SS St. Louis in 1939.

ing "the enemy," but the end of the Cold War threw into disarray who the enemy was.

The second is a design flaw: The global community saw refugees from World War II and those at the beginning of the Cold War as a short-term problem, and in the euphoria of triumph over evil, they did not foresee the waves of ethnic conflict that would erupt across Africa during the 1990s or the turmoil across the Middle East and many parts of the world today. Compared to today's intractable civil wars, World War II was brief. The global refugee regime is the strongest international law governing international migration, but it's myopic.

The third problem is that states can easily circumvent obligations to help those being persecuted. When people flee countries mired in conflict and plagued with broken economies and political repression, they are doing so for good reason. But, to qualify for resettlement, the specific reason for fleeing must be covered by the 1951 Convention Relating to the Status of Refugees and the 1967 Protocol. When those seeking a better economic future are mixed with those fleeing political persecution, as happened with the Rohingya from Myanmar, even liberal democracies claim grounds to deny them entry. There are other gaps, too. Although the media warns of impending waves of "climate refugees," climate change is not a qualifying reason for resettlement, and thus the term is inaccurate. Those facing natural disasters from climate change are more likely to be treated as economic migrants in search of a better life than as refugees. An arsenal of national and international laws address various aspects of immigration, but children often slip through the cracks. In 2014, the US Border Patrol apprehended more than 68,000 children trying to reach the United States without an adult—a 77 percent increase from the year before. Many of these children were fleeing gang violence in countries with the world's highest homicide rates. These children have generally sought asylum on those grounds, but they face a tough sell. Others are fleeing general poverty or abusive situations at home and are far outside the scope of asylum policy. Illegal migrants are technically law-breakers, so countries see them as perpetrators, but the many who have fled horrors and suffer exploitation are also victims. Advocates have argued for better safeguards for the maintenance of these child asylum seekers' well-being and rights, such as government-sponsored legal aid and child advocates. The large number of children fleeing Syria has demonstrated the continued importance of attention to this issue. And those gaps extend to adults as well. Throughout the autumn of 2018, the thousands of Central American emigrants who traveled northward in large groups trying to reach the southern US border, cross, and claim asylum faced significant issues justifying their claims under the 1951 and 1967 agreements.

Fourth, numbers used to be smaller. The USSR limited emigration, so absolute numbers of refugees and asylum seekers from the Soviet Union to Europe and other places was far smaller than the rush that happened after the Cold War, when conflicts erupted across Europe, Africa, and the Middle East. With 80 million forcibly displaced persons today, the numbers are overwhelming.

Fifth, terrorist attacks in Europe and 9/11 in the United States have securitized migration in general, but especially migration from conflict areas. (Securitization here means linking migration to existential threats to society.) Highly publicized terrorist events committed by people of immigrant backgrounds living in the West has fueled anti-immigrant sentiment, which in turn feeds the resentment of some migrants and their radicalization, perpetuating the cycle. Immigrants to liberal states increasingly come from states rife with conflict and that are hotbeds of extremism, giving rise to the perception that immigrants themselves are terrorists. This perception is reflected in policies. Although the United States has resettled more refugees than any other country since the creation of its federal Refugee Resettlement Program in 1980, under the Trump administration the number was drastically cut, to 18,000 in FY 2020 and 15,000 in FY 2021, and it was proclaimed that the United States would no longer take refugees from Syria. The Biden administration pledged to reraise the ceiling to 125,000 for FY 2022.

Given the variety of challenges—from legal wording, to political changes, to scale—we should expect a dismal fate for refugees, asylum seekers, and stateless persons. Since at least 1994, annual resettlement rates have never exceeded 1 percent of the global refugee population. The need for help is increasing, but no solution is coming.

• • •

We've seen significant resistance to migration. Policy makers wrongly see migration as a problem that can be dealt with by decreasing aspirations to migrate, rather than as an inevitable process driven by conflict, economic structures, and social networks. They promote development aid to sending countries as a panacea, but it takes generations of improved economic conditions for a country to become a net immigration rather than emigration country. After increased immigration in 2015, developed countries refocused efforts on deterring migration from less developed states by using development assistance. As scholars Michael Clemens and Hannah Postel argue, "Such policies seem intuitive: if there are more jobs and there is less violence at home, people may feel less compelled to move. However, these directives rarely rest on evidence that aid does, in fact, substantially deter migration." By way of increasing people's capabilities to migrate, aid (and the resulting development) tends to precipitate emigration—the opposite of what's intended. It's incredibly hard to figure out why people migrate, just as it is hard to identify one particular reason a couple might decide to have their first child, and so instituting policies to stop emigration is difficult. With the exception of closing borders—which is often effective—restrictive domestic policy does little to stop migration and makes it more dangerous. Such policies increase "irregular" (illegal) migration, encouraging the use of smugglers and closer ties to crime networks and creating incentives for permanent settlement among immigrants who might otherwise migrate seasonally for various economic opportunities, such as agricultural growing seasons. In addition, people with little reason to stay in their home countries aren't generally deterred from trying to migrate.

The Global Compact for Safe, Orderly, and Regular Migration, negotiated and signed in 2018 by all 193 UN Member States except for the United States, which pulled out in 2017, recognizes that while most of the world's approximately 250 million migrants emigrated deliberately and in an orderly way, there is a lack of regular—meaning legal—and safe pathways for *all* who want to migrate to do so. Yet, they do so anyway, and history repeats itself as the global community again faces a problem, a surprise, a crisis. To be sure, Europe's 2015 migrant crisis was a major impetus for the compact, both because it overwhelmed Europe and because it put the lives of so many migrants at risk, but that spike wasn't the first around the globe and it won't be the last.

There are significant pressures for greater migration governance, but there are several significant barriers to an effective global migration regime. While the Global Compact for Safe, Orderly, and Regular Migration is the first global agreement on all facets of migration, not just refugees, it is nonbinding. And therein lies the rub.

State sovereignty is still the highest principle in international relations. As crises over multiple policy areas lately have shown, even the European Union itself is tenuous, and migration policy further divides EU members. The original EU agreement left issues of migration in the hands of states. It was less than 20 years ago, through the Treaty of Amsterdam, that states of the Schengen Area in the European Union gave up their right to control immigration visas and asylum; those decisions are now made at the EU level. As Brexit and the rise of anti-immigrant parties in Europe have shown, states do not want to lose control over who passes across their borders, particularly in this age of high alert over terrorism. Binding international agreements over any issue are hard to come by, let alone issues such as migration that have such divergent interests among states.

Those conflicting interests prevent consensus on migration. Rich countries need labor from poorer countries but face domestic pressures to restrict immigration, while poorer countries need richer ones to remain open so their emigrants can send home remittances and to relieve pressure on their own labor markets. There is a general lack of global leadership on immigration issues, and international agreements are impossible without effective leadership, particularly of powerful states. The world's most powerful states benefit from the cheap labor and variety of skills that immigrants bring, and thus have no interest in regulating migration at an international level—they want to preserve the autonomy to decide who comes in and don't want standards of care imposed on migrants already in their country. That global power is mostly concentrated in the world's wealthiest states also constrains the ability of less developed states to represent their interests through global governance, as the paucity of signatures on the international conventions on migrant labor and migrant rights demonstrate (only 39 signatories in 2020, although adopted in 1990).

Scholar James Hampshire has also pointed out that few states openly embrace or codify a multicultural model (Canada is one of the few) and instead have significant nationalist pressures, something we'll see in greater detail in Chapter 6.

There is no reason to expect debates over immigrant integration to become more sanguine, because liberal states have inherent contradictions that prohibit effective immigration policies. On the one hand, capitalism and liberal values encourage openness, and on the other, national identity and public opinion press for closure.

In closing, states are highly unlikely to form global solutions to migration because they see their sovereignty as paramount, the issue lacks global leadership, and the interests of more and less developed countries conflict. Yet people will keep moving. The future of migration will look a lot like the past, dooming many to poverty, exclusion, or death, and forcing tough—but ultimately unproductive—conversations about moral responsibility within liberal states.

PART 2

• • ● • •

HOW POPULATION
TRENDS SHAPE
OUR WORLD

CHAPTER 5

Warfare and Wombfare

In its simplest definition, politics is about who gets what, when, where, and how. But how are such political decisions made? Historically, one of the most important tools has been demographic data, often in the form of a national census. Around the world and throughout time, the census is controversial because it makes official who is the majority and who is the minority, and when policy makers have access to such demographic data, they use it to distribute resources, such as schools and infrastructure, and even to apportion political offices and seats in the legislature. Different-sized groups get access to different amounts of political power, no matter where in the world we're talking about, so demography is universally at the heart of politics.

We see this vividly in Lebanon, home of one of the world's most controversial censuses. In fact, the only official census to take place in Lebanon occurred in 1932 while Lebanon was under the French-administered Mandate for Syria and Lebanon. That census revealed three major religious divisions—Maronite Christians, Shiite Muslims, and Sunni Muslims—and counted Christians as having the slightest numerical edge, with 28.8 percent of the population. Since that time, seats in Lebanon's parliament and appointed government positions, including president of the republic, the highest position of power, have been allocated using the outdated 1932 census. There is little doubt among demographers that Lebanon's demographics have shifted since the 1932 census, with a shrinking proportion of Christians because of emigration and low fertility. But despite their increasing numbers, Muslims remain a permanent minority because the Christian-based political parties have no incentive to undertake a new census that would more accurately reflect Lebanon's demographic reality. That's a problem for the "minority" sects, who argue that they aren't getting the resources or representation they deserve. Their exclusion has exacerbated resentment among this deeply divided country, which, although it has had some periods of sectarian harmony, has also experienced political crises, a violent civil war between religious sects, and 20 years without elections.

If there were a new census today, the resulting shift in political order could erupt into violence—arguably, the lack of a census preserves Lebanon's tenuous peace. As political demographer Håvard Strand and colleagues have found, the very act of publishing census data is dangerous in states with unstable regimes. The Rohingya Muslims of Myanmar, described in Chapter 4, are a prime example. After the 1983 census in Myanmar, the government reported the Muslim percentage of the population as 4 percent, even though most scholars estimate that it was more than twice that. It has only grown since then. Strand and colleagues argue, "This now creates a thorny situation for the current government, as accurately reporting the current number of Rohingyas would provide evidence for a three-fold increase in the Muslim population over the last 30 years and support the widespread belief among the Buddhist majority population that the country is being overrun by Muslims."

But demographics are no less controversial in stable regimes. That's because these demographic changes are at heart about identity politics. Varying rates of fertility, mortality, and migration among different ethnicities, races, or religions connect to competition for resources and influence. Groups with high fertility will grow faster than others; migration of one ethnic group into an area predominated by a different ethnic group changes the composition of that region. Identities are fluid and subjective, but they are also measured and observed and assigned and claimed—in short, they matter. Identity politics is here to stay, and if we track demographic trends, we gain a greater understanding of both violent identity conflicts, such as genocide, and nonviolent identity conflicts, such as right-wing populism. These conflicts are about more than just demographics, of course, but they can't be understood without appreciating the demographic dynamics that accompany them.

In Part I, we saw how policy interventions can shape fertility, mortality, and migration patterns. Here, we dig deeper to understand purposeful manipulation of population in order to gain political strength—a concept called demographic engineering. Two of the core scholars of demographic engineering, Myron Weiner and Michael Teitelbaum, define it as "the full range of government policies intended to affect the size, composition, distribution, and growth rate of a population." Others, such as Paul Morland of the University of London, define it more narrowly as the manipulation of demography by groups in conflict, often along ethnic lines. Either way, the purpose of demographic engineering is to gain advantage over an opposing group. Many attempts at demographic engineering are fairly benign, taking the form of carrots, such as tax breaks or monthly subsidies for those with children, while other attempts are more coercive—particularly when policies take the form of sticks instead of carrots. The most insidious form of demographic engineering is genocide, exterminating a rival group to achieve political ends.

Genocide is often interpreted as a conflict over identity. But identity itself is complicated. Although most of us probably think of identity—race or ethnicity in particular—as fixed, in reality it is fluid; identity groups are "imagined communities" that shift over time. A prime example is

Rwanda, a country infamous for its genocide and also one where social identities were worked and reworked throughout the twentieth century.

The Rwandan Genocide Memorial in Kigali vividly displays the creation and shifts of Rwanda's identity categories and the atrocities that resulted along ethnic lines along a winding timeline that covers history before, during, and after colonization. Before colonization, Rwandan society was structured into 19 clans to which both Tutsi and Hutu belonged. For most of the twentieth century, the categories Hutu, Tutsi, and Twa denoted socioeconomic classes within clans and were fluid. Ethnic identity was traced through the paternal line, but mixed marriages among the three main groups had been common for centuries. The groups all spoke the same language, Kinyarwanda, practiced the same Imana religion, and shared a culture. Those practical similarities met an official end at the hands of Belgian colonial administrators, and Rwandans are still dealing with the violent social upheaval nearly a century later.

These Belgian outsiders designated anyone with at least 10 cows as Tutsi and anyone with fewer than 10 as Hutu or Twa, depending on their profession, and decreed that such identity passed to their descendants. This new categorization removed the socioeconomic aspect and, by adding the designation to identity cards, made it racial and fixed. Even before the horrific genocide of 1994, Rwandan society grew more divided around these identities, both under the rule of the Belgians and after they left in 1962. Although they, and the German colonists before them, had favored the Tutsi minority, in the process of decolonization the Belgians shifted their support to the majority Hutu and thus abetted the 1959 Hutu revolution that toppled the Tutsi regime. Around 700,000 Tutsis were exiled between 1959 and 1973, including a very young Paul Kagame—who would become president in 2000—and his family. Subsequent killings were conducted under an independent government led by the architect of Hutu nationalism and first president of Rwanda, Grégoire Kayibanda.

Scholars have shown that it's a recipe for disaster when power is concentrated in the hands of a dominant minority; this was exactly the situation in Rwanda when the Belgians placed political dominance in the hands of the Tutsi minority, a common colonial tactic to avoid further empowering a demographic majority. As scholar Helen Hintjens explains, "By introducing Christianity and 'tidying up' Rwandan social groups, Belgian colonial administration cut across mechanisms of social cohesion, including the religious belief system and clan structures. This created a monolithic division between Hutu and Tutsi identities, and started to dissolve the ideological glue of Rwandan monarchical society." There were divisions not only among groups but also within them. In 1973 Juvénal Habyarimana, a Hutu from the north around the city of Gisenyi, executed a coup against his fellow Hutu, Kayibanda, whose government was dominated by Hutus from central Rwanda and excluded northern Hutu. Habyarimana then became president.

Starting in the late 1980s, economic crisis and a mounting trade deficit fed Hutu resentment of relative Tutsi success—the boundaries between identity groups further hardened. When the Habyarimana government refused to consider the return of exiled Tutsis, they invoked a different demographic excuse: Rwanda was too densely populated to allow anyone back. With this decision, the Rwandan Patriotic Front, a guerrilla army of about 5,000 to 10,000 of those previously exiled Tutsis, invaded in 1990, demanding political party representation and the right of exiles to return home, and plunged the country into a short-lived civil war. In the years that followed, corruption intensified as the price of coffee—Rwanda's chief export—plummeted in the international market, and public revenues dwindled. Society became more militarized, and the situation came to a head when the plane carrying President Habyarimana was shot down on the evening of April 6, 1994.

In mere weeks, between April 7 and July 15, 1994, the mass slaughter of up to a million Tutsis, Twa, and moderate Hutus ravaged the country—somewhere between 5 to 10 percent of the population was murdered. A national trauma survey by UNICEF estimated that 80 percent of Rwandan children experienced a death in their family in 1994, 70 percent witnessed someone being killed or injured, and 90 percent thought they would die. Two-thirds of the population was displaced. It was neither demographics nor the identity politics around those demographic groups that alone caused the genocide. Identities were a mask for political ends, which we know in part because of their relative fluidity during most of Rwanda's modern history leading up to the genocide. As with many such conflicts, the Rwandan genocide was more about power than about identity—the regime tried to hold onto power, and genocide was a means to that end. Conflicts preceding the genocide had a demographic veneer—ethnic divisions, arguments about population density—but they, too, were at heart about desire for political power. Yet, we cannot fully understand such events without understanding demographics.

As horrific as it is, this type of genocide is all too frequent and includes the atrocities of the Khmer Rouge in Cambodia between 1975 and 1979, of Croats and Serbs in Yugoslavia, of General Suharto in Indonesia in 1965, and other less well-known instances. Because of the mass nature of such killings, genocides often receive public, or at least scholarly, attention. It's the smaller-scale and more hidden forms of demographic engineering that attract less notice to which we now turn.

• • •

Polish Jewish jurist Raphael Lemkin coined the term *genocide* from the Greek prefix *genos-*, meaning "race," and the Latin suffix *-cide*, meaning "killing." The 1948 United Nations Genocide Convention includes as genocide trying to prevent births within a group—a clear case of demographic engineering. Since then, various groups have argued for an expanded definition and applied the term to a different set of cases. One such case is Canada, which has a sordid legacy of identity politics and demographic engineering that the government has acknowledged as cultural genocide.

For more than a hundred years, Canada took children from Indigenous families and sent them to Residential Schools to indoctrinate them
into the dominant Euro-Christian society. The government estimates
that at least 150,000 Indigenous children attended these schools, but the
violence and abuse of the system has reverberated for generations in the
form of higher levels of mental illness, alcohol abuse, suicide, poverty,
and even removal of Indigenous children into foster care, which some
have argued is a continuation of the Residential School system in a new
form. Canada's Truth and Reconciliation Commission, which investigated the Residential School system, states the impact bluntly, and it's
worth quoting at length:

> Cultural genocide is the destruction of those structures and prac-
> tices that allow the group to continue as a group. States that
> engage in cultural genocide set out to destroy the political and
> social institutions of the targeted group. Land is seized, and pop-
> ulations are forcibly transferred and their movement is restricted.
> Languages are banned. Spiritual leaders are persecuted, spiritual
> practices are forbidden, and objects of spiritual value are confis-
> cated and destroyed. And, most significantly to the issue at hand,
> families are disrupted to prevent the transmission of cultural
> values and identity from one generation to the next. In its dealing
> with Aboriginal people, Canada did all these things.

And Canada is not alone. Until its abolition in 1973, the White Australia policy endeavored to secure social cohesion through an assim-
ilationist strategy of accepting only White, Anglophone populations,
sourced largely from the United Kingdom, Ireland, and Europe, as
we saw in Chapter 4 on migration. A policy of "assimilation" sounds
benign, but Australia's was intended to rid the country of Black people, who were seen as inferior, either by natural elimination—meaning
hopes that they would die out—or by assimilating them into White

culture. Racial homogeneity thereby dominated the early conception of Australian-ness. Colonial settlers kidnapped Aboriginal and Torres Strait Islander children—Indigenous children—and used them as cheap labor. In the early twentieth century, the government took charge as "protector" of the Indigenous people, who were seen as unable to care for their own best interests. According to the Australian government: "In the name of protection Indigenous people were subject to near-total control. Their entry to and exit from reserves was regulated as was their everyday life on the reserves, their right to marry and their employment." "Protection" also meant that government officials began to forcibly remove Indigenous children and place them with adoptive families or in institutions to indoctrinate them into the majority White culture, similar to the "assimilation" of Indigenous populations in Canada. The goal was for those of mixed descent—Indigenous and European—to eventually merge with the European-origin population, which they felt was possible if given the right schooling and indoctrination. Sometimes children's names were changed, and they were forbidden to speak Indigenous languages. This social Darwinism favored those of lighter skin, who would theoretically stand a better chance of eventually joining the non-Indigenous society. Between 1910 and 1970, an estimated 10 to 33 percent of Indigenous children were removed from their families. They and their descendants have been termed Australia's Stolen Generations.

Examples of cultural genocide like these are too numerous to list, and historically they often overlapped with eugenics initiatives. "Improving the human race"—the goal of eugenics—was not always racial, but often was. Mexico's eugenic history, for example, includes efforts to "whiten" Indigenous children. From mass extermination to cultural elimination, we see how demographics are inseparable from politics as in-group and out-group dynamics shape the fortunes of people across the globe.

Physical territory is part of the story as well, as it can become a symbol of power and serve as a tool for extending political–demographic influence. The concept of *lebensraum* helps us understand how leaders justify such expansion through a demographic lens.

The term *lebensraum*, "living space" in German, was coined by the German geographer Friedrich Ratzel in the late nineteenth century. Before Hitler and the Nazi Party adopted the concept for their own nefarious purposes, *lebensraum* referred to Ratzel's Darwinistic theory that the development of any species is influenced by its ability to adapt to geographic circumstances. The most influential aspect of *lebensraum* was Ratzel's argument that in order to remain healthy (that is, survive and grow stronger), a species needs to continually expand its territory and, in the case of humans, establish agricultural hubs in the new territory.

The loose ideology of *lebensraum* supported campaigns for German settler colonialism in the 1880s and 1890s, then undergirded campaigns to conquer territory to Germany's east during World War I. It resonated even more in the aftermath of World War I and the devastating effects of the Treaty of Versailles, which disconnected millions of ethnic Germans from their German homeland. In addition, the precarious economic situation and hyperinflation in the early 1920s created "feelings of powerlessness" and "painful perceptions of social disintegration." Founded in the late nineteenth century, the Pan German League, a far-right nationalist political organization, set the stage for Hitler's own interpretation of *lebensraum*, demanding cultural homogenization, imperialist expansion, and "war as an historical necessity" to place Germany in a strong international position.

Adolf Hitler began his political career emphasizing the need for *lebensraum* and a revitalization of the German people and nation. Hitler, like many Germans at the time, viewed Germany as a victim of an unjust global order and viewed eastern expansion as Germany's "foundation of global power," "the defense against the 'economic death,'" and "the source of racial revitalization." The emphasis on *lebensraum* created a new conflict within Germany's borders: the ethnic, native Germans versus the "others" who lived in Germany "without entitlement to any land, or eventually, living space." Thus the Nazi Party turned its attention to expelling, whether by forcible removal or other violent means, anyone who did not fit its racial definition of German identity. With the outbreak of World War II in Eastern Europe, expulsions turned into mass extermination.

In the course of less than a century, Friedrich Ratzel's (mostly) harmless concept of *lebensraum* was transformed into a motive for some of the most violent actions the world has ever seen. Myron Weiner and Michael Teitelbaum urge us to differentiate between demography as explanation and demography as justification. Nazi *lebensraum* was clearly the latter.

The principle of sovereignty, which undergirds post–World War II international relations, means *lebensraum* is less of an issue today. But there are exceptions. Although we most often associate the Palestinian–Israeli conflict as territorial, it is demographic as well. Particularly within Israel, insecurities over territory and population together create the perception by each group that it faces an existential threat and drives the intractable fighting. The very founding of Israel as a permanent Jewish homeland reflects demographic insecurity, which was fresh on the heels of the Holocaust. Israel has seen tremendous population growth in its short official existence, growing more than 10 times its original population of 806,000 to 8.7 million by 2020, but composition changes are the heart of the political story. In 1948 at its founding, Israel was 82 percent Jewish and nearly all of the remainder Arab. By the beginning of 2021, the Jewish proportion had fallen to just under 74 percent, the Arab population had grown to 21 percent, and nearly 5 percent identified as an ethnic "other." Those changes stem from fertility and migration trends. For decades, immigration shaped Israel's demographics, as the possibility of a Jewish homeland attracted waves of Jews from around the world, particularly those liberated at the close of World War II, and later, those who were reshuffled at the end of the Cold War and the dissolution of the Soviet Union. For a long time, immigration played a prominent role in Israel's demographic composition. In 1950, only 35 percent of the Jews in Israel were born there, but by 2019, 78 percent were. Now, fertility is responsible for the majority (78 percent) of Israel's population growth. We've seen multiple times that immigration is political, but fertility is no less political, particularly in Israel, where Jews and Arabs have accused each other of a practice my colleague Monica Duffy Toft has termed "wombfare."

As Toft explains it, wombfare is a strategy to gain political edge, the intentional practice of using fertility to defeat an enemy under the assumption that more babies will give greater strength to an ethnic or religious group. Both the Jews and Arabs have accused the other of wombfare over the decades. Here's the short version of the story: At the turn of the twenty-first century, Muslim fertility was nearly two children higher than Jewish fertility—according to Israel's Central Bureau of Statistics, a total fertility rate (TFR) of 4.57 for Muslims and 2.67 for Jews. A solution to the Israeli–Palestinian conflict was nowhere in sight, and much of the media at the time noted that if Arabs bided their time, they would become the majority in Israel, the West Bank, and Gaza. Demographics were at the forefront of the conflict: Many media sources reported that Palestinian Liberation Organization leader Yasser Arafat had referred to Palestinian women as "biological bombs." But by 2019, the numbers had nearly equalized, to 3.16 for Muslims and 3.09 for Jews. Talk of wombfare has subsided, but new demographic issues have arisen. The drop in Muslim fertility is notable, but the increase in Jewish fertility is exceptional and driven by extremely high fertility among Israel's ultra-Orthodox Jewish population, the Haredi, which is 7.1 children per woman on average.

With fertility this high, Israel's composition is shifting to become not only more Jewish, but more Orthodox, as Figure 15 shows, which brings unique consequences. Orthodox men are excused from otherwise mandatory military service, receive special government subsidies, and are employed at far lower rates than are non-Orthodox men—51 percent to 87 percent in 2018. As their numbers grow, the economic

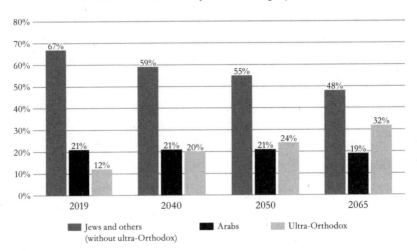

FIGURE 15. Israel's Projected Demographic Shift

and military strength of Israel could be at risk, some observers warn. As always, however, we need to take demographic projections with a grain of salt: Extrapolating future proportions from current fertility could inflate the numbers because not all children with Orthodox parents end up becoming Orthodox themselves—if they did, proportions of the Orthodox population would be much higher today. The social services and privileges offered to the ultra-Orthodox subgroup in some ways parallel those offered to older age groups in other developed states, as does fear that Israel will be unable to pay for an increasing proportion of dependents. As with aging states, though, such promises are political, not permanent, and can be taken away as the political winds shift.

Arabs also accuse the Israeli state of other forms of demographic engineering, including physically relocating population to build the Israeli nation. They say the Israeli state is using demography as a weapon by pushing Jewish Israelis further from population centers and into Arab regions of the territory. According to this view, Israeli settlement policy has intentionally tried to create "a physical Jewish presence in regions of conflict, enhancing territorial control, and contributing to demographic parity, and even majority." We can't understand the politics of Israel without understanding the confluence between population and territory. Those Palestinians living under Israeli control in the West Bank number somewhere between 1.5 million to 2.5 million, none of whom have voting rights in Israel, and their numbers are starting to dwindle. After decades of discussing high Arab Israeli fertility, the tide seems to have turned. Israeli Arabs and Palestinians number at most a third of Israel's current population. And fertility is not the only difference driving demographic divergence between Israel's Arabs and Jews: Between 2000 and 2010, life expectancy for Israeli Jews increased by 3.2 years but only 2 years for Israeli Arabs. According to Uri Sadot in *Foreign Policy* magazine, "This divergence was equivalent to a 2 percent increase to the Jewish population of Israel over that decade, equivalent to the arrival of 128,000 new immigrants." Sadot notes that Israel's leaders can use policy to influence political numbers as well: "If Israel simply matched its expatriate voting policies to those of the United States or Canada, it would add hundreds of thousands of additional voters to its electoral register." Given that Israel is a democracy, with proportional representation and a low threshold for seats (requiring a party to get only 3.25 percent of the votes to enter the Knesset), any of these demographic shifts will have major implications for Israel's domestic and foreign policy.

Like Israel, population, religion, and territory are also at the core of India's modern history. After 200 years of exercising dominion over the subcontinent, the British turned over governance of India at the stroke of midnight on August 15, 1947. Economically and physically devastated by World War II, Britain was eager to shed what had once been the jewel of its empire. When he arrived in Delhi in March 1947, Lord Louis Mountbatten, the new viceroy, acted quickly on his charge to hand over India with all haste and enlisted British lawyer Cyril Radcliffe to form a plan. In a mere 5 months, from the comfort of his office, Radcliffe drew the lines of what were to be two newly independent states. The result shaped the course of history.

By Radcliffe's design, the Indian territory would be divided into the state of India, which would be majority Hindu, and the state of Pakistan, which would be majority Muslim and spread into an east and west territory, separated by 1,000 miles of Indian territory in between (East Pakistan would become the independent country of Bangladesh in 1971). But of course not all Muslims already lived in the territory that would become Pakistan; likewise, there were Hindus in Pakistan's new territory. Half of India's Sikhs ended up on the Muslim side of partition. While theoretically there was no requirement for groups to move, many were terrified of staying put and being a demographic minority. Prior to partition, British India was three-quarters Hindu, and for many Muslims the idea that partition would allow them to escape Hindu domination was positive. And so about 14 million to 15 million people reshuffled across the new borders. The multi-religious population had long lived in relative peace, but partition ignited some of the worst violence the world had ever seen. Up to 1 million died in this traumatic and violent uprooting. As described by author Nisid Hajari, "Gangs of killers set whole villages aflame, hacking to death men and children and the aged while carrying off young women to be raped. British soldiers and journalists who had witnessed the Nazi death camps claimed Partition's brutalities were worse: pregnant women had their breasts cut off and babies hacked out of their bellies; infants were found roasted on spits."

Although the worst of the violence took place over only a short 6 weeks, it left a nasty legacy of fear, suspicion, and conflict among the populations. Demographic strains have continued to plague the Indian subcontinent. More recent releases of India's population figures have spurred a right-wing Hindu nationalist campaign indicting Indian Muslims for what is essentially wombfare. The "Love Jihad" campaign accuses Muslim men in India—referred to as "Love Romeos"—of waging jihad through romantic relationships with Hindu women, "swelling their numbers in an ongoing demographic war." There is little evidence Love Jihad is actually happening; rather, what we should notice about the story is the campaign of fear by right-wing Indian nationalists who perpetuate the myth. More often than not, it's fear of demographic change rather than actual change that motivates reactions. At the same time that Hindus are slightly shrinking in proportion to Muslims— falling from 80.5 percent in the 2001 census to 79.7 percent in the 2011 census, while Muslims increased from 13.4 percent to 14.2 percent of India's population—Hindu nationalism is enjoying a resurgence.

Those demographic fears pervade India's politics. On December 11, 2019, India passed the Citizenship Amendment Act, offering citizenship to immigrants from Afghanistan, Pakistan, and Bangladesh— as long as they weren't Muslim. The 2019 citizenship law effectively ascribes religious identity to bloodlines, seeing faith as patrilineal rather than individual. While advocates for Indian independence from Britain, including Mahatma Gandhi and Jawaharlal Nehru, had been adamant that India be a secular state where those from all religious backgrounds could flourish, the administration of Prime Minister Narendra Modi, who came to power in 2014, has insisted on Hindu dominance. How this will play out in coming years depends a lot on leadership, which has both the power to stoke demographic fears and the power to curtail them.

• • •

When groups within countries grow at different rates through natural increase or migration, conflicts over access to economic resources, political power, or cultural influence often arise. Ethnicity, race, and religion are used as in-group and out-group markers—ways of differentiating one's group from others—which creates a sense of community. Boundaries between these categories shift constantly, as we saw with Rwanda, but they remain, and remain important. These boundaries are tangible, but most scholars conceptualize ethnic communities as imagined communities that form around shared ancestry and history and where members differentiate themselves from other ethnic communities by markers such as language, custom, religion, or physical appearance. Ethnic communities are imagined, in that they are constructed, but are "often the very foundations on which embracing social systems are built" and the foundation of radical political changes.

Perhaps the most radical form of ethnic politics is civil war. In political science, we label the category of conflicts that stem from one group moving into another's territory "sons of the soil" conflicts. In these, members of the local or indigenous group are the "sons of the soil," meaning they claim some tie to the territory, and they are contrasted with recent migrants. Côte d'Ivoire is one of the most studied cases of sons of the soil conflicts and illustrates how ethnic differences became "imagined," but with deadly consequences.

The root of the problem in this West African country is money: The economy of Côte d'Ivoire has been shaped around cocoa production—it's still the world's largest single cocoa producer—and decades ago the government deliberately encouraged labor migration to the plantations in the western regions of the country. Hundreds of thousands of workers from neighboring countries such as Burkina Faso moved in and displaced native, autochthonous people, growing their ranks to somewhere between 50 and 60 percent of those local populations by the late 1980s. Local populations' economic fortunes slipped relative to the newcomers, and resentment started to show in the form of identity politics—an "us" versus "them." By the mid-1990s, an exclusionary identity, the Ivoirité, had bubbled up to divide the locals from the migrants, and in 1994 that identity found political expression in a law that said presidential candidates must not only be Ivoirians but also have parents who were born in Côte d'Ivoire. Policies stemming from this identity conflict threatened citizenship and land rights of both international and internal migrants, according to research by Isabelle Côté and Matthew Mitchell, and came to a physical head in violence, eventually a civil war outbreak in 2002.

Even with stable political institutions, big changes can knock at the door when ethnic politics is on the ballot. Whether we're talking about the community level or the national level, fear of being outnumbered is powerful. The 1927 Aliens Act was Sweden's first immigration law, timed as the exodus of Swedes—1 million to the United States and hundreds of thousands to other European countries between 1850 and 1930—came to a close. According to expert Admir Skodo, the law was originally meant to protect Swedish workers from foreign competition and ensure that people of undesirable races did not mix with Swedes. The influence of race and eugenic theories popular at the time was clear, as it was in other countries' immigration laws at the time, such as the United States' 1924 Johnson–Reed Act that excluded Asians.

Identity politics remains significant in stable democracies. A prime example is the near-secession of Quebec from the rest of Canada. Many outside of Canada forget that in 1995, the country nearly fractured along its Francophone and Anglophone fault lines. Quebec separatism is grounded in centuries-old differential demographic changes from both fertility and migration. In the eighteenth century, Quebec fertility rates were nearly the highest of recorded human history, second only to the religious Hutterites, but then during the 1960s and 1970s plummeted to one of the lowest in the world. During the late 1980s and early 1990s, the low fertility of Francophones in Quebec was coupled with the growth of English-speaking immigrants settling there and juxtaposed with relatively high fertility in the rest of Canada. Leaders of the Quebec separatist movement, including Parti Québecois founder René Lévesque, were alarmed at the prospect that Francophone Quebec could essentially disappear. Immigration helped boost the province's overall population numbers, and the fertility gap between Quebec and the rest of Canada narrowed in the 1980s and 1990s, as overall Canadian fertility fell. Strong nationalist movements fought what they perceived as creeping Anglophone influence, and tensions culminated in a 1995 referendum on secession where Quebec stayed by only the barest of margins: 50.58 percent voting to stay and 49.42 voting to leave. That Brexit occurred by a similar margin makes real that Canada was only a few tenths of a point away from a similarly dramatic exit.

As we've seen time and again throughout this book, rapid changes in population composition sometimes have the most drastic social and political consequences. For Britain, this drastic change happened after the European Union expanded in 2004, and Britain's prime minister Tony Blair allowed citizens of the eight newest Eastern European EU countries the right to work in the United Kingdom—the only major economy to do so. Prior to his decision, there were about 167,000 people from those eight countries in the United Kingdom; by 2011 there were nearly a million, and by 2014—just 10 years after the policy—there were 1.24 million. Other changes happened, too. The non-White share of Britain's population more than doubled in the 20 years between 1991 and 2011, from 7 to 14 percent. Then, in 2015 waves of asylum seekers arriving to the southern and eastern borders of the European Union boosted fears of the demographic changes accompanying open EU borders. In that year alone, there were almost 1.3 million asylum claims in the European Union.

These changes came to a head in a referendum on June 23, 2016, when Brits voted to leave the European Union by a majority of 1.3 million with a high 83 percent turnout. In the postmortem analysis, it seems clear that those who voted to leave were aware that there was little economic benefit to Brexit—it would clearly be onerous to negotiate trade and work agreements if Britain seceded. Yet, the Remain campaign mistakenly focused on the economic angle, hoping that appeals to economic rationality would win out. They did not. In a poll just 1 month prior to the vote, 95 percent of voters who favored Brexit thought the government should control borders at the cost of leaving the European Union, as did 60 percent of those who were undecided. The desire for greater border control wasn't about job competition from immigrants, even though the poor regions of Cornwall, Wales, and the northern Rust Belt had the highest Brexit vote; as scholar Sarah Harper argues, for many voters Brexit was about competition over culture and values. Although the United Kingdom's relationship with the European Union has always been complicated, and sovereignty was top of mind for some voters, Eric Kaufmann's research supports this claim. He finds that just mentioning how immigration will change the United Kingdom's ethnic composition by 2060 increases support for immigration restriction by 25 percentage points when compared with not mentioning such shifts. We saw this in the Brexit vote, too, as 84 percent of the voting districts in England's largest cities (London, Manchester, Birmingham, and Leeds)—which are diverse—voted to remain in the European Union, while 87 percent of those in rural areas voted to leave.

At the beginning of this chapter, we saw how dangerous the census can be in the context of sharp identity divisions, but absence of knowledge is often no better and can sometimes make the fear even worse. For example, the lack of religious census data in the United States and France has given fearmongers free rein to invent wild statistics about the growth of local Muslim communities. A 2016 survey of French citizens showed that they estimated France's Muslim population at about a third—31 percent—when in actuality it was more likely 7.5 percent, according to the Pew Research Center.

Reminiscent of the Canadian and Australian policies toward Indigenous people, in the French model of integration (also called the Republican model), immigrants are expected to contribute to the cohesion of society by "actively shedding former identities in favor of a single, exclusively French identity." We see the politics of this model vividly in the series of riots that broke out in 2005 in France's *banlieues*, districts predominated by those of immigrant background. The rioters were mostly young people from second and third generations of immigrants, many born in France with French citizenship, but who struggled with endemic unemployment and discrimination. This discrimination is clearly seen in the ways certain government officials, particularly then-president Nicolas Sarkozy, framed the situation. Scholar Marie des Neiges Léonard argues that Sarkozy was able to deny any forms of legitimacy or meaning to the riots through a racial frame that separated "the good white citizens, the victims of the riots" from the "immigrants, Muslims, 'scum' of the suburbs, delinquents" who were participating in the riots. In Sarkozy's mind, the banlieues are "prone to be violent and anti-institutions" and overrun with "a network of drug dealers, gang leaders or Islamists," thus contributing to the framing that associates ethnicity and immigrants with a culture of delinquency and urban violence.

When it comes to population data, you're damned if you do collect it, and you're damned if you don't. Contrast Lebanon, which has forestalled a census, and Israel, which regularly publishes official population estimates. In Lebanon, not knowing how proportions of the major ethnoreligious groups have shifted has fed resentment of outdated political apportionment. In Israel, shifts in composition are clear and cause tremendous political anxiety among subgroups who feel their fortunes slipping as others' grow. And we saw that in France, which does not collect and report data on religious composition, the average French person vastly overestimates the proportion of Muslims in the country—in the absence of official data, perception takes on even greater weight.

In this era of big data, we have the ability to collect and collate more population information than ever, stoking fears about Big Brother watching our every move. But knowing the composition of a state's population has always been powerful and is one reason why we have such good records on births and deaths historically. Still, decisions about what demographic information to collect and what to leave a mystery rise to the highest level of politics. The 2020 US census, for example, became embroiled in political controversy when the Trump administration pushed to add a question on citizenship to the form, ostensibly seeking to get a count of the number of illegal immigrants in the United States. The question was added in March 2018, but immigration advocates and others successfully argued for its removal, citing concerns that the government would be able to identify and deport those whom they identified as having illegal status, and that such data would be less accurate than current estimates because respondents would have little incentive to answer such a question honestly or might refuse to do so altogether. What data to collect and how much to trust the results is complicated.

• • •

Globalization, coupled with trends in fertility and migration, means we can be certain that ethnic composition will continue to shift in nation-states around the world in the decades to come. These changes will have political consequences, whether by empowering anti-immigrant political parties in democracies or fomenting violence in countries where conflicts are more often dealt with in the streets than at the polls. There are a few lessons we can take away from this review of composition change.

First, to promote social harmony, states need policies to deal with education, employment, and poverty, not just immigration and integration policies for new immigrants. In regions such as Europe and North America and countries such as Australia, those of migrant backgrounds need to be given a quality education, and they need access to and information about job networks. Without a chance to succeed, these marginalized populations grow increasingly resentful, as we saw with the 2005 French riots, and society further fractures as inequality grows. Those with an immigration background could also help shape policies in their favor if they could gain greater political representation.

Yet, even with representation, the relationship between demographics and democratization is not straightforward—our second lesson is that democracy is not one-size-fits-all. Political scientists have an ever-growing list of conditions under which ethnic composition matters, sometimes finding that greater fractionalization means higher chances of conflict, and at other times finding it means less chance. For example, federal structures, where national power is devolved away from the center (think the United States of America or Germany), are unstable in ethnically diverse countries, except when the majority group is without a home region or when the federal structure has been negotiated through consensus rather than either imposed externally or from above. Guaranteed representation can also help promote peace. As cases such as Northern Ireland (which suffered violent clashes between Protestants and Catholics) show, governance models that allow voices from various groups the equal chance of being heard often result from peace negotiations. These "consociational" models sometimes allocate seats in parliament to ethnic groups to ensure their representation in government, and the emphasis is on governance by consensus. So, just because a country is ethnically fragmented or diverse does not mean the country is unstable or more prone to violence. It also matters how salient, or meaningful, those ethnic identities are. For example, Argentina is considered an immigrant society, but cleavages run along ideological, not demographic, lines.

Third, we need to recognize that democratization in countries with delicate ethnoreligious balances can be fraught with conflict. Egypt's post–Arab Spring clashes between liberals and leftists on the one side and Islamists on the other is one example. Trying to democratize in the midst of ethnic conflict can be a disaster if authoritarian rulers try to hold on to power by manipulating ethnicity, as happened in Yugoslavia in the late twentieth century. Democracy is at heart about numbers, and democratization can displace dominant ethnic minorities who will fight to preserve their position.

Fourth, we shouldn't treat identity groups as monolithic. We saw with the example of Israel that just following the "Jewish" population would obscure that the most interesting and politically important dynamics are within the Jewish population, primarily secular versus Orthodox. The same can be said for analyzing the political preferences of less observant versus more observant Muslims in other political settings. Religious conflict can motivate believers across national borders, whereas ethnic conflict rarely does.

Finally, perception matters. Actual numbers aren't necessary for demographics to affect politics—we know that perception matters because just publishing identity data, such as censuses, increases risk of conflict onset. "Us" versus "them" dynamics are pervasive.

As the pace of demographic change accelerates—particularly ethnic, racial, and religious composition—we should expect identity conflicts to intensify. Whether they explode into violence or remain confined to the polls depends on the strength and functioning of the institutions in place.

The divide between the Global North and Global South is relevant here, too, as countries in the Global South have more fragile systems that fracture under demographic pressure. The Global North is more likely to see demographic pressures shift the relative power of political parties, strain communities, and flare up in isolated violence. In both, population matters.

CHAPTER 6

Malthus versus Marx

We've encountered numerous examples of governments trying to achieve what they see as an ideal population through pro-natalist or anti-natalist initiatives, health improvements, and migration policies. Some of this is in the name of identity politics, as we just saw in Chapter 5, but many times there's an economic motivation behind such measures. States are often chasing a demographic sweet spot known as the "window of opportunity." If high fertility leads to a youth population that is "too big" and low fertility leads to a working-age population that is "too small," how can states achieve population dynamics that are "just right" for conditions of economic growth and improvements in quality of life? In other words, how do demographics accelerate or hinder economic development? Age structure is one of the major factors that creates conditions for improvements in quality of life and economic growth. Population distribution between urban and rural areas is another. And these two demographic dynamics are tied, as those global regions with the youngest populations are for the most part the least urbanized.

Generally, we say that the demographic window of opportunity opens after a period of declining fertility when children under age 15 are less than 30 percent of the total population, and seniors age 65 and above are under 15 percent. During this time, median age is around 26 to 40 years. While the window is open states see a dividend in health, education, economic growth, and political stability. Commonly, scholars refer to the benefit that can result from this shift in age structure as the "demographic dividend," defined as when the productive population grows at a faster rate than the total population and the income per capita growth rate increases. Think about it as growth in the proportion of the population that is economically productive, pays taxes, participates in politics, and serves in the military, compared to the proportion that has aged out of (or is not yet in) the workforce and is possibly dependent. But as anyone who has a bank savings account knows, you only reap a dividend if you invest. The demographic dividend is no different.

Ireland had the right policies in place to take advantage of its window of opportunity, starting with a more open economy in the 1950s, when the government encouraged foreign direct investment (FDI) and promoted exports, and free secondary education starting in the mid-1960s. During its demographic bonus years, the "Irish Tiger" had relatively high per capita increases compared to other European economies—3.5 percent a year growth from 1960 to 1990 and 5.8 percent during the 1990s. Child mortality (under age 5) plummeted from 49 per 1,000 in 1950 to 7 by the end of the century.

The so-called Asian Tigers—Hong Kong, South Korea, Taiwan, and Singapore—are also classic cases of taking advantage of the window of opportunity. During the 1960s and 1970s, they instituted family-planning programs and invested in educating their shrinking number of children. Governments in China, Taiwan, South Korea, Thailand, and Indonesia promoted literacy and health care even before their population growth began to decline, and those states were well positioned to make the most of their window of opportunity. And taking advantage of the demographic transition hastened Asia's economic growth. One of the most well-known studies on the subject found that East Asia's demographic bonus between 1965 and 1990 (when the working-age population grew almost 10 times faster than the dependent population), along with changes in population density, explain one-third to one-half of East Asia's economic miracle. The mechanism seems straightforward: When the proportion of youth relative to workers declines, it "relieves pressure on child health and educational services, stimulates savings, contributes to productivity, and facilitates increased human capital investment and, ultimately, wage growth."

But what if the right policies aren't in place when the window opens? States can squander their dividend and let the chance for accelerated economic growth pass them by. While some East Asian states recorded per capita annual growth rates of 6.8 percent during the period 1975–1995, their demographic bonus years, Latin America's rate was only 0.7 percent during this period, even though its demographic structure was similar. Demographers have estimated that Latin America could have enjoyed a 1.7 percent a year boost to economic growth from its demographic dividend, but states in the region underinvested in their populations and failed to take full advantage of their favorable age structure.

A new crop of states is entering or is in their window, and investment now will make all the difference for how their economies emerge when the window closes. In fact, policy differences over the past few decades have already set some countries on the path toward greater quality of life. A comparison of East Pakistan (now Bangladesh) and West Pakistan (now just Pakistan), which officially split in 1971, shows how policy investments can make a difference in both the demographic transition itself and in reaping the demographic dividend that could follow. In the period 1975–1980, Bangladesh and Pakistan had nearly identical total fertility rates of 6.6, but soon after its independence, Bangladesh initiated community-based contraceptive distribution; the government worked in conjunction with the International Centre for Diarrheal Disease Research, Bangladesh (ICDDR/B), and the initiative was partially funded and supported by the United States Agency for International Development (USAID). Bangladesh's TFR declined sharply from 6.9 at independence to less than three children per woman on average just three decades later. Its TFR is projected to be 1.93 from 2020 to 2025, while Pakistan's TFR is projected to be 3.2. Likewise, Bangladesh's median age is nearly 5 years higher than Pakistan's, as is life expectancy at birth.

All of this bodes well for Bangladesh's economic prospects. Statistical models developed by Richard Cincotta and Elizabeth Leahy Madsen show that "by 2030 Bangladesh appears to have an even chance of reaching the [World] Bank's upper middle-income class (roughly US$4,000 to $12,000 per capita annually)." As they say, "For a country that Henry Kissinger famously dubbed 'a basket case' at independence in 1971, that prospect is impressive." Bangladesh's economy has been growing strongly, with rising exports and record remittances, which helped increase domestic demand and also helped with a decline in imports. Bangladesh has continued to shift from relying on agriculture to manufacturing and services. Exports grew, particularly orders of garments from China, agricultural products, and pharmaceuticals. Although foreign direct investment was incredibly low at the beginning of this century, it reached as high as $2.8 billion in 2015 and was $1.9 billion in 2019.

There are still needed reforms: The World Bank recommends adjustments to the financial sector and improvements in infrastructure to make doing business easier. With about 2 million people entering the workforce every year, Bangladesh needs even more investments in human capital. Bangladesh has been heavy in the textiles sectors and reliant on remittances, but will need to invest in developing a skills basis rich with workers who have managerial and technical expertise, according to the World Bank. College graduates, particularly female graduates, have a hard time finding jobs, yet employers are unable to fill high-skilled positions—there is an obvious mismatch of skills and needs.

Pakistan, like Bangladesh, is improving in terms of the markers of state fragility, such as economic inequality and human rights, but has a weaker foundation than Bangladesh when it comes to potential for reaping a demographic dividend. Not only is fertility much higher in Pakistan, only 67.5 percent of females aged 15 to 24 were literate in 2017, the last year for which data were available, compared with 94 percent of young women in Bangladesh that same year and 96 percent in 2019. Bangladesh's window of opportunity opened only recently and won't close until close to mid-century (depending on the pace of further fertility declines), so it's a country to watch during the next few decades. Pakistan's window of opportunity is not on track to open until around 2035, so the next few decades are key to getting the country on the right track.

Although not as far along the demographic transition as either Bangladesh or Pakistan, Ethiopia has been positioning to reap its potential demographic dividend. Life expectancy there is up, fertility is down, and the economy is growing. One pillar of Ethiopia's investment has been education: Ethiopia has built more schools and has increased enrollment. The country nearly erased its gender gap in literacy, which itself contributes to fertility decline, prepares women to work outside the home, and increases women's chances of obtaining small-business loans. In 2017, nearly 72 percent of women aged 15 to 24 were literate. While Ethiopia still struggles on rates of completing education, it has been headed in the right direction. A second pillar of Ethiopia's investment has been health. Ethiopia reduced infant and child mortality to speed up the first step of demographic transition—under-five mortality is less than half of what it was in 2000. Adult mortality is better in general, but the country still has a long way to go to improve maternal mortality— given the important role of mothers in the household, Ethiopia would be wise to dedicate efforts toward reversing that trend. Although it has fallen, Ethiopia's fertility is still close to four children per woman, and the country is not on pace to enter its window of opportunity until close to mid-century, but what it does now not only will accelerate fertility declines in the short and medium terms but also can prepare it to reap a demographic dividend in the long term.

• • •

The kinds of broad policies undertaken in Bangladesh and Ethiopia illustrate how to create conditions to reap a demographic dividend. States reap a dividend when their demographic structures work in harmony with their macroeconomic policies, education initiatives, and so on. But what happens when demographic and economic factors collide, when there's a mismatch between the labor market and the available labor?

Too few resources in a country with high population growth is clearly a recipe for disaster, but an abundance of natural resources coupled with high population growth is also problematic. Natural resource extraction can be profitable and can encourage an economic structure built entirely around that resource, failing to utilize another of the country's prime resources: labor. Natural resource extraction is often cheap, particularly in countries where the economy is underdeveloped and everything is "cheap" in comparison with rich countries. Oil-rich states surrounding the Persian Gulf are known for this model. Resource extraction can create something called rents—excess of revenue above costs—and lead societies to become rentier states, in essence living off of unearned wealth. That excess wealth can be used in lieu of taxing the population; it can also be used to pay the salaries of people employed by the state.

Saudi Arabia once promised a government job to every young man who wanted one. That worked for a while, until there were a whole lot more young men: Such a model is only sustainable when revenue growth exceeds population growth. In Saudi Arabia, that time is up. Saudi Arabia had fewer than 10 million people in 1980 but more than 20 million by 2000 and 34.8 million people in 2020. There's another demographic issue: A significant proportion of the working-age population was composed of foreigners, including oil workers from countries such as India and the Philippines, a situation similar to the other Persian Gulf states, where the government is able to use oil revenues to finance expenditures without taxing the population. For years, the Saudi government invited migrant workers to make up for skills missing in the native workforce, such as those of engineers or doctors, and to work jobs that Saudis were reluctant to perform, such as construction, while Saudis ended up in the public sector, a wealth of jobs funded by oil revenues that stemmed unemployment. In fact, 90 percent of workers in the private sector are foreign, and most of them are male as we see from the left side of Figure 16.

This economic structure, reliant as it is on oil revenues and foreign labor, is increasingly mismatched to Saudi Arabia's demographic realities and vulnerable to economic shocks, as when oil prices plummeted after 2014. There were more 20- to 29-year-old Saudis during the previous decade than ever before, and although their numbers peaked and started to decline between 2015 and 2020 (catching up to prior fertility declines), they still numbered 5.35 million in 2020. Saudi Arabia's population is set to have nearly doubled between 2000 and 2030, from 20.6

FIGURE 16. Saudi Arabia's Population in 2021

Male	Age Group	Female
	100+	
	95–99	
	90–94	
0.1%	85–89	0.1%
0.1%	80–84	0.2%
0.3%	75–79	0.3%
0.4%	70–74	0.4%
0.9%	65–69	0.7%
1.5%	60–64	0.8%
2.6%	55–59	1.2%
3.7%	50–54	1.7%
5.3%	45–49	2.8%
6.6%	40–44	3.7%
6.3%	35–39	3.8%
5.8%	30–34	4.1%
4.8%	25–29	3.9%
3.5%	20–24	3.2%
3.2%	15–19	3.1%
3.9%	10–14	3.7%
4.3%	5–9	4.2%
4.3%	0–4	4.2%

Percentage   Age Group   Percentage

million to 39.3 million. The CEO of Saudi ARAMCO said in 2010 that in order for the country to produce enough well-paying jobs for the large youth cohorts, the economy would have to grow at about 8 percent a year over the next 10 years, as opposed to the 3 to 5 percent rate at which it had been growing. Only rarely in the past two decades has Saudi Arabia's annual GDP per capita growth rate exceeded the overall population growth rate, and the economic indicator has often been negative.

Saudi Arabia's government seems to have finally recognized the unsustainability of its strategy. Since 2011, it has embarked on a "Saudization" of the labor force, particularly in the private sector, but the original reasons for bringing in foreign labor—unwillingness of Saudis to do certain menial jobs, skills shortages—haven't gone away. While youth unemployment is still estimated at 28.6 percent of those ages 15 to 24 years, those not in employment, education, or training is down from 20.6 percent in 2011 to an estimated 16.1 percent in 2020. The Saudi government sees youth unemployment, according to Omar Al-Ubaydli, the director of research at the Bahrain Center for Strategic, International and Energy Studies, "as a source of social instability, as well as a breeding ground for extremism."

Like Saudi Arabia, many other of today's youthful states face pressures to employ increasingly large youth cohorts, but their economic structures fail to create an adequate number of jobs. Natural resource–based economies are less labor-intensive than economies that are based on manufacturing and industry. Natural resource economies are also dependent on high global prices to create money for investment. In oil-based economies, revenues must go toward paying public salaries, leaving little left over for investment. Like Saudi Arabia, Nigeria, Sudan, South Sudan, and Iraq will remain youthful states vulnerable to oil-price fluctuations for the next several decades.

With leadership and vision, these youthful states can diversify their economies and can ensure that resource profits benefit the larger society. Botswana, rich in diamonds, is often lauded for successfully funneling its natural resource profits into education, infrastructure, and health care, helping the country transition to middle-income, although the population is still ravaged by HIV/AIDS. Botswana is on the cusp of its window of opportunity; its median age will be over 26 years by 2030. Because of their foresight during Botswana's youthful stage, Botswana's leaders have positioned the country to reap more of its potential demographic dividend.

The importance of age structure for economic growth was clear in the preceding examples, although the benefit is certainly not automatic. The relationships to population distribution, particularly the proportion of urban and rural populations, is more complicated. In theory, urban areas provide greater access to basic services such as education and health care and even to those elements that go beyond basic necessities to create a rich and full life, such as arts and entertainment. Urbanization reduces transaction costs, makes public investments in infrastructure and services worthwhile, and even promotes exchange of ideas. Cities can have outsized economic influence relative to their population. In Europe, secondary cities generate 40 percent of the European Union's GDP and have only 15 percent of the population.

In practice, urbanization sometimes fails to deliver those benefits.

According to the United Nations, "Today, an estimated 1.6 billion people live in inadequate housing globally, of which 1 billion live in slums and informal settlements. This means that about one in four people in cities live in conditions that harm their health, safety, prosperity and opportunities." Most of these 1.6 billion are in developing countries, but disaggregating this statistic paints an even bleaker picture of the global divide. More than 60 percent of Africa's urban population lacks clean water or sanitation and has unstable living conditions, both literally—as in falling-down houses—and with regard to insecure tenure.

One reason urbanization takes the form of growing slums is the high cost of housing. Relative to per capita GDP, the cost of food, housing, and transportation in Africa is 55 percent higher than in other regions. African cities are not alone. The rent-to-income ratio in Mumbai, India, is 6.8 percent, higher even than New York City, at 4.1 percent. Consulting firm McKinsey & Company has assessed that if current trends continue to 2025, an additional 110 million urban dwellers could be living in substandard housing or spend so much on putting a roof over their heads that it crowds out spending on other important things, such as health care.

It's hard to draw definitive conclusions about urbanization and quality of life. Infant mortality rates in Dhaka are lower than national rates, but the rural poor in Kenya are healthier than the urban poor there. Economist Edward Glaeser argues that urban slums are bad but rural poverty is worse, but Thomas Bollyky counters, "Congestion in Dhaka consumes 3.2 m working hours each day. That reduces the utility of that infrastructure, which deters investment and depresses wages." If we're thinking about quality of life, it's not immediately obvious that life in a poor but urban area is wildly better than life back on the family farm.

If it turns out that urbanization is a net positive, then it's problematic that some areas are failing to urbanize or failing to urbanize in the way earlier regions did. The pace of urbanization differs widely across the world, and with differing effects on economic growth and quality of life. In just 65 years, the proportion of Eastern Asia's urban population more than tripled, from 18 to 60 percent by 2015. In more developed regions, which urbanized first, the same growth took 80 years, from 1875 to 1955. Yet some areas have been urbanizing more slowly. The least urbanized are so because of low industrialization, overdependence on subsistence agriculture, poor land policies, lack of urban development strategies, legacies of colonial policies that discouraged rural-to-urban migration, lack of political will to urbanize, and dependence on natural resources.

Ethiopia, India, and Brazil are useful to compare. Pace-wise, as Figure 17 shows, India has urbanized far slower than Brazil. But there are data issues that keep us from getting a complete picture of India's

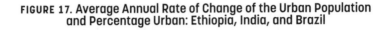

FIGURE 17. Average Annual Rate of Change of the Urban Population and Percentage Urban: Ethiopia, India, and Brazil

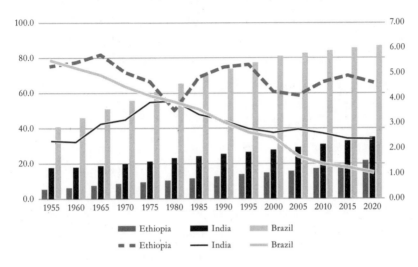

urbanization—India has been slow to reclassify some of its rural areas as urban. This is yet more reason we always need to consider contextual factors behind population numbers. Brazil's urbanization is basically saturated at 87 percent in 2020, while India's reported urbanization in 2020 is lower than Brazil's in 1955. Ethiopia's overall urbanization is still low, but four times higher than it was in 1955, and its average annual rate of change for urban areas has been above 3.5 percent for the past 70 years. While India's GDP per capita was only $2,099 in 2019, Brazil's was $8,717. As we would expect from its low level of urbanization, Ethiopia's was only $855, but that's up from $124 in 2000.

Africa is the least urbanized global region, with only 43 percent urban. Sub-Saharan Africa's experience with urbanization has thus far been faster than the historical experience of developed countries, just as it has been in Latin America and the Caribbean, East Asia, and West Asia. North Africa and South-Central Asia have urbanized slower than have developed countries, however. On the one hand, to point out Africa's lack of urbanization is to continue the centuries-long narrative of the continent's "backwardness," which motivated imperialists and capitalists to pillage the land and its people in the name of development. In another view, though, to see Africa's low levels of urbanization is to see an opportunity to shape growth with intention.

We tend to think of cities growing up as a country industrializes and people moving from rural areas where agriculture is the main business to cities where there are jobs such as in manufacturing. But many scholars have noted that urbanization today does not look the same as it once did, as cities develop in countries that don't have significant industry. Historically, Europe was the first major world region to urbanize. Increasing production and mechanization initially drove Europe's urban wave, which was coterminous with industrialization. High fertility meant that rural areas had an excess supply of labor, even as demand declined. Cities, with their new opportunities for manufacturing employment, were a draw, even if once new residents arrived life wasn't all sunshine and rainbows (more like smallpox and rats). The more recent cities, however, have experienced urbanization before jobs or infrastructure. Cities in the West attracted people because of jobs. But many in low-income countries are moving to cities and finding none there. For example, African economies have a much smaller manufacturing sector. As Rémi Jedwab notes from a 2012 World Bank Study, "In 2007, employment shares in industry and services were 10% and 26% for Africa, but 24% and 35% for Asia, and African labor productivity was 1.7 and 3.5 times lower in industry and services, respectively."

Studying urbanization patterns from 1960 to 2010, Douglas Gollin, Rémi Jedwab, and Dietrich Vollrath find that urbanization in those countries with heavy dependence on natural resource exports tends to take the form of what they term "consumption cities," which have economies primarily based on non-tradable services, such as those in Ghana and Côte d'Ivoire. In countries that don't have significant natural resource exports, however, urbanization takes the form of "production cities," which have more workers in tradable services, like finance, or in manufacturing and other industrial sectors. The issue is that the former, consumption cities, have more people living in slums and much higher poverty—the cities aren't wealthy areas of commerce. Their findings help explain the process of urbanization in Africa, where non-tradable manufacturing has increased urbanization but has not aided in growth or development. These cities aren't able to enter the world market because their economies are mostly localized, non-tradable manufacturing—making things for the local market—not internationally tradable goods. Urbanization and industrialization are no longer synonymous. Historically, urbanization has typically been driven by either an industrial revolution, which pulls labor to urban areas, or a green revolution in agriculture where higher output frees labor for other purposes and pushes it to cities. In Africa, when urbanization has happened, it's without either of those structural transformations. The resource curse, then, extends to the realm of urbanization—it's not automatic that urbanization drives economic growth and instead depends on the type of city.

Some regions are doing better than others. As World Bank researchers point out, Latin America and Asia—while still dealing with slums—have much higher capital investment and are much more open to the world. Unsurprisingly, many of the investment firms and other private-sector actors who track urbanization prescribe market-based solutions for the ills of urbanization. These include making sure land is made available for sale to developers, reducing construction costs by assembling some pieces off-location, and lowering financing costs for buyers and developers. To the extent that such policies deepen inequality, though, and inequality increases discontent, these cities may be trading one problem for another.

• • •

Demography is a structural force, and so far in this chapter we've talked about age composition and population distribution within countries and the connection of these to economic growth and improved quality of life. Global population distribution is also important, as it serves as both a release valve for excess labor and a source of income in the form of remittances.

Prosperous emigrants can provide a meaningful source of income for family back home and increase domestic consumption. India, Mexico, and the Philippines were the top receivers of remittances in 2019. In 2013, India received remittances that were almost three times as large as the investments of foreign firms. The vast majority of global remittances—71 percent—flow to middle-income countries, while the world's poorest countries only received 6 percent of remittances in 2013. These monetary flows are unsurprising, because citizens of low-income countries cannot afford to emigrate. However, remittances are a far more important source of revenue for low-income countries than for middle-income countries—composing 8 percent of revenue for the former versus 2 percent for the latter. Although we frequently compare India and China, in 2019 India received more than $83 billion in remittances, while China only received $18 billion—that's nearly 3 percent of India's GDP but only 0.1 percent of China's.

Remittances are such an important source of national income that the World Bank includes them in its measure of creditworthiness, underscoring the importance of freedom of population movement for low-income nations. Tajikistan's remittances peaked at around 44 percent of GDP in 2008 and 2013, falling after both years as economic troubles contracted labor markets. In 2019, remittances had declined as a share of GDP to just under 29 percent. While that might seem like good news, the decline was not because Tajikistan diversified and strengthened its economy, it was because of Russian economic troubles starting in 2014. For Tajikistan, a decline in remittances has contributed "to shrinking growth (from 7.4 percent in 2013 to 4.2 percent in 2015), slower poverty reduction, and a liquidity crisis within the banking sector." To show why we need to go beyond isolated data points, we can contrast Tajikistan's experience with that of Bangladesh. In 2019, remittances to Bangladesh were $18.3 billion, rising over time. Those remittances represented only 6 percent of GDP, though, down from more than 10.5 percent in 2012, meaning that as the actual value of remittances has increased, they've shrunk as a proportion of Bangladesh's economy, a sign of strength.

Remittances can be the differences between life and death for households in poor countries. Somalis abroad send $1.3 billion annually back home, an amount higher than humanitarian and development assistance, which helps families cover food and medication costs. Globally, remittances have been steadily trending upward for decades (with a small downturn in 2009 as a result of the global financial crisis), reaching half a trillion dollars by 2013 and $653 billion in 2019. We should expect a significant downturn any time there are crises, such as the COVID-19 pandemic that began in 2020, which underscores that diverse economies will be the most resilient.

Emigration has brought measurable benefits to countries such as the Philippines, but emigration can also be a massive drain on human capital, and thus a country's economy. In the early days of New World colonization, England was bleeding emigrants to places such as the North American colonies, forcing the English Parliament to outlaw emigration of skilled artisans in 1718. The effects of emigration can last a long time, as the massive Irish emigration in the nineteenth and twentieth centuries shows. During this wave, young Irish adults, mostly young men, started emigrating to the United States in increasing numbers throughout the early nineteenth century, from about 13,000 per year in 1821 to 93,000 per year by 1843. The 1845–1849 potato famine doubled that number. What began as a slow leak eventually drained Ireland's population: In 1891, 39 percent of Irish-born lived outside of Ireland. The country's population halved between 1841 and 1951, and it still hasn't recovered: Today, Ireland's population is still one-third less than its peak before the famine.

Naturally, because this is a book about people, a lot of our discussion of population and economics has been about labor, but the technologically minded reader may be wondering what the place of labor will be in the future workforce. Fears that automation will displace labor abound, what many call the "fourth industrial revolution." As it turns out, such fears have been around since the original Industrial Revolution, and the relationship between technology, labor, and the economy is still up for debate.

• • •

The reverend looked around the town square: It was practically crawling with babies. Bedraggled mothers chased rogue toddlers while three or four other urchins trailed in her wake like an army of ants. If things kept going like this, it seemed impossible that the human race would survive but a few more decades. Given how fast the population was growing, surely the end of humanity was nigh. After all, he knew two things to be absolutely certain: People need food and people need sex.

The year was 1798, and the reverend was one Thomas Robert Malthus, an English cleric and political economist. To Malthus, only emigration, famine, or pestilence could check population growth—humans' need for sex, and thus procreation, was too powerful. His central argument was simple: Population increased exponentially, but food production only increased linearly, so eventually (and sooner rather than later, he thought), population growth would outpace the ability of the land to provide. Malthus's ideas were immediately popular among the ruling classes in England who, like Malthus, saw England's Poor Laws as a colossal failure. Although intended to alleviate poverty, critics said the laws actually increased it by incentivizing employers to cut wages. In 1834, the Poor Laws were reformed and required those wanting relief to seek it through the "workhouse system"—the able-bodied were to leave behind their crafts and their farms and join the great machine of "Industrializing England."

Ah, Industrializing England. For a social scientist, there was no better laboratory for observing the confluence of urbanization, industrialization, youthful age structure, and improving mortality than mid-nineteenth century Britain. So, when Karl Marx landed there after being expelled from Paris in 1849, it's no wonder that what he saw and experienced then and there confirmed his theories about capitalism, the state, and the working class. For one, as he observed that great industrial machine, he felt even more strongly that the working class was not to blame for its lot. Malthus's ideas—still fresh, and popular among elites—were wrong. Marx criticized the reformed Poor Laws for ignoring the displacements caused by industrial capitalism. He thought that the laws combined Malthus's theory with a "bourgeois individualist and moralizing notion" that English families needed to curtail their fertility to match their means. In essence, the Poor Laws argued that it was reproduction that led people to be poor, not the evils of industrial capitalism.

Although it started centuries ago, the primary debate about population and the economy is at heart a debate about which one of these famous thinkers was right. The lenses of Malthus and Marx are still useful for trying to understand how urbanization, industrialization, youthful age structure (and increasingly older age structures), and improving mortality affect economic performance and individual fortunes.

Like economist Adam Smith (he of the market's invisible hand), Marx scoffed at the simplicity of Malthus's thesis and instead argued that other factors, such as human ingenuity and technology, would prevent the massive devastation Malthus foresaw. Today, many worry over automation displacing workers—exactly what Marx observed and discussed with respect to the industrial cotton industry displacing handweavers in the mid-nineteenth century.

Natural resource economies have challenges employing large numbers of youth; similarly, automation can close out opportunities to use a large labor force. One of the consequences Marx observed was the creation of an industrial surplus army of labor. Industrial capitalism displaced workers through productivity gains from automation, so firms could produce more goods with fewer workers. Technology can be a great leveler. Already by 2013, the World Bank and the African Development Bank reported 650 million mobile users in Africa, more than in the United States or Europe.

Mobile access allows economies to grow even without traditional infrastructure, such as reliable roads, electricity, or land-based phone lines. In fact, those same agencies reported that in some African countries, more people had "access to a mobile phone than to clean water, a bank account or electricity."

But there's an unknown side to technology; namely, the growing use of automation to replace labor in both developed and developing states. Already, in "middle-aged" countries it's challenging to provide jobs for a burgeoning workforce. The East Asian economies forged their path to astronomical growth through labor-intensive manufacturing and industrialization. It will be hard for emerging economies today to duplicate that path to growth—even though they have a similar bonus of workers, manufacturing is not the same. In South Asia and Africa, in particular, manufacturing is a much smaller share of the economy than it was for economic giants such as China.

Use of robotics, poor infrastructure, and changing consumer tastes mean that economies can no longer count on building strong manufacturing sectors to bring them out of the lowest rungs of poverty. Use of robotics is exploding and reducing the need for manufacturing labor even in India and China: According to the International Federation of Robotics, "Since 2010, demand for industrial robots has risen considerably due to the ongoing trend towards automation and continued technical innovations in industrial robots. From 2014 to 2019, annual installations increased by 11% on average each year." Asia is by far the biggest market. These economies, too, will need to chart a new course for future growth. Some argue that Africa can't rely on manufacturing for its development path. Economist Dani Rodrik calls this conundrum "premature deindustrialization." What this means for wage earners is that those making $10 to $20 a day, effectively the middle classes, in Southeast Asia and Africa have seen little expansion, even though these regions have abundant labor.

• • •

The start of the twenty-first century has been marked by a divide between developed aging countries and less developed youthful ones. The tremendous economic growth across Asia and in a handful of countries in other regions, such as Brazil and South Africa, was partly driven by favorable demographics and policies that took advantage of them, namely, high proportions of working-age people. Demographics aren't enough by themselves, and we could have reason to believe the stars aligned in a unique way that's highly unlikely for countries looking to develop today. Labor-intensive manufacturing, in particular, has a shaky future.

What's useful about the demographic transition is that it leads to a fairly predictable path along which age structure will travel from youthful to aged. Of course, depending on the pace of the demographic transition, those age-structure changes can vary in speed and intensity worldwide. China's median age went from 19 years to 30 years in just three decades (1970 to 2000). In India, in contrast, the pace of the demographic transition and thus the rise in median age has been much more gradual. What's certain, though, is that a country well into the demographic transition with a rising median age will one day be "old." That certainty means policy makers and businesses have the closest thing to an actual crystal ball where they can foresee the kinds of demographic pressures a country will face in the future.

As evidence from East Asia and Latin America shows, the demographic dividend is not automatic and requires laying groundwork early. East Asian states, in particular, invested in education and human capital and focused on shifting their economies away from agriculture, so that they were able to reap a greater dividend than did states in Latin America, which underinvested in those areas. The divergent experiences of these two regions demonstrates that states with intermediate age structures must invest in their populations in order to benefit from them, in turn. For the current group of countries in the window of opportunity, the prognosis is mixed. India has low levels of literacy, and some regions of the country are far behind others in terms of human development. States in the Middle East and North Africa will need to position themselves to take advantage of their favorable dependency ratios but thus far have underdeveloped labor markets and a mismatch between the population's skills and the types of jobs available.

While a country has the benefit of a relatively large labor force and relatively few dependents, the time is ripe to establish sustainable pension and retirement policies. Austere reforms are more likely to be palatable to a relatively younger population than to one that is close to receiving generous benefits. A country only reaps the benefit of a demographic dividend when it deliberately takes advantage of its population resources. Policies that make the labor market flexible, invest in health and education, and work toward gender equity, including in labor-force participation, will help provide conditions to reap a demographic dividend.

For example, Iran, whose median age will be 34 years in 2025, needs to reform its unsustainable pay-as-you-go social insurance system, which has already shown cracks, before more people enter their retirement years. Only about 17 percent of women participate in the labor force, despite their high levels of education.

As with age structure, the contribution of urbanization to economic growth is not automatic. Urbanization in natural resource–rich settings is qualitatively different than in settings where the urban population grows up around a rich industrial base. Connectivity between cities seems just as important as the cities themselves. Megaregions, such as China's Hong Kong–Shenzhen–Guangzhou megaregion and Brazil's São Paulo–Rio de Janeiro megaregion, account for 66 percent of the world's economic activity and are the breeding ground for 85 percent of all technological and scientific innovation. African cities, however, are "crowded, disconnected, and costly," in the words of the World Bank. Climate change is an additional challenge. A 2018 report from McKinsey & Company categorizes almost 1,700 cities today as under high chronic resource stress with respect to food, energy, or water and a further 951 as facing high acute environmental stress, such as drought, floods, and cyclones. Cities such as Lagos and Manila are driving much of their countries' economic growth but are projected to face intense stresses from climate change.

● ● ●

While the African Union named 2017 the year of the demographic dividend, some demographers and economists worry that prematurely employing rhetoric of the demographic dividend can cause us to gloss over serious institutional, structural, and population issues. Africa's economic issues are way bigger than labor issues alone. The unemployment rates among African youth are twice that of adults; in Eswatini, 43 percent of youth are unemployed, and more than half of South African youth are. Many of Africa's fastest growing economies are experiencing "jobless growth" and failing to employ their large youth bulges. In sub-Saharan Africa, on average, new entrants to the labor force increased by 3 percent a year between 2015 and 2020 and are projected to increase by 2.9 percent a year from 2020 to 2025. Even if fertility continues to decline, large numbers will enter the labor force in the future because they were born at a time when fertility was higher. Growth of the informal sector and lack of meaningful employment are also issues. One scholar, Christopher Cramer, has warned against policies that aim to provide jobs without considering the nature of the work. Cramer links motivations for violence among youth to rampant "demeaning and exploitative employment," which he says is just as much motivation for grievance as unemployment is. Such research has led the World Bank to conclude that "policy approaches that focus on plundering Africa's labor resources may well create more problems than solutions."

Most African countries are not yet at the beginning of their window of opportunity, but we can take a moment to recognize what it means for those countries currently in the window as it begins to close. Lower fertility and mortality create an "aging" country, but not yet aged. Any "dividend" comes only after the demographic transition, but the window eventually closes. After fertility and mortality decline during the demographic transition, the population assumes an intermediate age structure, with a bulge of people in working ages. This stopover between a youthful and mature age structure can last several decades or only a few, depending on the pace of fertility decline in individual states. With fertility on the decline, states such as Ethiopia have time to establish sustainable pension systems to prepare for eventual population aging.

Right now, many of the world's nearly 8 billion people live in countries whose populations are in the window of opportunity, with intermediate age structures, but as we know from Chapter 2, these countries are on their way to joining the club of aged states. Soon, windows in many will be closed for good. At the regional level, Central Asia, South Asia, and Central America are on the younger end of an intermediate age structure. Upper-middle income countries—a category that includes Mexico, Cuba, Costa Rica, and Turkey—are on average at the upper end of the intermediate age structure. To show how transitory this time is, by 2035, Latin America and the Caribbean will have aged beyond an intermediate structure to a mature one. What happens on the other side of the demographic dividend was made clear in the chapter on aging. The window will close.

CHAPTER 7

The Future of Global Population

Demography is a window into our past. It can help us understand political, social, and economic transitions and see patterns among them. Demography is also a window into our future—it is essential to a full picture of the world of tomorrow. Demographics are likely to come into more policy conversations as we collectively unwind from COVID-19 and climate change receives more attention across the public and private sectors. But, as we have learned, taking population numbers at face value and extrapolating from there is not the best way to use population numbers. Instead, we have to look at the forces in a society that amplify demographic trends and the forces that dilute them. Some of those include political institutions, for example, like electoral and political party systems. We also need to look closer at the demographic trends themselves. Although we have a diverse global population of nearly 8 billion, demographic trends often follow predictable patterns that can help us understand the global strategic environment. Once mortality declines, fertility generally follows. As fertility falls, a population's median age rises, and its proportions of young, mid-age, and older populations shift. With the right investments, Somalia may one day be lucky enough to face the problem of population aging, just like China, Iran, and many other countries that only recently had high fertility. When demographic dynamics diverge from expected patterns, we have the opportunity to deepen our understanding of the causes and effects of demographic change. How, then, can we make solid predictions about the direction of demographic trends, and how should we use demography to give us a fuller picture of the future?

As we consider how to make accurate or successful forecasts using demographics, we can take a tip from superforecaster Philip Tetlock, who argues that the process should be one of outside in, instead of inside out. The example he often uses for illustration is that of predicting a couple's likelihood of divorce. Imagine being at a wedding reception and the person next to you asks, their mouth full of cake, how likely you think the newly married couple is to divorce. The inside-out prediction would be to think of the vows the couple just made, their professions of love for each other, and the closeness of their bodies on the dance floor. Maybe you reply, "Oh, only 5 percent." That's the prediction that's in good taste, but if you were betting you'd probably lose.

The outside-in prediction would first take a look at the baseline divorce rates for the couple's socio-demographic group, which might be around 40 percent, then move to "inside" factors: how long they've known each other or dated, how often they fight and how they resolve disagreements, how well their life goals match, and so on. You'd move your prediction of the likelihood of divorce higher or lower from there. And, Tetlock cautions, you should frequently update your predictions because those "inside" factors often change.

How does this relate to demographics? Well, demographics are one of the best baseline, "outside" predictors we have. Knowledge of demographic trends and what they mean is a great first step in understanding how larger trends in violence and peace, democracy or repression, prosperity or poverty, are likely to play out on a global scale. Both because populations are the foundation of every society and because they are the best crystal ball we have for the future, they often play a prominent role in our assessments of the future.

But, demographic trends aren't the end-all. Or, to phrase it in parlance commonly used in this area, demography is *not* destiny. Historical context, geography, social dynamics, and so forth, are those "inside" factors that move our predictions up or down from the baseline. We learn a lot by focusing on one dynamic at a time, such as fertility rates, but there's never just one demographic trend characterizing a society at any one point in time. Even in a single country, some women, maybe of a certain ethnic or income group, are having lots of babies; others are having none. People with certain levels of education are moving from rural to urban areas; others are being uprooted and forced across borders by outbreaks of conflict.

Policies can change the trajectory of demographic trends, too. When famous doomsayer Paul R. Ehrlich published *The Population Bomb* in 1968, he followed in Malthus's footsteps and argued that humans were breeding themselves into extinction. Worried that global population was set to exceed Earth's carrying capacity, he advocated for strict family-planning measures, even flirting with coercion. Yet, here we are, with deaths from famine a fraction of what they were in Ehrlich's time. Ehrlich has had ample time to retract his predictions, yet he, and others, see value in his warnings, even though they did not come true, because they brought attention to poverty and famine in much of the world (granted, attention that sometimes led to human rights violations). People who dismiss him for his inaccurate forecasts miss the point. *Forecasts don't predict the future—they drive investments in the present. In other words, considering a range of demographic forecasts points you toward the investments you need to make today to shape the future you want tomorrow.* While we can be fairly certain that even in the absence of policy changes world population wouldn't have reached something like 30 billion, how much higher would global population have been without those drops in fertility? And, more important, how different might the quality of life have been for so many? When Ehrlich published *The Population Bomb*, global total fertility was 4.93—that's an average of nearly five children per woman. No wonder he and many others, particularly in the budding environmental movement, were worried. Twenty-five years later, global fertility had plummeted to only three children per woman and by 2020 was 2.47. How many policy investments in education, health-care infrastructure, and macroeconomics did it take to halve global fertility from Ehrlich's time? Asking such questions is more important than setting Ehrlich up as a strawman.

There's power in small population changes. Whenever you've seen population projections in this book, they're often using the United Nations medium projection because that's the standard used in most publications, but sometimes it's useful to explore a different projection and get a fuller picture of how policy interventions and other changes might alter the future demographic course. For the most accurate assessment of the future, we need to think through the range of projections and the implications across that range.

Let's apply the idea of a range of demographic forecasts to Nigeria

FIGURE 18. Median Age Scenarios for Nigeria: 2020–2100

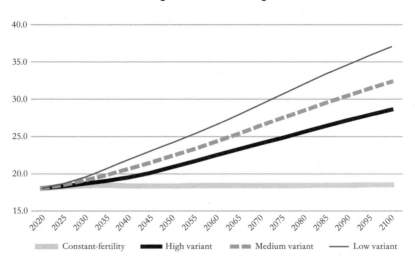

today. The rising median age shown in Figure 18 reflects that even the highest UN projection expects total fertility rate (TFR) in Nigeria to fall from 5.42 in 2020 to 4.06 by 2050 and 2.76 by 2100, and with that path Nigeria's median age would rise to 28.6 by the end of the century. If fertility drops faster, as in the medium scenario, Nigeria's median age would go from 18 in 2020 to 22.4 by mid-century. If it drops even faster, as in the low scenario, median age would be nearly 2 years higher by 2050.

Such scenarios are handy, but they're not the only possible paths— Nigeria may follow a totally different course. Botswana's path was actually even more accelerated than Nigeria's low scenario. As Figure 19 shows, Botswana's TFR fell from 6.7 children per woman on average in the period ending 1970 to about 3.5 by the turn of this century.

While Botswana had higher fertility than Nigeria in 1950, under the UN's high-fertility scenario Nigeria wouldn't achieve the fertility level of Botswana today (2.89) until after 2090, under the medium scenario until after 2065, and even under the low-fertility scenario until after 2050.

One conclusion from this exercise is we should be wary of using

FIGURE 19. Fertility Scenarios: Botswana and Nigeria

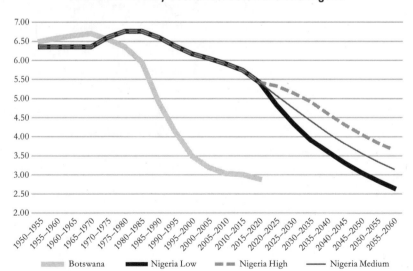

population projections more than two decades out for some planning purposes. Fertility drove a lot of the population changes we covered, especially in countries past the first stage of the demographic transition. But excess mortality from COVID-19, as in India and the United States, created demographic "surprises" outside of the projections we were all using. Two decades is still a long time, so nothing to lament, and certainly much longer than we could use political or economic projections. But even if ultimately inaccurate, looking at long-term projections is still useful when we're trying to understand how our decisions today drive tomorrow's reality. Anyone using demographic projections needs to ask: How plausible is it that fertility and mortality trends stay roughly the same as they are now? How likely are they to change? Instead of the medium variant, which is the one generally cited in the media, using the constant-fertility variant demonstrates what a country's demographic profile will look like without significant policy intervention or social shifts, and thus can help us understand the importance of short-term economic and political decisions on long-term population changes. When I'm trying to make a point to policy makers about the investments needed for high-fertility societies to move along the demographic transition, the constant fertility variant is the most powerful way to make my point. Mortality and migration projections for the constant-fertility variant are the same as for the UN's low-, medium-, and high-fertility projections, but as we've seen, those can change, too. As soon as US president Joe Biden took office in January 2021, for example, the pent-up demand at the southern US border started to spill over. The number of migrants US Customs and Border Protection encountered trying to enter the United States along the southwest border jumped 71 percent from February to March 2021. That includes 18,890 unaccompanied children from Central America, twice as many in March as in February.

• • •

Understanding that any demographic numbers for the future involve assumptions about fertility, mortality, and migration is the first step in making more accurate projections about their implications. The second step is checking our own assumptions. The danger in using demographics is that we often see what we want to see. Psychologists call this "desirability bias," and we need to avoid it. *When analyzing demographics, don't let your preferences cloud your judgment.*

When I speak to companies or policy makers, I try to convey that *the most important skills in demographic analysis are naming and being aware of your preferences, rethinking assumptions, and asking the right questions.* This includes our own assumptions as analysts. As the world's first "demographic billionaire," China's population growth and high fertility were criticized as a huge weakness, sure to undermine any of the communist government's efforts at global domination. Now, its aging population and low fertility are criticized as a liability. Can both criticisms be valid? Certainly, these contradictions make sense when we acknowledge that too often, the seer sees what he or she wants to see. I strongly caution against letting your goals drive your interpretation of demographic trends. If you're a competitor with China or with the United States and you let your desire to triumph in business or military power drive how you view the strengths and weaknesses of Chinese or American population trends, you're doing it wrong.

Desirability bias has also colored interpretations of Russia's demographic trends. Figure 20 is one of my favorite graphs because it says so much about how demographic assessments are driven by recent trends and how dangerous that practice can be. Focus on the two vertical black lines. Imagine first that the data endpoint was that left-most line, 2010. As I've written about elsewhere in this book, a lot of dire predictions about Russia's demographics were made right around the years 2009 and 2010, when Russia's depopulation was rapid and the country was on a clear downward slope. But what happened next? Russia saw a modest turnaround in fertility, and population began to rise. As we might expect, the result was a flood of news articles and policy analysis talking about Russia's miraculous turnaround in the birthrate. Sure, if we cut off our data at the right-most vertical black line, at 2020, we might indeed project that Russia is on the upswing. But we'd have an incomplete picture then, too.

Instead of these shortsighted views, a comprehensive picture of what fertility trends are like in countries such as Russia lets us know that they will be at sub-replacement fertility in the long run, and that intensive pro-natalist interventions only give modest rise to fertility, and generally only in the immediate term. Russia will need to prepare for its permanent shift to low fertility, population aging, and depopulation, absent significant immigration.

We also need to continually update our assessments. I'm not saying this just to keep myself in a job (although regular updates would ensure future editions of this book), but trends change. After all, we're trying to understand human behavior, not that of robots. While for decades the United States was an outlier in terms of higher fertility, the United States, China, and Russia are arguably more demographically alike than different, as Figure 21 shows. If you haven't updated your analysis and you're still considering the United States as an outlier, you're behind the

FIGURE 20. Population of the Russian Federation, 1990–2035

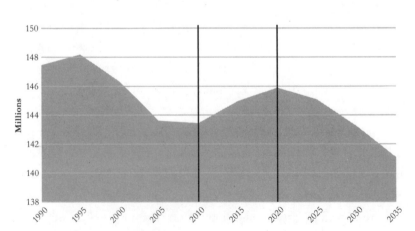

FIGURE 21. Population Statistics: United States, China, and Russia in 2020

2020	Russia	US	China
Total population	146	331	1,439m
Median age	37	38	38
Total fertility rate	1.82	1.6	1.7
Life expectancy at birth	70	80	77
Working age population	Peaked	Peaked	Peaked
Immigrants	12–13m	45m	Net sender

curve. More Americans are realizing that US population patterns are shifting, such as Matt Yglesias, who even before the results of the 2020 Census argued that America needed to dramatically expand its immigration to keep pace with China. What we should be asking is: What are the implications for global governance, global peace, and global economic growth when the world's leading powers are *all* aging?

• • •

Given these reminders about the utility and limitation of forecasts and the need for continually updating assumptions, is there anything we can say conclusively about demographics in a world of 8 billion? I think so and have gathered a list of what I see as the six most important takeaways as you go forth and analyze.

1. Size matters.

No matter how much technology has advanced or how postmodern our societies have become, population size still matters. And the primordial principle remains: the bigger the better. Some of this is literal, as we saw in the chapter on aging, as population size and age composition determine the number of potential soldiers. But a good deal of the issue is *perception*.

Tribes, states, and all the other assorted political units humans have organized themselves into throughout our history have always seen strength in their numbers. Their decline, on the other hand, has been perceived as weakness. Political–economic theories supported this thinking into the modern age. The economic philosophy of mercantilism, which saw the key to state power as accumulation of wealth, also included accumulation of people as a major source of wealth. Fundamentally, human capital is still a key factor when considering a nation's power, especially in regard to the nation's military and economics. The population of a society and its makeup directly influence all other factors of a society and will therefore weigh heavily in how groups perceive their own strength relative to that of others.

2. People move in somewhat predictable patterns.

It's certain that the world will continue to have migration "surprises" over the next few decades as conflicts and economic crises erupt. However, the *exact* situations that produce sudden displacements are impossible to predict. Migration for economic reasons (absent crisis) is more predictable. The global nature of capitalism means that capital moves to places where there's more bang for a buck, and labor moves to places where wages are higher. The majority of migrant workers go from smaller, middle-income economies to larger, high-income economies—in 2019 two-thirds of international migrants resided in high-income countries, with 29 percent in middle-income countries. Emigration from countries where GDP per capita is about $10,000, such as Jordan or the Philippines, is 2.5 times higher than in countries where it is only $1,000, such as Niger. As states move toward lower-middle incomes, more people in the country can afford to travel and have the skills and means to do so. Emigration rates slow when states achieve high-income status, what the World Bank defines as GDP per capita of $10,000 to $12,000, because at this point, there are generally attractive employment opportunities at home. We know from public opinion surveys that there's a high desire to emigrate among people in sub-Saharan Africa, but in many countries of that region income levels are too low for emigration en masse. As incomes rise, however, emigration is more likely.

Likewise, as levels of development increase, the population ages, and demand for labor rises, so states that cross the threshold to high income will begin to attract migrants in larger numbers. This includes both labor migration and conflict migration. As an example of the latter, as 2020 approached, the number of people applying for asylum in Mexico skyrocketed, an 11-fold increase between 2013 and 2017. Applications from Central Americans fleeing violence continued to go up in 2018, 2019, and the first three months of 2020, until COVID-19 drove border restrictions on entry into the country. While Mexico has historically been a source country of migrants to the United States, as incomes rise and the population ages Mexico is becoming a destination country in its own right.

3. The world is urban.

Given that the urban populations of the Western Hemisphere and Europe are saturated, the majority of future urban growth will come from Asia and Africa. African cities are growing at a much faster rate than cities did in the past. During the heyday of industrialization, from 1800 to 1910, London grew 2 percent a year, meaning the city's population doubled every 25 years. In contrast, the population of Kigali, Rwanda, grew 7 percent a year between 1950 and 2010, meaning it doubled every decade, according to researcher Greg Mills. India, alone, has 495 million urban dwellers, and China has 893 million. Going forward, India, China, and Nigeria will account for 35 percent of the growth in the world's urban population between 2018 and 2050. India will add 416 million urbanites, China 255 million, and Nigeria 189 million.

We can expect increasing urbanization of up to 70 percent of the world's population by 2050, most of which will take place in middle- and low-income countries. While today's developed countries saw the economic benefits of urbanization, some 800 million people worldwide are in slum areas, while "superstar" cities basically attract all the innovation, capital, talent, and investment. Urbanization is associated with tremendous economic benefits but also intersects with environmental change in ways that can undermine gains in income and quality of life. Urbanizing low-income and lower-middle-income countries are at risk of food insecurity, as their growing populations are heavily dependent on imports and subsistence agriculture still predominates. While we don't want to oversimplify and return to a strict Malthusian analysis, it is undeniable that climate change has already exacerbated droughts and floods, making these burgeoning urban areas vulnerable to such shocks.

4. An aging world is coming.

Although we may not live more years past age 122, more people are living to be centenarians than ever. That's been an interesting development in Japan, where the Japanese government had been in the practice of recognizing its new centenarians by gifting them with a sterling silver cup. The problem is that the number of centenarians—those at least age 100—has grown for 50 years in a row, from only 153 when the country started keeping records in 1963, to nearly 80,000 in 2020. Japanese centenarians are now so numerous that the government has switched from sterling silver to silver-plated to save money. That was a smart move, as centenarians there are expected to number 170,000 by 2027.

Of individuals, we often say that growing old is better than the alternative; to an extent the same sentiment is true for aging societies. We should continue to celebrate strides in increasing life expectancy at older ages and better child survival rates, which give people the confidence to have smaller families. But just as an individual feels the pains and strains of aging, so too do aging societies. By 2050, those ages 20 to 69 will shrink by 16.2 percent in South Korea, 14.9 percent in Taiwan, and 8.9 percent in China. If institutions don't change in states where the government has promised entitlements and early retirement, when those states age their economies will likely contract, and the governments will face a serious challenge in meeting their obligations. In countries where there are few long-term care facilities and low entitlements, the family will be strained to care for its aging members, likely depressing fertility even further. Retirement policies in most developed economies—the first wave of aging states—were shortsighted and expensive, because pay-as-you-go entitlement systems are unsustainable in aging states with shrinking workforces. Schemes that allow older people to skirt the system and exit early, such as through unemployment, are also costly. The most developed states have some hard political work ahead to reform policies in the face of extreme and unprecedented demographic aging. Policies to bring more women of all ages into the workforce and to allow older workers to stay in the workforce longer (getting rid of mandatory retirement age, for example) can increase the size of the workforce dramatically in societies where labor-force participation rates of those two groups are low (which is most developed countries). Those countries can also focus on supporting other factors that contribute to economic growth besides labor—productivity and efficiency, for example, can be improved by technology. Automation and immigration can offset some of the labor shortages that will come with increased aging, but never perfectly. Good health will also be key to thriving in an aging world to keep quality of life high, costs down, and productivity up.

5. Policies can shape the future we want.

Population is not like a tide that washes over us, taking us to various destinations no matter what we do—we can put policies in place that direct the flow. The good news is there are options: The causal arrow runs both ways between population on the one hand and politics, social relations, and economics on the other, meaning that actions on one side of the equation affect variables on the other. That's also the bad news. For countries to take full advantage of their demographic dividend, they have to put policies in place ahead of time to lay the groundwork for growth. That means everything from educating and training youth who will be of working age during the demographic window of opportunity, to creating macroeconomic policies conducive to foreign investment, to making sure the country is peaceful and stable enough for investors to take a risk. None of that is easy, but Merilee Grindle has discussed the aim of "good enough governance," which urges us to place stock in the power of small changes. Jack Goldstone and Larry Diamond state the menu of options succinctly: "making sensible investments in education, health, and infrastructure; supporting voluntary family planning; enforcing basic property rights; making economic growth more inclusive; and preventing diversion of too much national wealth and income to unproductive and corrupt ends."

If we've learned anything from the COVID-19 pandemic, it's that a good health foundation makes countries far more prepared for the unexpected. Studying what has worked then implementing those practices more widely can ensure that global health stays on the right track. While malaria still kills 430,000 a year, malaria cases were down 18 percent between 2010 and 2017, and deaths were down 28 percent. In 2019, Algeria and Argentina were declared malaria-free, and the first malaria vaccine was piloted in Ghana, Kenya, and Malawi. We've also seen tremendous gains in the global fight against HIV/AIDS. Until just a few years ago, in some southern African countries, HIV affected more than a third of the population and reduced life expectancy by up to 15 years. But the World Health Organization reports that between 2000 and 2018, the number of new HIV infections fell by 37 percent. The number of deaths related to infection also fell by 37 percent, and use of anti-retroviral therapy (ART) saved 13.6 million lives. Scholars have expressed concern that COVID-19 would redirect funds from other health areas, so gains in traditional areas of focus could be slower in the short term. It is too early to tell whether developed countries' efforts to prepare for pandemic readiness means they will devote fewer resources to health causes in less developed countries. Substituting pandemic preparedness for the fight against other diseases means trading one short-sighted and incomplete policy for another—instead, we need more funding for health overall so we can comprehensively address health challenges for the long term.

Policies also help determine the impact of population aging. Demographically speaking, Brazil is actually much younger than Russia or China. (China's median age is 38.4 and Brazil's is 33.5.) But, like China, Brazil is aging rapidly, and the most useful thing about demographics is that countries evolve along a fairly predictable path once they are well into the demographic transition. In other words, they know what's coming. Brazil's TFR is below replacement at 1.7 children per woman on average so Brazil's policy makers and business leaders are aware that the country is aging.

And yet.

During her first term in office, former Brazilian president Dilma Rousseff actually *increased* pension spending. Brazil spends a higher proportion of its GDP on pensions than does the world's oldest country, Japan. And whereas Japan's average age of exit from the workforce is 71 years for males, can you guess what it is in Brazil? Fifty-six. This is a very poor foundation to deal with population aging.

We should also consider India. Some talk about India and China in the same breath because they're big, they're neighbors, and they've sometimes recently seen similar economic growth. But, other than their size—together they compose 37 percent of the world's population—demographically, and in a lot of other respects, they couldn't be more different. The policies a country puts in place on everything from education, to urbanization, to pensions determine how demographic dynamics play out. India and China have a wide variety of policies that shape different outcomes for their demographic trends. Whereas literacy is nearly universal in China, in India only 66 percent of females are literate. China's massive urbanization drove much of its economic growth, while India is far behind the global average of 55.7 percent urban at only 35 percent in 2021 (possibly higher due to data issues, as mentioned in Chapter 6). China has been living up to its potential and making the most of its demography—India has not.

6. The demographic divide will shape the fortunes of countries.

Population data show that the divide between the developed and developing world continues to grow. More than 89 percent of the world's population growth between 2020 and 2050 will take place in lower-middle or low-income countries, while only 3 percent will take place in high-income countries. Sub-Saharan Africa is one of the fastest growing regions in the world, and the United Nations projects that the population will double by 2045, even if the subcontinent is able to reduce fertility from a current average of almost five children per woman to just over three. If fertility stays at its current level, the region's population will double a decade earlier, reaching more than 1.7 billion by 2035. On the other side of the divide, 42 percent of the world's population, mostly the developed world, lives in low-fertility countries. Of the world's 10 youngest countries, several stand out, including Somalia, the Democratic Republic of the Congo, and Uganda. These are not exactly countries known for being the world's most open, peaceful democracies with the most robust economic growth. Age structure doesn't tell us everything, but it gives pretty strong clues about political, social, and economic issues in various countries.

Given the ties between fertility and age structure, and between age structure and conflict or development, we can project that the economies of very low-fertility and high-fertility countries, which mostly have very mature or very young age structures, will face challenges meeting the needs of their dependents, while those of the middle ages—such as many rising powers—will experience high economic growth and a peace dividend. How these shifts translate to global power, peace, and prosperity will be something to watch. Globally, inequality will widen and deepen. The Middle East and North African (MENA) region illustrates this vast divide. While many states in the region, such as Iran and Tunisia, have relatively low fertility and aging populations, others, such as Yemen, still have high fertility and youthful age structures. The least developed countries continue to suffer from tremendous inequality internally, which can feed discontent and motivate political violence.

Climate change will bring additional challenges. Poor countries will be disproportionately affected, as will poor people even in developed countries; poor countries and poor communities will have less of an ability to adapt to higher temperatures and other extreme weather events. Continued population growth and rising incomes will mean continued rises in greenhouse gas emissions, barring radical change with clear leadership from the United States and China, in particular. Warming and changing climates also introduce diseases into new areas. Mosquitoes, for example, are increasing their range and bringing diseases such as yellow fever along with them.

● ● ●

This evening, somewhere in Upstate New York, a guy named Paul will celebrate his 50th birthday at home with his wife and two kids. He doesn't think of himself as old, especially as he probably needs to work another two decades before he can afford to retire. He and his wife have a second mortgage, their two sons' college to pay for, and a little bit of credit card debt from last year's family vacation to Hawaii. He just hopes he'll live long enough to retire. The doctor says his cholesterol is high and is worried Paul will develop diabetes from eating too much sugar.

Tonight, though, he'll indulge in a slice of German chocolate cake, just like his grandmother from the old country used to make, kiss the kids good night, crack open a beer, and settle in to watch television. His wife will go through the day's mail and toss an envelope on his lap before she returns to the kitchen to wash the dinner dishes. During the first commercial break, Paul will open his mail and get a punch in the gut. Inside the envelope is an unsolicited, personalized membership card to the powerful old-age lobbying group AARP. Happy birthday, Paul.

Across the world, in Somalia, on Africa's eastern horn, Faduma gets a sinking feeling in her stomach. How many days has it been since her last menstrual cycle? Her body has that ripe feeling of early pregnancy she went through with her first three children, and she's deathly afraid that even though her youngest is just a few months old and still nursing, she'll be adding another mouth to feed before long. She's only 22 and she's exhausted.

Paul's and Faduma's experiences are typical of their peers and representative of the great divide in population trends between richer and poorer countries today. I began studying demographics at the start of this century and have seen this divide deepen and become more resonant over these 20-plus years. In drafting this book, I returned to my first book, published a decade ago, and was pleased to see the assessments about demographic impact hold up—that's because the tools I've embraced and tried to relate in these pages really do work to help us understand *how* to use demographic projections and gain a deeper understanding of each other.

Our world of 8 billion will become a world of 9 billion, then 10 billion. While the pace at which global population is growing is slowing, we are still a world of 8 billion *and counting*. At any snapshot in time, these billions will comprise babies, children, workers, retirees, and those in the twilight of life. Just as an individual progresses through different ages and stages, societies that go through the various demographic transitions travel through ages and stages as well. The political opinions, consumer behaviors, and social abilities of generations of today have been (and will continue to be) shaped by their experiences with global recessions, pandemics, and wars, or stock market booms, flourishing peace, and technological revolutions. We are an interdependent, interconnected world, and the challenges that besiege one country easily touch us all: disease, climate change, economic crisis. But so do the good fortunes, as our interconnected economic world shows. The question we have before us is: How can we utilize the 8 billion people we have on the planet today to shape the world we want tomorrow?

ACKNOWLEDGMENTS

Parts of this book are about how incredibly hard it is to have young children at the same time as any semblance of a work or social life. To that end, my first thanks must be to the coterie of childcare workers who have supported my family and me through these long hours. Mallory McGolrick, especially, not only provided another set of caring hands for years, but also another set of ears to absorb all the worries and fears and another warm heart to love our babies. Thanks also to all of the other caregivers who made writing this book possible: Cammie Warren, Ebony Walker, Katie McBride, Betty Greene, Laura Gordon, and many more. I have the most supportive and loving husband imaginable, and none of my ambitions—personal or professional— would have been realized without him by my side. I love you, Paul. I'm also grateful for the patience of my friends as I fell off the radar for months—or longer—at a time. Daily venting sessions with Natalie Jones, Morgan Smith, and Jeni McBride were just the pressure release needed to keep going.

On the professional front I owe many debts of gratitude as well. Thanks to Duvall Osteen for an immediate yes to representing me and for believing that I can live out my childhood dream of being a writer. I'm grateful to the ace team at W. W. Norton who brought this book to life: Melanie Tortoroli, Mo Crist, Rachel Salzman, Meredith McGinnis, Dassi Zeidel, Devon Zahn, Chris Curioli, and Janine Barlow. Thanks also to Rimjhim Dey and Andy DeSio for helping me get this book out into the world.

A number of research assistants contributed case studies that made their way into this volume, including Clayton Getchell, Courtney Hornsby, Dylan Craddock, and Joon Hwang. Stuart Geitel-Basten, Anne Morse, Shadrack Nasong'o, Tait Keller, Esen Kirdis, and Jenny Wüstenberg provided feedback on small but significant points in the book. I would not have made it over the finish line without daily writing sessions via Zoom with Rebecca Tuvel, Courtenay Harter, and Vanessa Rogers. Rhodes College offered generous financial support for much of the research that made its way into this book; and the support of fabulous colleagues there, including Larryn Peterson, Katie White, and Laura Loth, was instrumental in balancing the teaching, service, research, and home-life demands that felt at times like they were pulling me apart at the seams.

Writing and publishing during a pandemic is its own kind of hell, but also an enormous privilege. I couldn't seriously study population trends without being aware of my own fortunate position, and it is my hope that this book at least shines a light on the diversity of experiences with family life around the globe. My sons, Rearden and Will, will hopefully live long enough to see a global population of likely 10 billion. I pray that such a world is more peaceful and prosperous than the one they were born into and that books like this one inspire us all to do better. As I say in the final chapter, we have to invest today to create the world we want tomorrow.

NOTES

Introduction

1 **300 million people:** Toshiko Kaneda and Carl Haub, "How Many People Have Ever Lived on Earth?" *PRB*, March 9, 2018, https://www.prb.org/howmanypeoplehaveeverlived onearth/.

1 **Those alive in 1750:** Kaneda and Haub, "How Many People."

2 **about 240 babies born:** US Census Bureau, "International Data Base," 2021, https://www.census.gov/data-tools/demo/idb/.

3 **the Japanese government projects:** Noriko O. Tsuya, *Low Fertility in Japan—No End in Sight* (Honolulu: East-West Center, June 2017), 2.

4 **Democratic Republic of the Congo (DRC):** World Bank, "World Development Indicators" (n.d.), https://data.worldbank.org.

5 **DRC saw 1.67 million:** "Democratic Republic of the Congo," International Displacement Monitoring Centre, 2019, https://www.internal-displacement.org/countries/democratic-republic-of-the-congo.

5 **cholera infects 5,000 of them:** "Cholera Count Reaches 500000 in Yemen," WHO News Release., August, 14, 2017, http://www.who.int/mediacentre/news/releases/2017/cholera-yemen-mark/en/.

5 **Economists have estimated:** World Bank, *Live Long and Prosper: Aging in East Asia and Pacific* (Washington, DC: World Bank, 2016).

6 **In a speech to Egypt's:** Hosni Mubarak, "President Hosni Mubarak on Egypt's Population," *Population & Development Review* 34, no. 3 (2008), 583–86.

9 **somewhere between 1 million and 2 million:** An ALNAP report says "more than 2 million" were "forced from their homes" (Katherine Haver, *Haiti Earthquake Response: Mapping and Analysis of Gaps and Duplications in Evaluations*. ALNAP-Active Learning Network for Accountability and Performance in Humanitarian Action, February 2011;

https://www.oecd.org/countries/haiti/47501750.pdf, p. 6). A Haitian government report, cited by DesRoches et al., says more than 1.3 million were displaced (Reginald DesRoches, Mary Comerio, Marc Eberhard, et al., "Overview of the 2010 Haiti Earthquake," *Earthquake Spectra* 27, no. S1 (2011): S1–S21, https://escweb.wr.usgs.gov/share/mooney/142.pdf.

9 **They brought cholera:** Liz Mineo, "Forcing the UN to Do Right by Haitian Cholera Victims," *Harvard Gazette* (2020), https://news.harvard.edu/gazette/story/2020/10/a-decade-of-seeking-justice-for-haitian-cholera-victims/.

9 **Haiti's infant mortality rate:** UNICEF, "UNICEF Data" (New York: UNICEF, May 5, 2020), https://data.unicef.org/country/hti/.

11 **Haiti's life expectancy at birth:** Population Reference Bureau, "2020 World Population Data Sheet" (Washington, DC: Population Reference Bureau, 2020), https://www.prb.org/wp-content/uploads/2020/07/letter-booklet-2020-world-population.pdf.

11 **This was the first decline:** Lenny Bernstein, "U.S. Life Expectancy Declines Again, a Dismal Trend Not Seen since World War I," *Washington Post*, November 28, 2018, https://www.washingtonpost.com/national/health-science/us-life-expectancy-declines-again-a-dismal-trend-not-seen-since-world-war-i/2018/11/28/ae58bc8c-f28c-11e8-bc79-68604ed88993_story.html.

11 **because of excessive deaths:** José Manuel Aburto, Jonas Schöley, Ilya Kashnitsky, et al., "Quantifying Impacts of the Covid-19 Pandemic through Life Expectancy Losses: A Population-Level Study of 29 Countries," *medRxiv* (2021), https://www.medrxiv.org/content/10.1101/2021.03.02.21252772v4.full-text.

11 **increasing in a predictable upward pattern:** Jim Oeppen and James W. Vaupel, "Broken Limits to Life Expectancy," *Science* 296, no. 5570 (2002), 1029–31.

11 **what Louis Dublin in 1928 forecasted:** Louis I. Dublin, *Health and Wealth* (New York: Harper, 1928).

12 **declined due in large part to:** Kimberly Singer Babiarz, Karen Eggleston, Grant Miller, and Qiong Zhang, "An Exploration of China's Mortality Decline under Mao: A Provincial Analysis, 1950-80," *Population Studies* 69, no. 1 (2015): 39–56. doi: 10.1080/00324728.2014.972432.

12 **from a life expectancy at birth of:** Nancy E. Riley, *Population in China* (Cambridge, UK: Polity Press, 2017). 2020 data from the United Nations.

12 **Even pedestrian improvements:** Riley, *Population in China*.

14 **from roughly 25 years to about 65:** Oeppen and Vaupel, "Broken Limits to Life Expectancy."

18 **Japan's today (71):** OECD, "Average Effective Age of Retirement Versus the Normal Age in 2018 in OECD Countries" (Paris: OECD, 2019).

18 **China only spends:** OECD, *Pensions at a Glance 2019: OECD and G20 Indicators* (Paris: OECD Publishing, 2019), https://doi.org/10.1787/b6d3dcfc-en, p. 203.

18 **Robert Gates even wrote that:** Robert M. Gates, "A Balanced Strategy: Reprogramming the Pentagon for a New Age," *Foreign Affairs* 88, no. 1 (2009).

19 **In December 2011:** "Syrian Regional Refugee Response: Inter-Agency Information Sharing Portal," UNHCR, updated April 30, 2021, https://data2.unhcr.org/en/situations/syria.

20 **nearly 80 million:** United Nations High Commissioner for Refugees, "Mid-Year Trends 2020," https://www.unhcr.org/statistics/unhcrstats/5fc504d44/mid-year-trends-2020.html.

20 **displaced people to remain so longer:** Colin Freeman and Matthew Holehouse, "Europe's Migrant Crisis Likely to Last for 20 Years, Says International Development Secretary," *Telegraph*, November 5, 2015, https://www.telegraph.co.uk/news/worldnews/europe/11977254/Warning-from-Justine-Greening-comes-as-new-EU-figures-say-three-million-migrants-could-arrive-in-next-two-years.html.

20 **50 percent of the world's refugees:** UNICEF, "Child Displacement," April 2020,https://data.unicef.org/topic/child-migration-and-displacement/displacement/.

20 **1 in every 97 persons:** United Nations High Commissioner for Refugees, *1 Per Cent of Humanity Displaced: UNHCR Global Trends Report*, June 18, 2020, https://data.unicef.org/topic/child-migration-and-displacement/displacement/.

20 **As of March 2017:** "Amid Humanitarian Funding Gap, 20 Million People across Africa, Yemen at Risk of Starvation, Emergency Relief Chief Warns Security Council," United Nations Press Release, March 10, 2017, https://www.un.org/press/en/2017/sc12748.doc.htm.

20 **The United Nations estimates:** "The United Nations in Yemen," United Nations, 2021, https://yemen.un.org/en/about/about-the-un.

20 **In just two months of 2017:** United Nations, Office for the Coordination of Humanitarian Affairs, "Under-Secretary-General for Humanitarian Affairs/Emergency Relief Coordinator Stephen O'Brien: Statement to the Security Council on Missions to Yemen, South Sudan, Somalia and Kenya and an Update on the Oslo Conference on Nigeria and the Lake Chad Region," ReliefWeb, March 10, 2017, https://reliefweb.int/report/yemen/under-secretary-general-humanitarian-affairsemergency-relief-coordinator-stephen-o.

20 **In Nigeria, the fight against:** Council on Foreign Relations, "Boko Haram in Nigeria," last modified March 2, 2021, https://www.cfr.org/global-conflict-tracker/conflict/boko-haram-nigeria.

20 **driven 2.9 million:** United Nations High Commissioner for Human Rights, "Regional Response – Nigeria Situation," last modified February 28, 2021, https://data2.unhcr.org/en/situations/nigeriasituation#_ga=2.155809531.1973709748.1571844796-1590759838.1571844796.

20 **Venezuela's economic and political:** "Venezuela Situation," UNHCR (n.d.), https://www.unhcr.org/en-us/venezuela-emergency.html.

21 **In 2019, two-thirds of all:** United Nations, Department of Economic and Social Affairs, *International Migration Report 2017: Highlights* (New York: United Nations, 2017); Jeanne Batalova, Mary Hanna, and Christopher Levesque, "Frequently Requested Statistics on Immigrants and Immigration in the United States," Migration Policy Institute, February 11, 2021, https://www.migrationpolicy.org/article/frequently-requested-statistics-immigrants-and-immigration-united-states-2020#refugees-asylum.

21 **Eighty-eight percent of:** United Nations, Department of Economic and Social Affairs, Population Division, "International Migrant Stock 2019" (United Nations database, POP/DB/MIG/Stock/Rev.2019), https://www.un.org/en/development/desa/population/migration/data/estimates2/estimates19.asp.

21 **Turkey, Jordan, Palestine:** United Nations, Department of Economic and Social Affairs, Population Division, "International Migrant Stock 2019."

21 **Just behind Asia:** United Nations, Department of Economic and Social Affairs, Population Division, "International Migrant Stock 2019."

21 **On average during 2015:** Author's own calculations from European Stability Initiative,

The Refugee Crisis through Statistics: A Compilation for Politicians, Journalists and Other Concerned Citizens, 15 (Berlin, Brussels, Istanbul: European Stability Initiative, 2017), https://www.esiweb.org/pdf/ESI%20-%20The%20refugee%20crisis%20through%20statistics%20-%2030%20Jan%202017.pdf.

21 **The population of the 27:** Eurostat, "EU Population in 2020: Almost 448 Million," Eurostat News Release, July 10, 2020, https://ec.europa.eu/eurostat/documents/2995521/11081093/3-10072020-AP-EN.pdf/d2f799bf-4412-05cc-a357-7b49b93615f1.

21 **British voters in 2016:** David Coleman, "A Demographic Rationale for Brexit," *Population & Development Review* 42, no. 4 (2016): 681–92.

22 **In the year 1800:** Thomas J. Bollyky, *Plagues and the Paradox of Progress: Why the World Is Getting Healthier in Worrisome Ways* (Cambridge, MA: MIT Press, 2018), 107.

22 **Even in 1950:** United Nations, Department of Economic and Social Affairs, *The World's Cities in 2018* (New York: United Nations, 2018).

22 **There's no standard international definition:** United Nations, Department of Economic and Social Affairs, *United Nations Demographic Yearbook 2018* (New York: United Nations, 2019), 120–23.

22 **Almost half of the world's urban:** United Nations, Department of Economic and Social Affairs, "Key Facts: World Urbanization Prospects: The 2018 Revision" (New York: United Nations, 2018), https://population.un.org/wup/Publications/Files/WUP2018-KeyFacts.pdf.

23 **Tokyo is projected to lose:** Department of Economic and Social Affairs, "World Urbanization Prospects," United Nations, 2018, https://population.un.org/wup/DataQuery/.

23 **A stark public-radio story:** Erik German and Solana Pyne, "Dhaka: Fastest Growing Megacity in the World," *The World* (2010), https://www.pri.org/stories/2010-09-08/dhaka-fastest-growing-megacity-world.

23 **some researchers are arguing:** Bollyky, *Plagues and the Paradox of Progress,* 108.

23 **"planet of slums":** Mike Davis, *Planet of Slums* (London: Verso, 2006).

25 **Monica Duffy Toft:** Monica Duffy Toft, *The Geography of Ethnic Violence* (Princeton, NJ: Princeton University Press, 2003).

25 **The age-structural transition:** Richard Cincotta, "The Age-Structural Theory of State Behavior," *Oxford Research Encyclopedia of Politics,* August 2017, https://doi.org/10.1093/acrefore/9780190228637.013.327.

26 **Countries with a young age structure:** Richard Cincotta, "Iran's Chinese Future," *Foreign Policy,* June 25, 2009, https://foreignpolicy.com/2009/06/25/irans-chinese-future/.

26 **A generation, or cohort:** Michael Dimock, "Defining Generations: Where Millennials End and Post-Millennials Begin," Pew Research FactTank, March 1, 2018, https://www.pewresearch.org/fact-tank/2019/01/17/where-millennials-end-and-generation-z-begins/.

27 **In the United States today, millennials:** Pew Research Center, *The Whys and Hows of Generations Research* (Washington, DC: Pew Research Center, 2015), http://www.people-press.org/2015/09/03/the-whys-and-hows-of-generations-research/.

Chapter 1: From the Cradle

31 **Romania was falling behind:** Michael S. Teitelbaum and Jay Winter, *A Question of Numbers: High Migration, Low Fertility, and the Politics of National Identity* (New York: Hill and Wang, 1998), 109–18.

32 **a national family-planning program:** Rebecca Jane Williams, "Storming the Citadels of Poverty: Family Planning under the Emergency in India, 1975–1977," *The Journal of Asian Studies* 73, no. 2 (2014), 471–92.

32 **foreign pressure from America:** Sanjan Ahluwalia and Daksha Parmar, "From Gandhi to Gandhi: Contraceptive Technologies and Sexual Politics in Postcolonial India, 1947-1977," in *Reproductive States: Global Perspectives on the Invention and Implementation of Population Policy*, ed. Rickie Solinger and Mie Nakachi (New York: Oxford University Press, 2016), 129.

32 **Teachers who declined sterilization:** Phillipa Levine, *Eugenics: A Very Short Introduction*. Very Short Introductions (New York: Oxford University Press, 2017).

32 **in June 1975:** Williams, "Storming the Citadels of Poverty."

33 **massive, labor-intensive campaigns:** Judith Shapiro, *Mao's War against Nature: Politics and the Environment in Revolutionary China* (Cambridge, UK: Cambridge University Press, 2001).

33 **which took effect in 1979:** Tyrene White, "China's Population Policy in Historical Context," in *Reproductive States: Global Perspectives on the Invention and Implementation of Population Policy*, ed. Rickie Solinger and Mie Nakachi (New York: Oxford University Press, 2016), 329–68.

35 **women in Chad:** Central Intelligence Agency, "Mother's Mean Age at First Birth," in *The World Factbook* (Langley, VA: Central Intelligence Agency, 2021).

35 **Fertility declines were earliest:** United Nations, Department of Economic and Social Affairs, Population Division, *World Urbanization Prospects: The 2018 Revision* (New York: United Nations, 2019).

36 **In Zimbabwe, for example:** Population Reference Bureau, "Family Planning Data" (Washington, DC: Population Reference Bureau, n.d.), https://www.prb.org/fpdata.

36 **in some states of the Middle East:** World Bank, "World Development Indicators" (Washington, DC: World Bank, 2021), https://databank.worldbank.org/source/world-development-indicators.

36 **Gender is also a factor:** Population Reference Bureau, "Family Planning Data."

36 **Sub-Saharan Africa lags:** John Bongaarts, "Can Family Planning Programs Reduce High Desired Family Size in Sub-Saharan Africa?" *International Perspectives on Sexual and Reproductive Health* 37, no. 4 (2011): 209–16.

37 **South Africa, Botswana:** Lyman Stone offers an alternative view, saying demographers and development experts have overreacted and the fertility trend is still downward so Africa is where it should be. Lyman Stone, "African Fertility Is Right Where It Should Be," Institute for Family Studies, October, 29, 2018, https://ifstudies.org/blog/african-fertility-is-right-where-it-should-be.

37 **In 2004, the United Nations projected:** United Nations, Department of Economic and Social Affairs, Population Division, *United Nations: World Population Prospects: The 2004 Revision* (New York: United Nations, 2005), http://pratclif.com/demography/unitednations-world-population%20rev%202004.htm.

38 **Demographer John Bongaarts found:** John Bongaarts, "Africa's Unique Fertility Transition," *Population and Development Review* 43 (2017): 55.

38 **"The problem of Africa":** "Speech: President Museveni's National Address," Uganda Media Centre Blog, updated September 9, 2018, https://ugandamediacentreblog.wordpress.com/2018/09/09/speech-president-musevenis-national-address/.

38 **Magufuli said in 2018:** "Magufuli Advises against Birth Control," *The Citizen*, September 10, 2018, https://www.thecitizen.co.tz/News/Magufuli-advises-against-birth-control/1840340-4751990-4h8fqpz/index.html.

38 **some African leaders resist:** John F. May, "The Politics of Family Planning Policies and Programs in Sub-Saharan Africa," *Population & Development Review* 47 (2017): 308–29.

39 **Even in antiquity:** Deborah R. McFarlane and Richard Grossman, "Contraceptive History and Practice," in *Global Population and Reproductive Health*, ed. Deborah R. McFarlane (Burlington, MA: Jones & Bartlett, 2015), 143–70.

39 **abortions and natural family planning:** John M. Riddle (ed.), *Contraception and Abortion from the Ancient World to the Renaissance* (Cambridge, MA: Harvard University Press, 1992).

40 **"limited choice of methods":** Riddle (ed.), *Contraception and Abortion*.

40 **Starting in the late 1980s:** "Youth, Women's Rights, and Political Change in Iran," Population Reference Bureau, 2009, http://www.prb.org/Articles/2009/iranyouth.aspx.

40 **"By 2000, about 90 percent":** Richard Cincotta and Karim Sadjadpour, *Iran in Transition: The Implications of the Islamic Republic's Changing Demographics* (Washington, DC: Carnegie Endowment for International Peace, 2017), 6.

40 **Free family-planning services:** Richard Cincotta, "Emulating Botswana's Approach to Reproductive Health Services Could Speed Development in the Sahel," New Security Beat, January 27, 2020, https://www.newsecuritybeat.org/2020/01/emulating-botswanas-approach-reproductive-health-services-speed-development-sahel/; Population Reference Bureau, "2019 World Population Data Sheet" (Washington, DC: Population Reference Bureau, 2019).

40 **while Botswana's TFR is:** Population Reference Bureau, "2020 World Population Data Sheet" (Washington, DC: Population Reference Bureau, 2020), https://www.prb.org/wp-content/uploads/2020/07/letter-booklet-2020-world-population.pdf.

41 **10 percent using any method:** Deborah R. McFarlane, "Population and Reproductive Health," in *Global Population and Reproductive Health*, ed. Deborah R. McFarlane (Burlington, MA: Jones & Bartlett, 2015), 11.

41 **In 2019 there were:** World Health Organization, "Family Planning/Contraception Methods," World Health Organization, https://www.who.int/news-room/fact-sheets/detail/family-planning-contraception.

41 **Ten percent of women:** World Health Organization, "Family Planning/Contraception Methods."

41 **Fewer than 15 percent:** Population Reference Bureau, "Family Planning Data."

41 **In Libya:** Population Reference Bureau, "2019 World Population Data Sheet."

41 **Globally, the unintended pregnancy rate:** Jonathan Bearak, Anna Popinchalk, Leontine Alkema, and Gilda Sedgh, "Global, Regional, and Subregional Trends in Unintended Pregnancy and Its Outcomes from 1990 to 2014: Estimates from a Bayesian Hierarchical Model," *Lancet Global Health* 6, no. 4 (2018): E380–89.

42 **China's SRB was 107.2:** Sharada Srinivasan and Shuzhuo Li, "Unifying Perspectives on Scarce Women and Surplus Men," in *Scarce Women and Surplus Men in China and India: Macro Demographics Versus Local Dynamics*, ed. Sharada Srinivasan and Shuzhuo Li (New York: Springer, 2018), 2.

42 **In South Korea, for example:** Quanbao Jiang, Qun Yu, Shucai Yang, and Jesús J. Sánchez-Barricarte, "Changes in Sex Ratio at Birth in China: A Decomposition by Birth Order," *Journal of Biosocial Science* 49, no. 6 (2017): 826–41.

43 **In China, 2010 data:** Ibid. Jiang et al., "Changes in Sex Ratio at Birth in China."

43 **in China and in India:** Simon Denyer and Annie Gowen, "Too Many Men," *Washington Post* (April 18, 2018), https://www.washingtonpost.com/graphics/2018/world/too-many

-men/?noredirect=on&utm_campaign=42d302f32e-newsletter_12_07_17&utm
_medium=email&utm_source=Jocelyn%20K.%20Glei%27s%20newsletter&utm
_term=.23aa9d7dc5a4.

43 **Some scholars frame the issue:** Denyer and Gowen, "Too Many Men."

44 **"even if a sizeable proportion":** Nancy E. Riley, *Population in China* (Cambridge, UK: Polity Press, 2017).

44 **"In South Korea, although":** Valerie M. Hudson, Andrea M. Den Boer, and Jenny Russell, "China's Mismatched Bookends: A Tale of Birth Sex Ratios in South Korea and Vietnam," Presented at the *International Studies Association Annual Conference*, New Orleans, Louisiana, 2015.

45 **Neither a strong state:** Valerie Hudson and Andrea M. den Boer, "Patrilineality, Son Preference, and Sex Selection in South Korea and Vietnam," *Population & Development Review* 43, no. 1 (2017): 119–47.

45 **significant pressures on both genders:** Valerie M. Hudson, "Sex, Demographics, and National Security," in *A Research Agenda for Political Demography*, ed. Jennifer D. Sciubba (Cheltenham, UK: Edward Elgar, 2021).

45 **as Hudson's latest work does:** Valerie M. Hudson, Donna Lee Bowen, and Perpetua Lynne Nielsen, *The First Political Order: How Sex Shapes Governance and National Security Worldwide* (New York: Columbia University Press), 2020.

45 **"crude evolutionary theories":** Kaz Ross, "An 'Army of Bachelors'? China's Male Population as a World Threat," *Journal of Asia Pacific Studies* 1, no. 2 (2010): 354.

45 **"the re-surfacing of fear":** Ross, "An 'Army of Bachelors'?" 338.

45 **larger fears about China's population:** Ross, "An 'Army of Bachelors'?" 339.

47 **Presumably, his question:** "How a Slap Sparked Tunisia's Revolution," *60 Minutes*, February 22, 2011, https://www.cbsnews.com/news/how-a-slap-sparked-tunisias-revolution-22-02-2011/.

48 **Henrik Urdal found that:** Henrik Urdal, "The Demographics of Political Violence: Youth Bulges, Insecurity, and Conflict," in *Too Poor for Peace? Global Poverty, Conflict, and Security in the 21st Century*, ed. Lael Brainard and Derek Chollet (Washington, DC: Brookings Institution Press, 2007), 90–100.

50 **more than 18 percent of voters:** Sebastian Doerr, Stefan Gissler, Jose-Luis Peydro, and Hans-Joachim Voth, "From Finance to Fascism," SSRN, November 3, 2020, https://ssrn.com/abstract=3146746.

52 **Researcher Eric Hooglund's 1977 fieldwork:** Eric Hooglund, "Rural Participation in the Revolution," *MERIP Reports*, no. 87 (1980): 4.

52 **by 1979 those aged 15 to 19:** Author's calculations using United Nations, Department of Economic and Social Affairs, Population Division, *World Population Prospects: The 2019 Revision* (New York: United Nations, 2019).

52 **under the shah, 25 percent:** Jerald A. Combs, *The History of American Foreign Policy*, Vol. II, 3rd ed. (Armonk, NY: M.E. Sharpe, 2008).

52 **World War I was started:** Herbert Moller, "Youth as a Force in the Modern World," *Comparative Studies in Society and History* 10, no. 3 (1968): 237–60.

53 **In May 2018, Nigerian youth:** "Nigeria Lowers Minimum Ages for Office in Victory for Youth Campaign," *Reuters*, June 1, 2018, https://www.reuters.com/article/ozatp-uk-nigeria-politics-youth-idAFKCN1IX410-OZATP.

53 **Youth also played an important role:** Olena Nikolayenko, "The Revolt of the Post-Soviet

Generation: Youth Movements in Serbia, Georgia, and Ukraine," *Comparative Politics* 39, no. 2 (2007): 169.

53 **As political scientist Graeme B. Robertson:** Graeme B. Robertson, *The Politics of Protest in Hybrid Regimes: Managing Dissent in Post-Communist Russia* (Cambridge, UK: Cambridge University Press, 2011), 4.

53 **Robertson argues:** Robertson, *The Politics of Protest in Hybrid Regimes* [Kindle locations 834–39].

54 **Singapore's median age at first marriage:** "Median Age at First Marriage of Grooms and Brides by Educational Qualification, Annual," Government of Singapore, 2019, https://data.gov.sg/dataset/median-age-at-first-marriage-of-grooms-and-brides-by-educational-qualification-annual.

54 **In 1968, French university students:** Dorothy Pickles, "France in 1968: Retrospect and Prospect," *World Today* 24, no. 9 (1968): 393–402.

54 **In the 10 years prior, France's:** David Caute, *The Year of the Barricades: A Journey through 1968* (New York: Harper & Row, 1988), 212–13.

54 **Young workers:** Caute, *The Year of the Barricades*, 233.

54 **Soviet tanks rolled into Prague:** Mark Kurlansky, *1968: The Year That Rocked the World* (New York: Ballentine Books, 2004), Loc. 667.

55 **"What was unique about 1968":** Kurlansky, *1968: The Year That Rocked the World*, Loc. 62.

55 **"a generation that felt":** Kurlansky, *1968: The Year That Rocked the World*, Loc. 71.

56 **Measuring youth risk factor:** Many measures of risk associated with youth bulge measure those ages 15 to 24 or 29 as a proportion of total population or total adult population, as Bricker and Foley point out. Noah Q. Bricker and Mark C. Foley, "The Effect of Youth Demographics on Violence: The Importance of the Labor Market," *International Journal of Conflict and Violence* 7, no. 1 (2013): 179–94.

56 **According to research by Richard Cincotta:** Richard Cincotta, "The Age-Structural Theory of State Behavior," *Oxford Research Encyclopedia of Politics*, August 2017, https://doi.org/10.1093/acrefore/9780190228637.013.327.

56 **According to Cincotta's research:** Richard Cincotta, "Forecasting in Age-Structural Time," in *A Research Agenda for Political Demography*, ed. Jennifer D. Sciubba (Cheltenham, UK: Edward Elgar, 2021).

56 **Cincotta and his colleague John Doces:** Richard P. Cincotta and John Doces, "The Age-Structural Maturity Thesis: The Impact of the Youth Bulge on the Advent and Stability of Liberal Democracy," in *Political Demography: How Population Changes Are Reshaping International Security and National Politics*, ed. Jack A. Goldstone, Eric P. Kaufman, and Monica Duffy Toft (Boulder: Paradigm Publishers, 2012).

58 **Yet critiques of this view:** Daniela Huber, "Youth as a New 'Foreign Policy Challenge' in Middle East and North Africa: A Critical Interrogation of European Union and US Youth Policies in Morocco and Tunisia," *European Foreign Affairs Review* 22, no. 1 (2017): 117.

58 **The transition to adulthood:** TongFi Kim and Jennifer Dabbs Sciubba, "The Effect of Age Structure on the Abrogation of Military Alliances," *International Interactions* 41, no. 2 (2015): 279–308.

Chapter 2: Gray Dawn

59 **In his sci-fi short story:** Kurt Vonnegut, "Tomorrow and Tomorrow and Tomorrow," in *Welcome to the Monkey House* (New York: Dial Press, 2006).

62 **According to the OECD:** Jaewon Kim, "No Country for Old Koreans: Moon Faces Senior Poverty Crisis," *Nikkei Asian Review*, January 29, 2019, https://asia.nikkei.com/Spotlight /Asia-Insight/No-Country-For-Old-Koreans-Moon-faces-senior-poverty-crisis.

62 **"The generation of South Koreans":** Kim, "No Country for Old Koreans."

63 **In the late 1960s:** Gavin Thompson, Oliver Hawkins, Aliyah Dar, and Mark Taylor, "Olympic Britain: Social and Economic Change since the 1908 and 1948 London Games" (London: House of Commons Library, 2012), 18.

63 **her contemporary waits until 29:** OECD, "Sf2.3: Age of Mothers at Childbirth and Age-Specific Fertility" (Paris: OECD, 2017).

63 **So, how many babies did women:** Tomáš Sobotka, "Post-Transitional Fertility: The Role of Childbearing Postponement in Fueling the Shift to Low and Unstable Fertility Levels," *Journal of Biosocial Science* 49, no. S1 (2017): S20–S45.

64 **Births in the United States:** Brady E. Hamilton, Joyce A. Martin, and Michelle J.K. Oster-man, *Births: Provisional Data for 2020* (US Department of Health and Human Services, Centers for Disease Control and Prevention, May 2021), https://www.cdc.gov/nchs/data/vsrr /vsrr012-508.pdf.

64 **In Italy, England, and the Netherlands:** Valeriy Elizarov and Victoria Levin, "Family Policies in Russia: Could Efforts to Raise Fertility Rates Slow Population Aging?," in *Russian Federation Aging Project* (Washington, DC: World Bank Group, 2015).

64 **fewer women are having second:** Elizarov and Levin, "Family Policies in Russia."

65 **The average age of first marriage:** US Census Bureau, "Historical Marital Status Tables," US Census Bureau, December 2020, https://www.census.gov/data/tables/time-series /demo/families/marital.html.

65 **As author Rebecca Traister reports:** Rebecca Traister, *All the Single Ladies: Unmarried Women and the Rise of an Independent Nation* (New York: Simon & Schuster, 2016).

65 **1967 *Teen Guide to Homemaking* textbook:** Marion S. Barclay and Frances Champion, *Teen Guide to Homemaking*, 2nd ed. (St. Louis: McGraw-Hill, 1967).

66 **Sociologist Arlie Hochschild tried:** Arlie Hochschild, *The Second Shift: Working Families and the Revolution at Home* (New York: Penguin, 2012).

66 **Researchers Mary Brinton and Dong-Ju Lee find:** Mary C. Brinton and Dong-Ju Lee, "Gender-Role Ideology, Labor Market Institutions, and Post-Industrial Fertility," *Population & Development Review* 42, no. 3 (2016): 405–33.

66 **2009 survey by the East-West Center:** United Nations, Department of Economic and Social Affairs, *Government Response to Low Fertility in Japan* (UNDESA, Population Division & East-West Center, 2015).

67 **many South Koreans cannot afford:** Sotaro Suzuki, "South Korean Population on Cusp of Steep Decline," *Nikkei Asian Review*, March 29, 2019, https://asia.nikkei.com/ Economy/South-Korean-population-on-cusp-of-steep-decline.

67 **interaction between gender norms:** Brinton and Lee, "Gender-Role Ideology," 424–25.

67 **Countries that have more flexible:** Brinton and Lee, "Gender-Role Ideology," 424–26.

67 **the unemployment rate:** OECD, *Investing in Youth: Korea* (Paris: OECD, 2019).

67 **TFR hit a record low:** Young-sil Yoon, "S. Korea's Total Fertility Rate Falls Below 1,"

BusinessKorea, August 29, 2019, http://www.businesskorea.co.kr/news/articleView.html ?idxno=35471.

67 **In the United States, women held:** Claire Cain Miller, "Women's Gains in the Work Force Conceal a Problem," *New York Times*, January 21, 2021), https://www.nytimes .com/2020/01/21/upshot/womens-gains-in-the-work-force-conceal-a-problem.html.

68 **COVID-19 lockdowns:** Claire Ewing-Nelson, "All of the Jobs Lost in December Were Women's Jobs," National Women's Law Center, January 2021, https://nwlc.org/wp-content /uploads/2021/01/December-Jobs-Day.pdf.

68 **Women of color were hit:** Ewing-Nelson, "All of the Jobs Lost in December Were Women's Jobs."

68 **Among OECD countries:** OECD, "Sf2.4: Share of Births Outside of Marriage" (Paris: OECD, 2016), 1.

69 **Births out of wedlock:** OECD, "OECD Family Database" (Paris: OECD, 2020), https:// www.oecd.org/els/family/database.htm.

70 **Japan's National Institute:** "Population Projections for Japan (2016-2065): Summary," National Institute of Population and Social Security Research, accessed May 3, 2021, http://www.ipss.go.jp/pp-zenkoku/e/zenkoku_e2017/pp_zenkoku2017e_gaiyou.html.

70 **the United Nations projects that:** Benedict Clements, Kamil Dybczak, Vitor Gaspar, et al., "The Fiscal Consequences of Shrinking Populations," in *Staff Discussion Notes* (Washington, DC: International Monetary Fund, 2015), 5.

70 **from the 1840s to the 1950s:** David Coleman and Robert Rowthorn, "Who's Afraid of Population Decline? A Critical Examination of Its Consequences," *Population & Development Review* 37, Supplement (2011): 227.

70 **first population declines:** Coleman and Rowthorn, "Who's Afraid of Population Decline?," 222.

71 **The average age of French senators:** "German MPs Are Younger Than French MPs," *L'Observatoire des Senioi*, April 12, 2017, https://observatoire-des-seniors.com/en/les -deputes-allemands-ont-en-moyenne-497-ans-et-les-francais-628-ans/.

74 **German men today:** OECD, "Average Effective Age of Retirement Versus the Normal Age in 2018 in OECD Countries" (Paris: OECD, 2019).

75 **In Germany, about 56 percent:** Christoph Merkle, Philipp Schreiber, and Martin Weber, "Framing and Retirement Age: The Gap between Willingness-to-Accept and Willingness-to-Pay," *Economic Policy* 32 (2017): 760. Citing FRA (Deutsche Rentenversicherung, 2015).

75 **Across the OECD:** OECD, *Ageing and Employment Policies—Statistics on Average Effective Age of Retirement*, 2018, https://www.oecd.org/els/emp/average-effective-age-of-retirement .htm.

75 **In the United States:** "Historical Background and Development of Social Security," US Social Security Administration, accessed November 4, 2020, https://www.ssa.gov/history /briefhistory3.html.

75 **Even the fiscally conservative Peter G. Peterson:** "What Effect Does Social Security Have on Poverty?," Fiscal Blog. Peter G. Peterson Foundation, September 10, 2018, https://www .pgpf.org/blog/2018/09/what-effect-does-social-security-have-on-poverty.

76 **some have estimated that the European Union:** Sarah Harper, "The Important Role of Migration for an Ageing Nation," *Population Ageing* 9 (2016): 185.

76 **Out of the 34 OECD countries:** OECD, *Pensions at a Glance: 2017* (Paris: OECD Publishing, 2017), 10.

76 **Cutting benefits:** Liliana Michelena, "Protests against President Disrupt Brazil's Major Cities," *Associated Press*, June 30, 2017, https://apnews.com/article/michel-temer-brazil -rio-de-janeiro-caribbean-strikes-b35d78ac7c4645a895adfc4eff7851f9.

77 **Japanese women and men hold:** "Global Health Observatory Data," World Health Organization, 2021, https://www.who.int/data/gho.

77 **From 2000 to 2016, the employment rate:** OECD, *Pensions at a Glance: 2017*, 125.

77 **"Flexible retirement":** OECD, *Pensions at a Glance: 2017*.

78 **director of the Massachusetts Institute of Technology's:** Joseph F. Coughlin, *The Longevity Economy: Unlocking the World's Fastest-Growing, Most Misunderstood Market* (New York: PublicAffairs, 2017).

78 **peak of America's baby boom:** "Vital Statistics of the United States, 2003, Volume I, Natality," Centers for Disease Control and Prevention, 2005, https://www.cdc.gov/nchs /products/vsus/vsus_1980_2003.htm. The timing of Seuss's publications was pointed out by Bruce Handy, *Wild Things: The Joy of Reading Children's Literature as an Adult* (New York: Simon & Schuster, 2017), 110.

78 **In the United States in 2015:** Coughlin, *The Longevity Economy*, 7.

79 **in democracies such as the United States and Japan:** William H. Frey, "2018 Voter Turnout Rose Dramatically for Groups Favoring Democrats, Census Confirms," Brookings Institution, 2019, https://www.brookings.edu/research/2018-voter-turnout-rose -dramatically-for-groups-favoring-democrats-census-confirms/.

79 **world's three oldest:** Jennifer Dabbs Sciubba, "Rhetoric and Action on Aging in Germany, Italy, and Japan: Party Platforms and Labor Policies in the World's Oldest Democracies," in *Ageing Population in Postindustrial Democracies*, ed. Pieter Vanhuysse and Achim Goerres (Abingdon, UK: Routledge, 2011), 54–78.

79 **the $179 billion that American grandparents:** Patty David and Brittne Nelson-Kakulla, "Grandparents Embrace Changing Attitudes and Technology." *AARP Research*, April 2019, https://www.aarp.org/research/topics/life/info-2019/aarp-grandparenting-study.html.

80 **story in *BusinessInsider*:** Mark Abadi, "Elderly People in Japan Are Getting Arrested on Purpose Because They Want to Go to Prison," *BusinessInsider* March 19, 2018, https:// www.businessinsider.com/japan-aging-prison-2018-3

81 **In the Netherlands:** Tiffany R. Jansen, "The Nursing Home That's Also a Dorm," *CityLab*. *Bloomberg*, October 2, 2015, https://www.citylab.com/equity/2015/10/the-nursing-home -thats-also-a-dorm/408424/.

81 **In Italy, Milan's:** Emma Charlton, "Students in Milan Are Moving in with the Elderly to Fight Loneliness and Save Money," WeForum [blog], November 2018, https:// www.weforum.org/agenda/2018/11/why-some-students-in-milan-are-moving-in -with-elderly-people/.

81 **In an academic study of:** Jennifer Dabbs Sciubba and Chien-Kai Chen, "The Politics of Aging in Singapore and Taiwan," *Asian Survey* 57, no. 4 (2017): 642–64.

81 **In China, sons are still:** Nancy E. Riley, *Population in China* (Cambridge, UK: Polity Press, 2017), 133.

81 **in Singapore the elderly:** Ann Biddlecom, Napaporn Chayovan, and Mary Beth Ofstedal, "Intergenerational Support and Transfers," in *The Well-Being of the Elderly in Asia: A Four-Country Comparative Study*, ed. Albert I. Hermalin (Ann Arbor: University of Michigan Press, 2002), 202.

82 **the government, children, and parents:** Riley, *Population in China*, 186.

83 **In 2010, an *Asahi*:** Chico Harlan, "Strict Immigration Rules May Threaten Japan's Future," *Washington Post*, July 28, 2010, http://www.washingtonpost.com/wp-dyn/content/article /2010/07/27/AR2010072706053.html.

83 **Even with issuing visas:** Justin McCurry, "The Changing Face of Japan: Labour Shortage Opens Doors to Immigrant Workers," *The Guardian*, November 8, 2018, https://www .theguardian.com/world/2018/nov/09/the-changing-face-of-japan-labour-shortage -opens-doors-to-immigrant-workers.

83 **In Shinzo Abe's words:** Anthony Kuhn, "As Japan Tries Out Immigration, Migrant Workers Complain of Exploitation," NPR, January 15, 2019, https://www.npr.org/2019 /01/15/683224099/as-japan-tries-out-immigration-migrant-workers-complain-of -exploitation.

84 **Germany since 2017 has desired to increase:** "German Army Recruits More Minors Than Ever Before: Report," *TheLocal.de*, January 9, 2018, https://www.thelocal.de/2018 0109/german-army-recruits-more-minors-than-ever-before-report/.

84 **immigrants from other European Union:** "German Army Floats Plan to Recruit For-eigners," *Reuters*, December 27, 2018, https://www.reuters.com/article/us-germany -military-foreigners/german-army-floats-plan-to-recruit-foreigners-idUSKCN1OQ14L.

84 **South Korea's government projects:** Statistics Korea, *Population Projections for Korea (2017~2067)*, Statistics Korea, March 28, 2019, http://kostat.go.kr/portal/eng/press Releases/8/8/index.board?bmode=read&bSeq=&aSeq=375684&pageNo=1&rowNum =10&navCount=10&currPg=&searchInfo=&sTarget=title&sTxt=.

84 **South Korea's population would shrink:** Anthony Fensom, "Korea's Future Is Dying (Thanks to Demographics)," *National Interest*, August 31, 2019, https://nationalinterest .org/blog/korea-watch/koreas-future-dying-thanks-demographics-77206.

85 **South Korea has about 625,000:** Fensom, "Korea's Future Is Dying."

85 **China's defense spending:** M.P. Funaiole, B. Chan, and B. Hart, "Understanding China's 2021 Defense Budget," Critical Questions, CSIS, March 5, 2021, https://www.csis.org /analysis/understanding-chinas-2021-defense-budget.

85 **In 2006, President Vladimir Putin:** Vladimir Putin, "Vladimir Putin on Raising Russia's Birth Rate," *Population & Development Review* 32, no. 2 (2006): 385–88.

86 **Power transition theory:** Jennifer Dabbs Sciubba, "Coffins Versus Cradles: Russian Pop-ulation, Foreign Policy, and Power Transition Theory," *International Area Studies Review* 7, no. 2 (2014): 205–21.

Chapter 3: A Billion Ways to Die

91 **"The idea of microscopic germs":** Steven Johnson, *The Ghost Map: The Story of London's Most Terrifying Epidemic—and How It Changed Science, Cities, and the Modern World* (New York: Riverhead Books, 2006). [Kindle iOS version, 60.]

91 **In his 1840 essay:** John M. Barry, *The Great Influenza: The Story of the Deadliest Pandemic in History* (New York: Penguin Books, 2005). [Kindle iOS version, 51.]

91 **Two decades later, French scientist:** "Louis Pasteur," Science History Institute, 2020, https://www.sciencehistory.org/historical-profile/louis-pasteur.

92 **In 1882, German doctor Robert:** "Robert Koch 1843-1910," Science Museum Group, 2020, http://broughttolife.sciencemuseum.org.uk/broughttolife/people/robertkoch.

92 **In Europe, the practice was documented:** World Health Organization, *Bugs, Drugs &*
Smoke: Stories from Public Health (Geneva: World Health Organization, 2011), 5.

92 **This practice, called variolation:** Barry, *The Great Influenza*, 20.

92 **Today, pharmaceutical giant Merck's:** Thomas J. Bollyky, *Plagues and the Paradox of Prog-*
ress: Why the World Is Getting Healthier in Worrisome Ways (Cambridge, MA: MIT Press, 2018),
84.

92 **The COVID-19 vaccines:** Walter Isaacson, *The Code Breaker: Jennifer Doudna, Gene Editing,*
and the Future of the Human Race (New York: Simon & Schuster, 2021).

92 **A study of 428 parents:** Metin Yigit, Aslinur Ozkaya-Parlakay, and Emrah Senel, "Evaluation of Covid-19 Vaccine Refusal in Parents," *Pediatric Infectious Disease Journal* 40, no. 4
(2021): e134–136. doi: 10.1097/INF.0000000000003042.

93 **vaccine refusals "due to misinformation":** World Health Organization, *Polio Endgame*
Strategy 2019-2023: Eradication, Integration, Certification and Containment (Geneva: World
Health Organization, 2019), 1, https://polioeradication.org/wp-content/uploads/2019/06
/english-polio-endgame-strategy.pdf.

93 **UN secretary-general António Guterres:** "Secretary-General Calls Vaccine Equity Biggest Moral Test for Global Community, as Security Council Considers Equitable Availability of Doses," United Nations News Release, February 14, 2021, https://www.un.org/
press/en/2021/sc14438.doc.htm.

94 **In Yemen, cholera vaccines sat:** Frederik Federspiel and Mohammad Ali, "The Cholera
Outbreak in Yemen: Lessons Learned and Way Forward," *BMC Public Health* 18, no. 1 (2018),
1338.

94 **more than 2.5 million cases:** World Health Organization, *Cholera Situation in Yemen* (Cairo,
Egypt: World Health Organization, Regional Office for the Eastern Mediterranean,
December 2020).

94 **world's poorest countries:** World Health Organization, "World Health Statistics Overview 2019: Monitoring Health for the SGDs, Sustainable Development Goals" (Geneva:
World Health Organization, 2019), 4.

94 **it alone kills one child:** "Malaria Vaccine Pilot Launched in Malawi," WHO News Release,
April 23, 2019, https://www.who.int/news-room/detail/23-04-2019-malaria-vaccine
-pilot-launched-in-malawi.

94 **In 2016, the gap in life:** World Health Organization, "World Health Statistics 2020:
Monitoring Health for the SDGs" (Geneva: World Health Organization, 2020), vii–1.

95 **new diseases that infect humans:** World Health Organization, *Bugs, Drugs & Smoke*, 128.

95 **Knowledge of the origins of COVID-19:** Amy McKeever, "We Still Don't Know the
Origins of the Coronavirus. Here Are 4 Scenarios," *National Geographic*, April 2, 2021,
https://www.nationalgeographic.com/science/article/we-still-dont-know-the-origins
-of-the-coronavirus-here-are-four-scenarios.

96 **During the recent war, Yemen's:** Federspiel and Ali, "The Cholera Outbreak in Yemen."

96 **In 2017, only one-third:** World Health Organization, "World Health Statistics 2020," 3.

96 **At the start of Liberia's 2014 Ebola:** Sara Jerving, "Why Liberians Thought Ebola Was
a Government Scam to Attract Western Aid," *The Nation*, September 16, 2014, https://
www.thenation.com/article/archive/why-liberians-thought-ebola-was-government
-scam-attract-western-aid/.

96 **in poor countries the equivalent:** *Diarrhea: Common Illness, Global Killer,* US Department

of Health and Human Services, Centers for Disease Control and Prevention, https://www
.cdc.gov/healthywater/pdf/global/programs/Globaldiarrhea508c.pdf.

96 **Between 2000 and 2017, yearly deaths:** "Diarrhoea," UNICEF, 2021, https://data
.unicef.org/topic/child-health/diarrhoeal-disease/.

96 **has saved 50 million people:** "Cholera," World Health Organization, February 5, 2021,
https://www.who.int/news-room/fact-sheets/detail/cholera.

97 **According to the Institute:** Institute for Health Metrics and Evaluation, "Japan," 2020,
http://www.healthdata.org/japan.

98 **According to the WHO:** World Health Organization, "World Health Statistics 2020," vii.

98 **in only two regions of the world:** Bollyky, *Plagues and the Paradox of Progress*, 10.

98 **Of the 15 million deaths:** World Health Organization, "World Health Statistics 2020," vii.

98 **exposed severe issues:** Shikha Dalmia, "How Foreign Aid Screwed up Liberia's Ability to Fight Ebola," *The Week*, October 24, 2014, https://theweek.com/articles/442800
/how-foreign-aid-screwed-liberias-ability-fight-ebola.

98 **saw between 300 and 400:** World Health Organization Africa, "The Ebola Outbreak
in Liberia," World Health Organization Africa, https://www.afro.who.int/news/ebola
-outbreak-liberia-over.

98 **Nigeria saw only 19:** World Health Organization, "WHO Declares End of Ebola Outbreak in Nigeria," WHO News Release, October 20, 2014, https://www.who.int/
mediacentre/news/statements/2014/nigeria-ends-ebola/en/.

98 **Because of a lack of health infrastructure:** Joseph Akwiri and Maggie Fick, "In Kenya,
Covid-19's Rural Spread Strains Creaky Healthcare," *Reuters*, December 7, 2020, https://
www.reuters.com/article/us-health-coronavirus-kenya/in-kenya-covid-19s-rural-spread
-strains-creaky-healthcare-idUSKBN28H0J0.

99 **Europe's demographic transition:** Bollyky, *Plagues and the Paradox of Progress*, xiii.

99 **Niger has seen:** Bollyky, *Plagues and the Paradox of Progress*, 147.

100 **Globally, 808 women die:** *Maternal Mortality: Levels and Trends 2000 to 2017* (WHO,
UNICEF, UNFPA, World Bank Group, & UN Population Division, 2019), https://www
.who.int/reproductivehealth/publications/maternal-mortality-2000-2017/en/.

100 **A 15-year-old girl in Chad:** *Maternal Mortality*, 38.

100 **high-income countries:** *Maternal Mortality*.

100 **Some scholars have calculated:** L. Chola, S. McGee, A. Tugendhaft, et al., "Scaling Up
Family Planning to Reduce Maternal and Child Mortality: The Potential Costs and Benefits of Modern Contraceptive Use in South Africa," *PLoS ONE* 10, no. 6 (2015): e0130077.

100 **HIV-positive women:** E. Lathrop, D.J. Jamieson, and I. Danel, "HIV and Maternal Mortality," *International Journal of Gynaecology and Obstetrics* 127, no. 2 (2014): 213–15.

100 **Three-fourths of all maternal:** V. Filippi, D. Chou, C. Ronsmans, et al., "Levels and
Causes of Maternal Mortality and Morbidity," in *Reproductive, Maternal, Newborn, and Child
Health: Disease Control Priorities*, ed. R.E. Black, R. Laxminarayan, M. Temmerman, et al.,
Vol. 2, 3rd ed., chap. 3 (Washington, DC: The International Bank for Reconstruction
and Development / The World Bank, 2016), https://www.ncbi.nlm.nih.gov/books/
NBK361917/doi: 10.1596/978-1-4648-0348-2_ch3.

101 **two-thirds of those are in:** *Maternal Mortality*.

101 **A Black woman in the United States:** Nina Martin and Renee Montagne, "Nothing Protects Black Women from Dying in Pregnancy and Childbirth," *ProPublica*,
December7,2017,https://www.propublica.org/article/nothing-protects-black-women
-from-dying-in-pregnancy-and-childbirth.

101 **"a black woman with an advanced":** Linda Villarosa, "Why America's Black Mothers and Babies Are in a Life-or-Death Crisis," *New York Times Magazine*, April 11, 2018, https://www.nytimes.com/2018/04/11/magazine/black-mothers-babies-death-maternal-mortality.html.

102 **According to UNICEF:** UNICEF, *Ending Child Marriage: A Profile of Progress in Ethiopia* (New York: UNICEF, 2018), https://www.unicef.org/ethiopia/sites/unicef.org.ethiopia/files/2018-10/Child%20Marriage%20Ethiopia-%20online%20version_0.pdf.

102 **Rwanda was one:** World Health Organization, "Trends in Maternal Mortality: 1990 to 2015: Estimates by WHO, UNICEF, UNFPA, World Bank Group and the United Nations Population Division" (Geneva: World Health Organization, 2015).

102 **the WHO has reported that:** Guillaume Cohen and Michal Shinwell, "How Far Are OECD Countries from Achieving SDG Targets for Women and Girls?: Applying a Gender Lens to Measuring Distance to SDG Targets." OECD Statistics Working Papers, No. 2020/02 (Paris: OECD Publishing, 2020).

103 **life expectancy decreased rapidly:** World Health Organization, *Alcohol Policy Impact Case Study. The Effects of Alcohol Control Measures on Mortality and Life Expectancy in the Russian Federation* (Copenhagen: WHO Regional Office for Europe, 2019).

103 **A 1-year old Russian boy:** The life expectancy at age 1 for a Russian male in 2020 was 66.24 years, while the life expectancy of a Russian female at age 1 in 1955 was 67.23 years. Vladimir Starodubov, Laurie B. Marczak, Elena Varavikova, et al. [GBD 2016 Russia Collaborators], "The Burden of Disease in Russia from 1980 to 2016: A Systematic Analysis for the Global Burden of Disease Study 2016," *Lancet* 392, no. 10153 (2018): 1138–46.

104 **In 2016, the global gap was:** "World Health Statistics Overview 2019."

104 **it's 67.5 years for women:** *Healthy Life Expectancy (Hale) - Data by Country*. Edited by World Health Organization, Geneva, 2020.

104 **Russians over age 15 consume:** World Health Organization, *Alcohol Policy Impact Case Study*.

104 **for those aged 15 to 49 years:** Starodubov et al., "The Burden of Disease in Russia from 1980 to 2016."

104 **Ischemic heart disease:** Starodubov et al., "The Burden of Disease in Russia from 1980 to 2016."

104 **"an increased risk of circulatory":** Starodubov et al., "The Burden of Disease in Russia from 1980 to 2016."

105 **comparing Russia to the Baltic states:** Starodubov et al., "The Burden of Disease in Russia from 1980 to 2016."

105 **Russia's "abortion culture":** Vyacheslav Karpov and Kimmo Kääriäinen, "'Abortion Culture' in Russia: Its Origins, Scope, and Challenges to Social Development," *Journal of Applied Sociology* 22, no. 2 (2005): 13–33.

105 **in 1965, abortions were:** Amie Ferris-Rotman, "Putin's Next Target Is Russia's Abortion Culture," *Foreign Policy*, October 3, 2017, https://foreignpolicy.com/2017/10/03/putins-next-target-is-russias-abortion-culture/.

105 **In 2009, Russia registered:** Guy Faulconbridge, "Russia Says Population Up for First Year since 1995," *Reuters India*, January 19, 2010, http://in.reuters.com/article/idINTRE60I2KM20100119.

105 **Compared with the United States and Germany:** Ferris-Rotman, "Putin's Next Target Is Russia's Abortion Culture."

105 **Making sure alcohol isn't:** World Health Organization, *Alcohol Policy Impact Case Study*.

105 **between 2003 and 2016:** World Health Organization, *Alcohol Policy Impact Case Study.*

105 **Highly dangerous binge drinking:** World Health Organization, *Alcohol Policy Impact Case Study.*

106 **In 1960, the United States had:** *Health, United States, 2017: With Special Feature on Mortality,* (Hyattsville, MD: National Center for Health Statistics, 2018).

106 **In the case of the United States:** Steven H. Woolf and Laudan Aron, "Failing Health of the United States," *British Medical Journal* 360 (2018): k496.

106 **Improvements in some factors:** Christopher J.L. Murray, "The State of US Health, 1990-2016: Burden of Diseases, Injuries, and Risk Factors among Us States," *Journal of the American Medical Association* 319, no. 14 (2018): 1461.

106 **severity of the COVID-19 pandemic:** Elizabeth Arias, Betzaida Tejada-Vera, and Farida Ahmad, "Provisional Life Expectancy Estimates for January through June, 2020," NVSS Vital Statistics Rapid Release, US Department of Health and Human Services, Centers for Disease Control and Prevention, National Center for Health Statistics, National Vital Statistics System, 2021.

106 **greatest disparities are at the state:** Murray, "The State of US Health, 1990-2016," 1461.

107 **spends more on:** Roosa Tikkanen and Melinda K. Abrams, "U.S. Health Care from a Global Perspective, 2019: Higher Spending, Worse Outcomes?" Commonwealth Fund, https://www.commonwealthfund.org/publications/issue-briefs/2020/jan/us-health -care-global-perspective-2019.

107 **2013 study:** D. Squires and C. Anderson, "U.S. Health Care from a Global Perspective: Spending, Use of Services, Prices, and Health in 13 Countries," *Issue Brief (Commonwealth Fund)* 15 (2015): 1–15.

107 **Physical activity was up:** Murray, "The State of US Health, 1990-2016"; Woolf and Aron, "Failing Health of the United States."

108 **one-third of Europeans died:** Bollyky, *Plagues and the Paradox of Progress,* 23.

108 **Children and poor working-age cohorts:** John B. Henneman, Jr., "France: A Fiscal and Constitutional Crisis," in *The Black Death: A Turning Point in History?,* ed. William M. Bowsky (New York: Holt, Rinehart and Winston, 1971), 86–88.

108 **serious problems for European economies:** David Herlihy, *The Black Death and the Transformation of the West* (Cambridge, MA: Harvard University Press, 1997), 42.

108 **During 2006, the average:** Bollyky, *Plagues and the Paradox of Progress,* 144.

108 **2020 COVID-19 pandemic exacerbated income:** Mohamad A. El-Erian and Michael Spence, "The Great Unequalizer: The Pandemic Is Compounding Disparities in Income, Wealth, and Opportunity," *Foreign Affairs,* 2020, https://www.foreignaffairs.com/articles/ united-states/2020-06-01/great-unequalizer.

108 **West African Ebola outbreak in 2015:** Global Preparedness Monitoring Board, "A World at Risk: Annual Report on Global Preparedness for Health Emergencies" (Geneva: World Health Organization, 2019), 4, https://apps.who.int/gpmb/assets/annual_report/GPMB _annualreport_2019.pdf.

108 **That breaks down to:** Global Preparedness Monitoring Board, "A World at Risk."

109 **World Bank's estimate:** "What Is the Economic Cost of Covid-19?" *The Economist,* January 7, 2021, https://www.economist.com/finance-and-economics/2021/01/09/what-is -the-economic-cost-of-covid-19.

109 **estimate of the International Monetary Fund:** Larry Elliott, "IMF Estimates Global

Covid Cost at \$28tn in Lost Output," *The Guardian*, October 13, 2020, https://www
.theguardian.com/business/2020/oct/13/imf-covid-cost-world-economic-outlook.

109 **consulting group Deloitte Canada:** "Covid-19: Managing Supply Chain Risk and Disruption," Deloitte Canada, https://www2.deloitte.com/global/en/pages/risk/articles/
covid-19-managing-supply-chain-risk-and-disruption.html.

109 **Epidemics can also depress fertility:** David Herlihy, "Malthus Denied," in *The Black
Death: A Turning Point in History?*, ed. William M. Bowsky (New York: Holt, Rinehart and
Winston, 1971), 63.

109 **Decisions to abstain from:** Tomáš Sobotka, "Fertility in Central and Eastern Europe after
1989: Collapse and Gradual Recovery," *Historical Social Research* 36, no. 2 (2011): 246–96.

110 **At the World Health Assembly in 1966:** World Health Organization, "Statue Commemorates Smallpox Eradication," WHO News Release, May 17, 2010, https://www.who.int
/mediacentre/news/notes/2010/smallpox_20100517/en/.

110 **"pays homage to all those":** World Health Organization, "Statue Commemorates Smallpox Eradication."

111 **On 21 February 2003:** World Health Organization, *Bugs, Drugs & Smoke*, 135.

111 **Russia—as the Soviet Union:** Judy Twigg, "Vaccine Dreams and Russian Reality,"
ThinkGlobalHealth.org, August 12, 2020, https://www.thinkglobalhealth.org/article/
vaccine-dreams-and-russian-reality.

111 **Coalition for Epidemic Preparedness was founded:** Global Preparedness Monitoring
Board, "A World at Risk," 9.

111 **On May 29, 2020:** Jason Beaubien, "President Trump Announces That U.S. Will Leave
WHO," NPR, May 29, 2020, https://www.npr.org/2020/05/29/865685798/president
-trump-announces-that-u-s-will-leave-who.

111 **largest funder:** "United Kingdom of Great Britain and Northern Ireland," United
Nations Population Fund (n.d.), https://www.unfpa.org/data/donor-contributions/
united-kingdom.

111 **Because of COVID-related budget:** Natalia Kanem, "Statement on UK Government
Funding Cuts," UNFPA News Release, April 28, 2021, https://www.unfpa.org/press
/statement-uk-government-funding-cuts.

112 **polls showed that even Russians had lower:** "Putin's Trust Rating Falls to New Low
Amid Far East Protests," *Moscow Times*, July 29, 2020, https://www.themoscowtimes
.com/2020/07/29/putins-trust-rating-falls-to-new-low-amid-far-east-protests-a71012.

112 **only 16 percent:** Twigg, "Vaccine Dreams and Russian Reality."

112 **"what was true of ships":** World Health Organization, *Bugs, Drugs & Smoke*, 124.

112 **the Spanish flu is so named:** Mark Honigsbaum, *The Pandemic Century: One Hundred Years
of Panic, Hysteria, and Hubris* (New York: Norton, 2019), 26; Barry, *The Great Influenza*, 4.

113 **In Afghanistan and Pakistan:** Global Preparedness Monitoring Board, "A World at Risk," 15.

113 **Some Liberians were skeptical:** Jerving, "Why Liberians Thought Ebola Was a Government Scam to Attract Western Aid."

113 **there were 1,282 cases:** "Measles Cases and Outbreaks," Centers for Disease Control and
Prevention, updated May 3, 2021, https://www.cdc.gov/measles/cases-outbreaks.html.

113 **To prevent measles from spreading:** World Health Organization, *Bugs, Drugs & Smoke*, 9.

113 **Thirty-one percent of parents:** Gillian K. SteelFisher, Robert J. Blendon, Mark M.
Bekheit, and Keri Lubell, "The Public's Response to the 2009 H1N1 Influenza Pandemic,"
New England Journal of Medicine 310, no. 3 (2010): e65.

114 **"for this approach to work":** Michael T. Osterholm and Mark Olshaker, "Chronicle of a Pandemic Foretold: Learning from the Covid-19 Failure—before the Next Outbreak Arrives," Foreign Affairs, May/June 2020, https://www.foreignaffairs.com/articles/united-states/2020-05-21/coronavirus-chronicle-pandemic-foretold.

114 **Thabo Mbeki, president of:** Pride Chigwedere, George R. Seage, III, Sofia Gruskin, et al., "Estimating the Lost Benefits of Antiretroviral Drug Use in South Africa," *Journal of Acquired Immune Deficiency Syndrome* 49, no. 4 (2008): 410–14.

114 **Because South Africa did not:** Chigwedere et al., "Estimating the Lost Benefits of Antiretroviral Drug Use in South Africa," 412.

114 **"a triumph of management":** World Health Organization, *Bugs, Drugs & Smoke*, 20.

114 **Of those paying large sums:** "World Health Statistics 2020" 4.

115 **The World Bank and the WHO:** Global Preparedness Monitoring Board, "A World at Risk" 21.

115 **Eradicating smallpox meant savings:** World Health Organization, "Statue Commemorates Smallpox Eradication."

115 **the number of males using tobacco:** "Global Health Bright Spots 2019," World Health Organization, 2019, https://www.who.int/news-room/feature-stories/detail/global-health-bright-spots-2019.

115 **This blood delivery system:** World Health Organization, "Drones Take Rwanda's National Blood Service to New Heights," World Health Organization, https://www.who.int/news-room/feature-stories/detail/drones-take-rwandas-national-blood-service-to-new-heights.

116 **with COVID-19 those in the youngest:** Farida B. Ahmad, Jodi A. Cisewski, Arialdi Miniño, and Robert N. Anderson, "Provisional Mortality Data—United States, 2020," *Morbidity and Mortality Weekly Report* 70, no. 14 (2021), 519–22.

116 **The CDC estimates:** Centers for Disease Control and Prevention, "2009 H1N1 Pandemic (H1N1pdm09 Virus)," Centers for Disease Control and Prevention (n.d.), https://www.cdc.gov/flu/pandemic-resources/2009-h1n1-pandemic.html.

116 **refugees from the fight for:** World Health Organization, *Bugs, Drugs & Smoke*, 39.

117 **As COVID-19 became widespread:** Hans Henri P. Kluge, Zsuzsanna Jakab, Jozef Bartovic, et al., "Refugee and Migrant Health in the Covid-19 Response," *Lancet* 395, no. 10232 (2020): 1238.

117 **Ebola only spills over:** Honigsbaum, *The Pandemic Century: One Hundred Years of Panic, Hysteria, and Hubris*, 8.

117 **The geographic distribution of diseases:** Hina Asad and David O. Carpenter, "Effects of Climate Change on the Spread of Zika Virus: A Public Health Threat," *Reviews on Environmental Health* 33, no. 1 (2018): 31–42.

Chapter 4: People on the Move

119 **refugee women Hedren was working with:** Kimberly Pham, "The Vietnamese-American Nail Industry: 40 Years of Legacy," *Nails Magazine*, December 29, 2015, https://www.nailsmag.com/vsarticle/117757/the-vietnamese-american-nail-industry-40-years-of-legacy.

120 **Vietnamese-dominated nail industry today:** Karen Grigsby Bates, "Nailing the American Dream, with Polish." NPR, June 14, 2012, https://www.npr.org/2012/06/14/154852394/with-polish-vietnamese-immigrant-community-thrives.

121 **sub-Saharan Africa hosts:** UNHCR, "Africa: African Union," UNHCR (n.d.), https://www.unhcr.org/en-us/africa.html.

121 **individual choices about whether:** Stephen Castles, Mark J. Miller, and Hein de Haas, *The Age of Migration*, 5th ed. (New York: Guilford Press, 2014).

121 **push–pull model:** Everett S. Lee, "A Theory of Migration," *Demography* 3, no. 1 (1966): 47–57.

123 **The presence of some Vietnamese:** Susan Eckstein and Thanh-Nghi Nguyen, "The Making and Transnationalization of an Ethnic Niche: Vietnamese Manicurists," *International Migration Review* 45, no. 3 (2011): 639–74.

123 **The same is true of:** Clark Gray, "Climate Change and Migration," presentation to the Climate Change and Population Dynamics webinar, 21 September 2021, https://iussp.org/sites/default/files/IUSSP-PERN_Webinar_Gray-Climate%20Change%20%26%20Population%20Dynamics_2021.pdf.

123 **In 2013, less than 3:** Christopher Inkpen, "7 Facts About World Migration," Pew Research FactTank, September 2, 2014, http://www.pewresearch.org/fact-tank/2014/09/02/7-facts-about-world-migration/.

124 **According to the United Nations:** "The Number of International Migrants Reaches 272 Million, Continuing an Upward Trend in All World Regions, Says UN," United Nations News Release, September 17, 2019, https://www.un.org/development/desa/en/news/population/international-migrant-stock-2019.html.

124 **High-income countries are home:** Ellen Berg and Douglas J. Besharov, "Patterns of Global Migration," in *Adjusting to a World in Motion: Trends in Global Migration and Migration Policy*, ed. Douglas J. Besharov and Mark H. Lopez (New York: Oxford University Press, 2016), 58–80.

124 **Between 2000 and 2010, the migration:** United Nations, Department of Economic and Social Affairs, Population Division, *International Migration Report 2013* (New York: United Nations, 2013), https://www.un.org/en/development/desa/population/publications/pdf/migration/migrationreport2013/Full_Document_final.pdf.

124 **by 2019 the China–US "corridor":** International Organization for Migration, *World Migration Report 2020*, ed. Marie McAuliffe and Binod Khadria (Geneva: IOM, 2019), https://publications.iom.int/books/world-migration-report-2020.

125 **In just 6 months of 2019:** Claire Dennis S. Mapa, "Total Number of OFWs Estimated at 2.2 Million," Philippine Statistics Authority, 2020, https://psa.gov.ph/content/total-number-ofws-estimated-22-million.

125 **"the acquisition of people":** UN Office on Drugs and Crime, "Human Trafficking and Migrant Smuggling," UN Office on Drugs and Crime (n.d.), https://www.unodc.org/unodc/human-trafficking/.

125 **Africa experienced negative population growth:** N. Nunn, "The Long-Term Effects of Africa's Slave Trades," *Quarterly Journal of Economics* 123, no. 1 (2008), 139–76, https://doi.org/10.1162/qjec.2008.123.1.139.

125 **Today's slavery is most often:** United Nations Office on Drugs and Crime, *Global Report on Trafficking in Persons 2020* (Vienna: United Nations Office on Drugs and Crime, 2020).

126 **In 2018, the number of recorded:** United Nations Office on Drugs and Crime, *Global Report on Trafficking in Persons 2020*.

126 **Syria experienced a "rapid increase":** UN Office on Drugs and Crime, *Global Report on Trafficking in Persons* (New York: United Nations, 2016), 10.

127 **internally displaced, more than 55 million:** UNHCR, "Internally Displaced People," UNHCR (n.d.), https://www.unhcr.org/en-us/internally-displaced-people.html.

127 **An additional 26 million:** UNHCR, "Figures at a Glance," UNHCR (n.d.), https://www.unhcr.org/en-us/figures-at-a-glance.html.

128 **79.5 percent of the people forcibly:** UNHCR, "Figures at a Glance."

128 **Turkey, gateway to Europe:** UNHCR, "Figures at a Glance."

129 **In 1950:** "Who We Are," United Nations Relief and Works Agency for Palestine Refugees in the Near East, 2021, https://www.unrwa.org/who-we-are.

129 **More than one in five:** Statistics Canada, "Immigrant Population in Canada, 2016 Census of Population," Statistics Canada, October 25, 2017, https://www150.statcan.gc.ca/n1/pub/11-627-m-11-627-m2017028-eng.htm.

130 **"were not interested":** Eric Kaufmann, *Whiteshift: Populism, Immigration and the Future of White Majorities* (London: Allen Lane, 2018), 275.

130 **Australia was already 45 percent:** Castles et al., *The Age of Migration*, 245.

130 **Australia's 2016 census:** "Barely Half of Population Born in Australia to Australian-Born Parents," *The Guardian*, June 26, 2017, https://www.theguardian.com/australia-news/2017/jun/27/australia-reaches-tipping-point-with-quarter-of-population-born-overseas.

130 **37.5 percent in Switzerland:** "Population by Migration Status," Federal Statistical Office, Switzerland, https://www.bfs.admin.ch/bfs/en/home/statistics/population/migration-integration/by-migration-status.html.

131 **32.5 percent in Canada:** *Focus on Geography Series, 2016 Census* (Ottawa, Ontario: Statistics Canada, 2017), https://www12.statcan.gc.ca/census-recensement/2016/as-sa/fogs-spg/Facts-can-eng.cfm?Lang=Eng&GK=CAN&GC=01&TOPIC=7.

131 **20 to 30 percent in Sweden:** "Population Statistics," Statistics Sweden, Population and Economic Welfare Statistics Unit, 2021, https://www.scb.se/en/finding-statistics/statistics-by-subject-area/population/population-composition/population-statistics/.

131 **In Germany, only one parent:** "Year-on-Year Increase of 4.4% in the Population with a Migrant Background in 2017," Statistisches Bundesamt News Release, August 1, 2018, https://www.destatis.de/EN/PressServices/Press/pr/2018/08/PE18_282_12511.html.

131 **between 1850 and 1914:** Thomas J. Bollyky, *Plagues and the Paradox of Progress: Why the World Is Getting Healthier in Worrisome Ways* (Cambridge, MA: MIT Press, 2018), 152.

131 **Europe is relatively new:** Castles et al., *The Age of Migration*.

131 **Muslims are increasing:** Pew Research Center, *Europe's Growing Muslim Population* (Washington, DC: Pew Research Center, 2017).

132 **Muslims composed almost 5 percent:** Pew Research Center, *Europe's Growing Muslim Population*, 12.

132 **Even if the refugee flows:** Pew Research Center, *Europe's Growing Muslim Population*.

132 **Germany was one of the most:** OECD (n.d.), "OECD Databases on Migration" (Paris: OECD).

132 **Germany has a large number of:** Pew Research Center, *Europe's Growing Muslim Population*.

132 **Pew Research Center's projections to 2050:** Pew Research Center, *Europe's Growing Muslim Population*.

133 **world's highest number:** Jeanne Batalova, Mary Hanna, and Christopher Levesque, "Frequently Requested Statistics on Immigrants and Immigration in the United

States," Migration Policy Institute, February 11, 2021, https://www.migrationpolicy.org/article/frequently-requested-statistics-immigrants-and-immigration-united-states-2020#refugees-asylum.

133 **As of 2018:** Randy Capps, J. Gelatt, A.G.R. Soto, and J. Van Hook, *Unauthorized Immigrants in the United States*. Migration Policy Institute, December 2020, https://www.migrationpolicy.org/sites/default/files/publications/mpi-unauthorized-immigrants-stablenumbers-changingorigins_final.pdf.

133 **top global destination for migrants:** International Organization for Migration, *World Migration Report 2020*.

133 **If trends in new arrivals:** Gustavo Lopez and Kristen Bialik, "Key Findings About U.S. Immigrants," Pew Research FactTank, May 3, 2017, http://www.pewresearch.org/fact-tank/2017/05/03/key-findings-about-u-s-immigrants/.

134 **The Persian Gulf states have:** United Nations, Department of Economic and Social Affairs, Population Division, *World Population Prospects 2019 Highlights* (New York: United Nations, 2019).

134 **Europe's population would shrink:** Pew Research Center, *Europe's Growing Muslim Population*, 7.

134 **More than 75 percent of the people:** "Asylum Statistics" (Luxembourg: Eurostat, updated April 27, 2021), https://ec.europa.eu/eurostat/statistics-explained/index.php?title=Asylum_statistics#Age_and_gender_of_first-time_applicants.

134 **research in other settings:** James Hampshire, *The Politics of Immigration* (Cambridge, UK: Polity Press, 2013); Castles et al., *The Age of Migration*.

135 **Sweden's Muslim population:** Pew Research Center, *Europe's Growing Muslim Population*, 8.

136 **It seems to me:** L. Frank Baum, *The Emerald City of Oz* (Champaign, IL: Project Gutenberg, n.d.).

137 **first modern wave of boats:** Janet Phillips, *Boat Arrivals and Boat 'Turnbacks' in Australia since 1976: A Quick Guide to the Statistics* (Sydney: Commonwealth of Australia, 2017), https://www.aph.gov.au/About_Parliament/Parliamentary_Departments/Parliamentary_Library/pubs/rp/rp1617/Quick_Guides/BoatTurnbacks.

137 **the "Pacific Solution":** Fiona H. McKay, Samantha L. Thomas, and Susan Kneebone, "'It Would Be Okay if They Came through the Proper Channels': Community Perceptions and Attitudes Towards Asylum Seekers in Australia," *Journal of Refugee Studies* 25, no. 1 (2012): 113–33.

137 **poor island of Nauru:** Peter Dauvergne, *Environmentalism of the Rich* (Cambridge, MA: MIT Press, 2018), 6.

137 **In 2013 Australia went even:** Anthea Vogl, "Over the Borderline: A Critical Inquiry into the Geography of Territorial Excision and the Securitisation of the Australian Border," *UNSW Law Journal* 38, no. 1 (2015): 114.

138 **a refugee is someone who:** UN General Assembly, "Draft Convention Relating to the Status of Refugees" (New York: UN General Assembly, 1950).

138 **leaders from Thailand, Malaysia, Indonesia:** Indonesia did accept some but started turning others away. Scott Neuman, "Why No One Wants the Rohingyas," NPR, May 15, 2015, http://www.npr.org/sections/thetwo-way/2015/05/15/407048785/why-no-one-wants-the-rohingyas.

139 **"I'm sorry. If you want":** Shalailah Medhora, "'Nope, Nope, Nope': Tony Abbott Says Australia Will Take No Rohingyha Refugees," *The Guardian*, May 20, 2015, http://www

.theguardian.com/world/2015/may/21/nope-nope-nope-tony-abbott-says-australia-will
-take-no-rohingya-refugees.

139 **Caroline Moorehead:** Caroline Moorehead, *Human Cargo: A Journey among Refugees* (New York: Picador, 2006).

140 **children often slip through:** Amy Risley, *The Youngest Citizens: Children's Rights in Latin America*. Latin American Tópicos, ed. Michael LaRosa (New York: Routledge, 2019).

140 **In 2014, the US Border Patrol:** US Customs and Border Protection, "Southwest Border Unaccompanied Alien Children Fy2014," US Customs and Border Protection, updated November 24, 2015, http://www.cbp.gov/newsroom/stats/southwest-border-unaccompanied-children/fy-2014.

141 **Throughout the autumn:** Kate Smith, "Asylum Denials Hit Record-High in 2018 as Trump Administration Tightens Immigration Policy," *CBS News*, December 4, 2018, https://www.cbsnews.com/news/asylum-seekers-asylum-denials-hit-record-high-in-2018-as-trump-administration-tightens-immigration-policy-as-the-caravan-arrives/.

141 **United States has resettled more:** Lopez and Bialik, "Key Findings about U.S. Immigrants."

141 **18,000 in FY2020:** Jeanne Batalova, Mary Hanna, and Christopher Levesque, "Frequently Requested Statistics on Immigrants and Immigration in the United States," Migration Policy Institute, February 11, 2021, https://www.migrationpolicy.org/article/frequently-requested-statistics-immigrants-and-immigration-united-states-2020#refugees-asylum.

142 **Since at least 1994:** David Scott FitzGerald, *Refuge Beyond Reach: How Rich Democracies Repel Asylum Seekers* (New York: Oxford University Press, 2019), 3.

142 **"Such policies seem intuitive":** Michael A. Clemens and Hannah M. Postel, "Deterring Emigration with Foreign Aid: An Overview of Evidence from Low-Income Countries," *Population & Development Review* 44, no. 4 (2018): 667.

144 **James Hampshire has also pointed:** Hampshire, *The Politics of Immigration*.

Chapter 5: Warfare and Wombfare

147 **the only official census:** "Census and Sensibility," *The Economist*, November 5, 2016, https://www.economist.com/middle-east-and-africa/2016/11/05/census-and-sensibility.

148 **Muslims remain a permanent minority:** Muhammad A. Faour, "Religion, Demography, and Politics in Lebanon," *Middle Eastern Studies* 43, no. 6 (2007): 909–21.

148 **Håvard Strand and colleagues:** Håvard Strand, Henrik Urdal, and Isabelle Côté, "Ethnic Census Taking, Instability, and Armed Conflict," in *People Changing Places: New Perspectives on Demography, Migration, Conflict, and the State*, ed. Isabelle Côté, Matthew I. Mitchell, and Monica Duffy Toft (London: Routledge, 2019), 66–85.

148 **"This now creates a thorny":** Strand et al., "Ethnic Census Taking, Instability, and Armed Conflict," 68.

149 **"the full range of government":** Myron Weiner and Michael S. Teitelbaum, *Political Demography, Demographic Engineering* (New York: Berghahn Books, 2001).

149 **manipulation of demography:** Paul Morland, *Demographic Engineering: Population Strategies in Ethnic Conflict*. International Population Studies, ed. Philip Rees (London: Routledge, 2014).

150 **Before colonization:** Tor Sellström and Lennart Wohlgemuth, *Historical Perspective: Some*

Explanatory Factors. Joint Evaluation of Emergency Assistance to Rwanda (1996), https://www.oecd.org/derec/unitedstates/50189653.pdf.

150 **These Belgian outsiders designated:** Helen M. Hintjens, "Explaining the 1994 Genocide in Rwanda," *Journal of Modern African Studies* 37, no. 2 (1999): 241–86.

150 **Around 700,000 Tutsis:** Author's visit to Kigali Genocide Museum, Kigali, Rwanda, November 10, 2018.

150 **including a very young:** Colin M. Waugh, *Paul Kagame and Rwanda: Power, Genocide and the Rwandan Patriotic Front* (Jefferson, NC: McFarland & Company, 2004).

151 **"By introducing Christianity":** Hintjens, "Explaining the 1994 Genocide in Rwanda," 254.

151 **When the Habyarimana:** Sellström and Wohlgemuth. *Historical Perspective.*

151 **In mere weeks:** Hintjens, "Explaining the 1994 Genocide in Rwanda," 241.

152 **national trauma survey:** Author's visit to Kigali Genocide Museum, Kigali, Rwanda, November 10, 2018.

153 **For more than a hundred years:** Ashifa Kassam, "Ratio of Indigenous Children in Canada Welfare System Is 'Humanitarian Crisis'," *The Guardian*, November 4, 2017, https://www.theguardian.com/world/2017/nov/04/indigenous-children-canada-welfare-system-humanitarian-crisis.

153 **Cultural genocide is the destruction:** Truth and Reconciliation Commission of Canada, "Honouring the Truth, Reconciling for the Future: Summary of the Final Report of the Truth and Reconciliation Commission of Canada," 2015, 1, https://publications.gc.ca/site/eng/9.800288/publication.html.

154 **"In the name of protection":** Commonwealth of Australia, *Bringing Them Home*, 23.

154 **"Protection" also meant that:** "The Stolen Generations," Australians Together (n.d.), https://australianstogether.org.au/discover/australian-history/stolen-generations/.

154 **Mexico's eugenic history:** Phillipa Levine, *Eugenics: A Very Short Introduction.* Very Short Introductions (New York: Oxford University Press, 2017).

155 **The term *lebensraum*:** Vejas Gabriel Liulevicius, *War Land on the Eastern Front: Culture, National Identity, and German Occupation in World War I* (Cambridge, UK: Cambridge University Press, 2000); Jeremy Noakes, "Hitler and 'Lebensraum' in the East," *BBC*, March 30, 2011, http://www.bbc.co.uk/history/worldwars/wwtwo/hitler_lebensraum_01.shtml.

155 **The loose ideology of *lebensraum*:** Shelley Baranowski, *Nazi Empire: German Colonialism and Imperialism from Bismarck to Hitler* (New York: Cambridge University Press, 2011), 122.

155 **Founded in the late nineteenth century:** Baranowski, *Nazi Empire*, 27.

155 **Adolf Hitler began his political:** Baranowski, *Nazi Empire*, 142, 152.

155 **The emphasis on *lebensraum* created:** Rob K. Baum, "Deconstruction of National Identity in the Third Reich: *Naziprache* and *Geopolitik*," *National Identities* 8, no. 2 (2006): 98.

156 **Thus the Nazi Party turned:** Weiner and Teitelbaum, *Political Demography, Demographic Engineering*, 69.

156 **Myron Weiner and Michael Teitelbaum:** Weiner and Teitelbaum, *Political Demography, Demographic Engineering*, 54.

156 **The very founding of Israel:** David Newman, "Population as Security: The Arab-Israeli Struggle for Demographic Hegemony," in *Redefining Security: Population Movements and National Security*, ed. Nana Poku and David T. Graham (Westport, CT: Praeger, 1998), 164.

156 **Israel has seen tremendous population:** "Population of Israel on the Eve of 2021," Israel

Central Bureau of Statistics, News Release, December 31, 2020, https://www.cbs.gov.il/en/mediarelease/pages/2020/population-of-israel-on-the-eve-of-2021.aspx.

156 **In 1950:** "Jews, by Country of Origin and Age," Israel Central Bureau of Statistics, 2020, https://www.cbs.gov.il/he/publications/doclib/2020/2.shnatonpopulation/st02_08x.pdf.

157 **fertility is responsible for:** "Sources of Population Growth," Israel Central Bureau of Statistics, updated September 15, 2020, https://www.cbs.gov.il/he/publications/doclib/2020/2.shnatonpopulation/st02_12.pdf.

157 **As Toft explains it:** Monica Duffy Toft, "Wombfare: Religious and Political Dimensions of Fertility and Demographic Change," in *Political Demography: Interests, Conflict and Institutions*, ed. Jack A. Goldstone, Monica Duffy Toft, and Eric Kaufmann (Basingstoke, UK: Palgrave Macmillan, 2011), 213–25.

157 **At the turn of the twenty-first century:** Israel Central Bureau of Statistics, *Statistical Abstract of Israel 2020* (Jerusalem: Israel Central Bureau of Statistics, 2020).

157 **Many media sources reported:** See, for example, Douglas Davis, "Biological Warfare," *The Spectator*, September 6, 2003, https://www.spectator.co.uk/article/biological-warfare.

157 **But by 2019, the numbers:** Israel Central Bureau of Statistics, *Statistical Abstract of Israel 2020*.

157 **driven by extremely high:** Meirav Arlosoroff, "Haredim Are Leaving the Fold, but the Community Is Growing," *Haaretz*, November 13, 2019, https://www.haaretz.com/israel-news/.premium-haredim-are-leaving-the-fold-but-the-commmunity-is-growing-1.8121764.

157 **Orthodox men are excused:** Gilad Malach and Lee Cahaner, 2019 Statistical Report on Ultra-Orthodox Society in Israel: Highlights, (Jerusalem: Israel Democracy Institute, 2019).

157 **economic and military strength:** Arlosoroff, "Haredim Are Leaving the Fold."

158 **"a physical Jewish presence":** Newman, "Population as Security: The Arab-Israeli Struggle for Demographic Hegemony," 168.

159 **"This divergence was equivalent":** Uri Sadot, "Israel's 'Demographic Time Bomb' Is a Dud," *Foreign Policy*, December 18, 2013, http://foreignpolicy.com/2013/12/18/israels-demographic-time-bomb-is-a-dud/.

159 **"If Israel simply matched":** Sadot, "Israel's 'Demographic Time Bomb' Is a Dud."

159 **requiring a party:** Evan Gottesman, "Crossing the Threshold: Israel's Electoral Threshold Explained," *Israel Policy Forum*, February 19, 2019, https://israelpolicyforum.org/2019/02/19/crossing-the-threshold-israels-electoral-threshold-explained/.

160 **Half of India's Sikhs:** Nisid Hajari, *Midnight's Furies: The Deadly Legacy of India's Partition* (Gloucestershire: Amberley Publishing, 2015).

160 **While theoretically there was no:** Hajari, *Midnight's Furies*.

160 **More recent releases of India's:** Mohan Rao, "Love Jihad and Demographic Fears," *Indian Journal of Gender Studies* 18, no. 3 (2011): 425.

160 **There is little evidence Love:** Rao, "Love Jihad and Demographic Fears."

161 **Hindus are slightly shrinking:** "Population by Religious Community," Office of the Registrar General & Census Commissioner, India, Ministry of Home Affairs, Government of India, http://censusindia.gov.in/2011census/C-01.html; "Distribution of Population by Religion," Office of the Registrar General & Census Commissioner, India, Ministry of Home Affairs, Government of India, http://censusindia.gov.in/Census_And_You/religion.aspx.

162 **"often the very foundations":** Fredrik Barth, "Introduction," in *Ethnic Groups and Boundaries: The Social Organization of Cultural Difference*, ed. Fredrik Barth (Long Grove, IL: Waveland Press, 1998), 10.

162 **the economy of Côte d'Ivoire:** Isabelle Côté and Matthew Mitchell, "Elections and 'Sons of the Soil' Conflict Dynamics in Africa and Asia," *Democratization* 23, no. 4 (2015): 657–77.

162 **By the mid-1990s:** Côté and Mitchell, "Elections and 'Sons of the Soil' Conflict Dynamics," 661.

163 **The 1927 Aliens Act:** Admir Skodo, "Sweden: By Turns Welcoming and Restrictive in Its Immigration Policy," Migration Policy Institute, December 6, 2018, https://www.migrationpolicy.org/article/sweden-turns-welcoming-and-restrictive-its-immigration-policy.

163 **in 1995, the country:** Michael S. Teitelbaum and Jay Winter, *A Question of Numbers: High Migration, Low Fertility, and the Politics of National Identity* (New York: Hill and Wang, 1998).

163 **Leaders of the Quebec separatist:** Weiner and Teitelbaum, *Political Demography, Demographic Engineering*, 38–40.

164 **there were about 167,000:** David Coleman, "A Demographic Rationale for Brexit," *Population & Development Review* 42, no. 4 (2016): 681–92.

164 **non-White share:** Stephen Jivraj, "How Has Ethnic Diversity Grown 1991-2001-2011?," in *The Dynamic of Diversity: Evidence from the 2011 Census* (Manchester, UK: Center on Dynamics of Ethnicity, University of Manchester, 2012).

164 **1.3 million asylum claims:** "Asylum Statistics" (Luxembourg: Eurostat, last updated April 27, 2021), https://ec.europa.eu/eurostat/statistics-explained/index.php?title=Asylum_statistics#Age_and_gender_of_first-time_applicants.

164 **In a poll just 1 month:** Coleman, "A Demographic Rationale for Brexit."

164 **The desire for greater border:** Sarah Harper, "The Important Role of Migration for an Ageing Nation," *Population Ageing* 9 (2016): 184.

165 **He finds that just mentioning:** Eric Kaufmann, "Why Culture Is More Important Than Skills: Understanding British Public Opinion on Immigration," LSE British Politics and Policy Blog, London School of Economics and Political Science, January 30, 2018, https://blogs.lse.ac.uk/politicsandpolicy/why-culture-is-more-important-than-skills-understanding-british-public-opinion-on-immigration/.

165 **84 percent of the voting districts:** Philip Auerswald and Joon Yun, "As Population Growth Slows, Populism Surges," *New York Times*, May 22, 2018, https://mobile.nytimes.com/2018/05/22/opinion/populist-populism-fertility-rates.html.

165 **lack of religious census data:** Pamela Duncan, "Europeans Greatly Overestimate Muslim Population, Poll Shows," *The Guardian*, December 13, 2016), https://www.theguardian.com/society/datablog/2016/dec/13/europeans-massively-overestimate-muslim-population-poll-shows; Conrad Hackett, "5 Facts About the Muslim Population in Europe," Pew Research FactTank, November 29, 2017, https://www.pewresearch.org/fact-tank/2017/11/29/5-facts-about-the-muslim-population-in-europe/.

165 **"actively shedding former identities":** Yvonne Yazbeck Haddad and Michael J. Balz, "The October Riots in France: A Failed Immigration Policy or the Empire Strikes Back?," *International Migration* 44, no. 2 (2006): 26.

165 **Marie des Neiges Léonard argues:** Marie des Neiges Léonard, "The Effects of Political Rhetoric on the Rise of Legitimized Racism in France: The Case of the 2005 French Riots," *Critical Sociology* 42, no. 7–8 (2015): 1087–1107.

166 **In Sarkozy's mind:** Léonard, "The Effects of Political Rhetoric," 1095.

166 **The 2020 US census:** Hansi Lo Wang, "How the 2020 Census Citizenship Question Ended up in Court," NPR, November 4, 2018, https://www.npr.org/2018/11/04/661932989/ how-the-2020-census-citizenship-question-ended-up-in-court.

167 **Political scientists have an ever-growing:** Mark R. Beissinger, "A New Look at Ethnicity and Democratization," *Journal of Democracy* 19, no. 3 (2008): 85–97.

168 **less observant versus more observant:** Eric P. Kaufmann and Vegard Skirbekk, " 'Go Forth and Multiply': The Politics of Religious Demography," in *Political Demography: How Population Changes Are Reshaping International Security and National Politics*, ed. J.A. Goldstone, E.P. Kaufmann, and M. Duffy Toft (New York: Oxford University Press, 2012), 194–212.

Chapter 6: Malthus versus Marx

172 **more open economy:** David E. Bloom, David Canning, and Jaypee Sevilla, *The Demographic Dividend: A New Perspective on the Economic Consequences of Population Change.* Population Matters (Santa Monica: RAND Corporation, 2003).

172 **During the 1960s and 1970s:** Megan Catley-Carlson, "Foreword," in *Do Population Policies Matter? Fertility and Politics in Egypt, India, Kenya, and Mexico*, ed. Anrudh Jain (New York: Population Council, 1998).

172 **Governments in China, Taiwan:** Jennifer Dabbs Sciubba, *The Future Faces of War: Population and National Security* (Santa Barbara: Praeger Security International/ABC-CLIO, 2011), 64.

172 **One of the most well-known:** David E. Bloom, David Canning, and Pia N. Malaney, *Demographic Change and Economic Growth in Asia* (Cambridge, MA: Center for International Development at Harvard University, 1999).

173 **"relieves pressure on":** Richard P. Cincotta, "Half a Chance: Youth Bulges and Transitions to Liberal Democracy," *Environmental Change and Security Program*, no. 13 (2009): 11.

173 **Demographers have estimated:** Ronald Lee and Andrew Mason, "What Is the Demographic Dividend?" *Finance and Development* 43, no. 3 (2006), http://www.imf.org/external /pubs/ft/fandd/2006/09/basics.htm.

173 **Bangladesh initiated:** Richard Cincotta and Elizabeth Leahy Madsen, "Bangladesh and Pakistan: Demographic Twins Grow Apart," New Security Beat, October 10, 2018, https://www.newsecuritybeat.org/2018/10/bangladesh-pakistan-demographic -twins-grow/.

174 **Statistical models developed by:** Cincotta and Madsen, "Bangladesh and Pakistan: Demographic Twins Grow Apart."

174 **Although foreign direct investment:** World Bank, "World Development Indicators," 2021, https://databank.worldbank.org/source/world-development-indicators.

174 **The World Bank recommends:** Bernard James Haven, Nazmus Sadat Khan, Zahid Hussain, et al., *Bangladesh Development Update: Tertiary Education and Job Skills* (Washington, DC: World Bank Group, 2019).

175 **state fragility:** Fund for Peace, "Fragile States Index: 2020" (Washington, DC: The Fund for Peace, 2021), https://fragilestatesindex.org/data/.

175 **only 67.5 percent of females:** World Bank, "World Development Indicators."

175 **Ethiopia has built:** Assefa Admassie, Seid Nuru Ali, John F. May, et al., *The Demographic*

Dividend: An Opportunity for Ethiopia's Transformation (Washington, DC: Population Reference Bureau and Ethiopian Economics Association, 2015).

175 **In 2017, nearly 72 percent:** World Bank, "World Development Indicators," World Bank, accessed 5 May 2020, https://data.worldbank.org.

177 **government is able to use:** Thaddeus Baklinski, "Saudi Arabian King Asked to Consider Implementing Population Control," *LifeSite*, January 12, 2015, https://www.lifesitenews.com/news/saudi-arabian-king-asked-to-consider-implementing-population-control.

177 **For years, the Saudi government invited:** "What's Behind Saudi Arabia's Pivot Away from Foreign Workers," *World Politics Review*, August 16, 2019, https://www.worldpoliticsreview.com/insights/28129/pushing-for-a-saudization-of-its-workforce-saudi-arabia-pivots-away-from-foreign-workers.

177 **90 percent of workers:** Caryle Murphy, "Saudi Arabia's Youth and the Kingdom's Future," Occasional Paper Series (Washington, DC: Middle East Program, Woodrow Wilson International Center for Scholars, 2011), 3.

178 **The CEO of Saudi ARAMCO:** Murphy, "Saudi Arabia's Youth and the Kingdom's Future," 3.

178 **While youth unemployment:** "Share of Youth Not in Employment, Education or Training (Neet) by Sex—ILO Modelled Estimates, Nov. 2019: Annual," ed. International Labour Organization (ILOSTAT database, 2020); "Unemployment Rate by Sex and Age—ILO Modelled Estimates Nov. 2019 (%): Annual," ed. International Labour Organization (ILOSTAT database, 2020).

178 **"as a source of social":** "What's Behind Saudi Arabia's Pivot Away from Foreign Workers."

178 **Botswana, rich in diamonds:** James A. Robinson. "Botswana as a Role Model for Country Success," in *Achieving Development Success: Strategies and Lessons from the Developing World*, ed. Augustin K. Fosu (Oxford: Oxford University Press, 2013), 187–203.

179 **In Europe, secondary cities:** Thomas Farole, Soraya Goga, and Marcel Ionescu-Heroiu, *Rethinking Lagging Regions: Using Cohesion Policy to Deliver on the Potential of Europe's Regions* (Washington, DC: World Bank, 2018).

179 **According to the United Nations:** UN-HABITAT, *Concepts and Definitions* (Nairobi: UN-HABITAT, October 2020), https://unstats.un.org/sdgs/metadata/files/Metadata-11-01-01.pdf.

179 **More than 60 percent:** Somik Vinay Lall, J. Vernon Henderson, and Anthony J. Venables, *Overview—Africa's Cities: Opening Doors to the World* (Washington, DC: World Bank, 2017).

179 **Relative to per capita GDP:** Lall, Henderson, and Venables, *Overview*.

180 **The rent-to-income ratio:** Tanza Loudenback, "Here's How Much It Would Cost You to Live in the 10 Largest Megacities around the World," *BusinessInsider*, October 20, 2017, https://www.businessinsider.com/worlds-largest-cities-megacity-cost-of-living-2017-10.

180 **Consulting firm McKinsey & Company:** Jonathan Woetzel, "Tackling the World's Affordable Housing Challenge," McKinsey & Company, 2014.

180 **Infant mortality rates:** Thomas J. Bollyky, *Plagues and the Paradox of Progress: Why the World Is Getting Healthier in Worrisome Ways* (Cambridge, MA: MIT Press, 2018), 129–30.

180 **"Congestion in Dhaka":** Bollyky, *Plagues and the Paradox of Progress*, 133.

180 **In just 65 years:** United Nations, Department of Economic and Social Affairs, Population Division, "The Speed of Urbanization around the World," in *POPFACTS* (New York: United Nations, 2018), 2.

180 **there are data issues:** Jedwab, "Urbanization without Structural Transformation."

181 **While India's GDP per capita:** World Bank, "World Development Indicators."

181 **Africa is the least:** United Nations, Department of Economic and Social Affairs, Population Division, *The Speed of Urbanization around the World* (New York: United Nations, 2018), https://www.un.org/development/desa/pd/sites/www.un.org.development.desa .pd/files/files/documents/2020/Jan/un_2018_factsheet1.pdf.

182 **urbanization today does not look:** Kingsley Davis, "The Urbanization of the Human Population," *Scientific American* 213, no. 3 (1965): 40–53.

182 **African economies have:** Lall, Henderson, and Venables, *Overview*, 8.

182 **As Rémi Jedwab:** Rémi Jedwab, "Urbanization without Structural Transformation: Evidence from Consumption Cities in Africa," Working paper, 2013.

182 **Studying urbanization patterns:** Douglas Gollin, Rémi Jedwab, and Dietrich Vollrath, "Urbanization with and without Industrialization." *Journal of Economic Growth* 21, no. 1 (2016): 35–70.

183 **urbanization has typically:** Jedwab, "Urbanization without Structural Transformation."

183 **As World Bank researchers point out:** Woetzel, "Tackling the World's Affordable Housing Challenge."

184 **India, Mexico, and the Philippines:** Stephen Castles, Mark J. Miller, and Hein de Haas, *The Age of Migration*, 5th ed. (New York: Guilford Press, 2014).

184 **The vast majority of global remittances:** World Bank, "World Development Indicators," World Bank, https://data.worldbank.org.

184 **Tajikistan's remittances:** World Bank, "World Development Indicators," https:// databank.worldbank.org/source/world-development-indicators.

184 **"to shrinking growth":** Edward Lemon, "Dependent on Remittances, Tajikistan's Long-Term Prospects for Economic Growth and Poverty Reduction Remain Dim," Migration Policy Institute, November 14, 2019, https://www.migrationpolicy.org/article/dependent -remittances-tajikistan-prospects-dim-economic-growth.

185 **In 2019, remittances to Bangladesh:** World Bank, "World Development Indicators," https://databank.worldbank.org/source/world-development-indicators.

185 **Somalis abroad send $1.3 billion:** "Remittances to Somalia," Oxfam, https:// policy-practice.oxfamamerica.org/work/in-action/remittances-to-somalia/.

185 **Globally, remittances have been steadily:** World Bank, "World Development Indicators," https://data.worldbank.org.

185 **In the early days of New World:** Roger White, *Immigration Policy and the Shaping of U.S. Culture: Becoming America* (Cheltenham, UK: Edward Elgar, 2018), 26–27.

185 **During this wave, young Irish:** Bollyky, *Plagues and the Paradox of Progress*, 152.

186 **"fourth industrial revolution":** Klaus Schwab, *The Fourth Industrial Revolution* (New York: Crown Business, 2016).

186 **In 1834, the Poor Laws:** Ronald L. Meek (ed.), *Marx and Engels on the Population Bomb: Selections from the Writings of Marx and Engels Dealing with the Theories of Thomas Robert Malthus* (London: Ramparts Press, 1953), 8–9.

187 **"bourgeois individualist":** Simon Szreter, "Marx on Population: A Bicentenary Celebration," *Population & Development Review* 44, no. 4 (2018): 752.

188 **Already by 2013:** Jocelyne Sambira, "Africa's Mobile Youth Drive Change," *Africa Renewal* (May 2013), https://www.un.org/africarenewal/magazine/may-2013/africa's-mobile -youth-drive-change.

188 **Use of robotics:** Raymond Zhong, "For Poor Countries, Well-Worn Path to Development Turns Rocky," *Wall Street Journal*, November 24, 2015, http://www.wsj.com/articles/for-poor-countries-well-worn-path-to-development-turns-rocky-1448374298?tesla=y.

188 **According to the International Federation:** Christopher Müller and Nina Kutzbach, "World Robotics 2020," Industrial Robots, IFR Statistical Department, VDMA Services GmbH, Frankfurt am Main, Germany, 2020.

188 **Economist Dani Rodrick:** Dani Rodrick, *Premature Deindustrialization* (Cambridge, MA: National Bureau of Economic Research, 2015), https://www.nber.org/system/files/working _papers/w20935/w20935.pdf.

189 **those making $10:** Bollyky, *Plagues and the Paradox of Progress*, 103.

190 **Iran, whose median age:** Richard Cincotta and Karim Sadjadpour, *Iran in Transition: The Implications of the Islamic Republic's Changing Demographics* (Washington, DC: Carnegie Endowment for International Peace, 2017), 14.

190 **Only about 17 percent:** Cincotta and Sadjadpour, *Iran in Transition*, 14.

190 **Megaregions, such as China's:** UN-HABITAT, *State of the World's Cities 2010/2011: Bridging the Urban Divide* (London: Earthscan for UN-HABITAT, 2010).

191 **"crowded, disconnected, and costly":** Lall, Henderson, and Venables, *Overview*.

191 **A 2018 report from McKinsey:** Joe Frem, Vineet Rajadhyaksha, and Jonathan Woetzel, "Thriving Amid Turbulence: Imagining the Cities of the Future," McKinsey & Company Public Sector, October 2018.

191 **The unemployment rates:** *Jobs for Youth in Africa: Catalyzing Youth Opportunity across Africa*, African Development Bank Group, March 2016, https://www.afdb.org/fileadmin/uploads /afdb/Images/high_5s/Job_youth_Africa_Job_youth_Africa.pdf.

191 **in Eswatini:** World Bank, "World Development Indicators," https://data.worldbank.org.

191 **Many of Africa's fastest growing:** Kate Meagher, "The Scramble for Africans: Demography, Globalisation and Africa's Informal Labour Markets," *Journal of Development Studies* 52, no. 4 (2016): 484.

191 **In sub-Saharan Africa:** Author's calculations from United Nations, Department of Economic and Social Affairs, Population Division, *World Population Prospects: The 2019 Revision* (New York: United Nations, 2019).

192 **"policy approaches that focus":** Meagher, "The Scramble for Africans," 494; C. Cramer, "Unemployment and Participation in Violence." World Development Report 2011 Background Paper (Washington, DC: World Bank, 2010).

Chapter 7: The Future of Global Population

194 **superforecaster Philip Tetlock:** Philip Tetlock and Dan Gardner, *Superforecasting: The Art and Science of Prediction* (New York: Crown Publishers, 2016).

198 **much longer than we could use:** Nathan Keyfitz, "The Limits of Population Forecasting," *Population & Development Review* 7, no. 4 (1981): 579–93.

198 **As soon as US president Joe Biden:** Rebecca Morin and Matthew Brown, "Migrant Encounters Up 71% in March as Biden Administration Grapples with Border," *USA Today*, April 8, 2021, https://www.usatoday.com/story/news/politics/2021/04/08/migrants -border-were-up-march-biden-grapples-immigration/7130399002/.

201 **Matt Yglesias:** Matthew Yglesias, *One Billion Americans: The Case for Thinking Bigger* (New York: Portfolio/Penguin, 2020).

202 **Tribes, states, and all the other:** Jay Winter and Michael Teitelbaum, *The Global Spread of Fertility Decline: Population, Fear, and Uncertainty* (New Haven, CT: Yale University Press, 2013).

202 **Political–economic theories:** David Coleman and Robert Rowthorn, "Who's Afraid of Population Decline? A Critical Examination of Its Consequences," *Population & Development Review* 37, Supplement (2011): 217.

202 **in 2019 two-thirds:** International Organization for Migration, *World Migration Report 2020*, ed. Marie McAuliffe and Binod Khadria (Geneva: IOM, 2019), https://publications. iom.int/books/world-migration-report-2020.

202 **Emigration from countries where:** Michael Clemens, *The Emigration Life Cycle: How Development Shapes Emigration from Poor Countries* (Washington, DC: Center for Global Development, 2020), https://www.cgdev.org/publication/emigration-life-cycle-how -development-shapes-emigration-poor-countries.

203 **We know from public opinion:** According to Gallup public opinion surveys between 2007 and 2010 of more than 350,000 people in 148 countries that comprise 95 percent of the world's population, desire to migrate was greatest in sub-Saharan Africa. In the results of this survey, 36 percent of respondents said they would prefer to move permanently to another country if given the chance. Source: Neli Esipova, Rajesh Srinivasan, and Julie Ray, "Adjusting to a World in Motion," in *Adjusting to a World in Motion: Trends in Global Migration and Migration Policy*, ed. Douglas J. Besharov and Mark H. Lopez (New York: Oxford University Press, 2016), 21–57.

203 **as 2020 approached:** Kirk Semple, "Mexico Once Saw Migration as a U.S. Problem. Now It Needs Answers of Its Own," *New York Times*, December 5, 2018, https://www.nytimes .com/2018/12/05/world/americas/mexico-migrants.html.

203 **During the heyday of industrialization:** Greg Mills, "Strategic Dilemmas: Rewiring Africa for a Teeming, Urban Future," *PRISM* 6, no. 4 (2017): 46–63.

203 **India, alone, has 495 million:** United Nations, Department of Economic and Social Affairs, Population Division, "Key Facts: World Urbanization Prospects: The 2018 Revision" (New York: United Nations, 2018).

204 **While today's developed countries:** Richard Florida, *The New Urban Crisis: How Our Cities Are Increasing Inequality, Deepening Segregation, and Failing the Middle Class—and What We Can Do About It* (New York: Basic Books, 2017).

204 **climate change has already exacerbated:** *Global Trends 2040: A More Contested World* (Washington, DC: National Intelligence Council, 2021), 20.

204 **number of centenarians:** "Centenarians Top 80,000 for First Time in Rapidly Aging Japan," *Japan Times*, September 15, 2020, https://www.japantimes.co.jp/news/2020/09/15 /national/centenarians-80000-japan-aging/.

204 **government has switched from sterling silver:** Justin McCurry, "Japanese Centenarian Population Edges Towards 70,000," *The Guardian*, September 14, 2018, https://www .theguardian.com/world/2018/sep/14/japanese-centenarian-population-edges-towards -70000.

206 **Merilee Grindle has discussed:** Merilee Grindle, "Good Enough Governance Revisited," *Development Policy Review* 25, no. 5 (2007): 533–74.

206 **Jack Goldstone and Larry Diamond state the menu:** Jack A. Goldstone and Larry Diamond, "Demography and the Future of Democracy," *Perspectives on Politics* 18, no. 3 (2020): 867–80.

206 **While malaria still kills:** "Global Health Observatory Data," World Health Organization, https://www.who.int/gho/malaria/en/.

206 **In 2019, Algeria and Argentina:** "Global Health Bright Spots 2019," World Health Organization, 2019, https://www.who.int/news-room/feature-stories/detail/global-health-bright-spots-2019; "Malaria Vaccine Pilot Launched in Malawi," WHO News Release, April 23, 2019, https://www.who.int/news-room/detail/23-04-2019-malaria-vaccine-pilot-launched-in-malawi.

206 **Until just a few years ago:** Thomas J. Bollyky, *Plagues and the Paradox of Progress: Why the World Is Getting Healthier in Worrisome Ways* (Cambridge, MA: MIT Press, 2018), 62.

206 **But the World Health Organization reports:** World Health Organization, *HIV/AIDS Key Facts* (Geneva: World Health Organization, November 30, 2020), https://www.who.int/news-room/fact-sheets/detail/hiv-aids.

206 **Scholars have expressed:** Stephen Brown, "The Impact of Covid-19 on Development Assistance," *Journal of Global Policy Analysis* (2021), https://journals.sagepub.com/doi/full/10.1177/0020702020986888.

207 **Japan's average age of exit:** OECD, "Average Effective Age of Retirement Versus the Normal Age in 2018 in OECD Countries" (Paris: OECD, 2019); Jens Arnold and Alberto González Pandiella, "Towards a More Prosperous and Inclusive Brazil," OECD [blog], February 28, 2018, https://oecdecoscope.blog/2018/02/28/towards-a-more-prosperous-and-inclusive-brazil/.

208 **literacy is nearly universal in China:** "Literacy Rate, Adult Female (% of Females Aged 15 and Above)," World Bank, updated September 2020, https://data.worldbank.org/indicator/SE.ADT.LITR.FE.ZS?name_desc=false.

208 **India is far behind the global average:** "Urban Population (% of Total Population)," World Bank, 2018, https://data.worldbank.org/indicator/SP.URB.TOTL.IN.ZS.

208 **More than 89 percent:** Author's own calculations from United Nations, Department of Economic and Social Affairs, Population Division, *World Population Prospects: The 2019 Revision* (New York: United Nations, 2019).

BIBLIOGRAPHY

"2020 Internal Displacement." Global Internal Displacement Database. Geneva: Internal Displacement Monitoring Centre. Accessed 22 October 2021, https://www.internal-displacement.org/database/displacement-data.

Abadi, Mark. "Elderly People in Japan Are Getting Arrested on Purpose Because They Want to Go to Prison." *BusinessInsider*, March 19, 2018, https://www.businessinsider.com/japan-aging-prison-2018-3.

Aburto, José Manuel, Jonas Schöley, Ilya Kashnitsky, et al. "Quantifying Impacts of the Covid-19 Pandemic through Life Expectancy Losses: A Population-Level Study of 29 Countries." *medRxiv* (2021), https://www.medrxiv.org/content/10.1101/2021.03.02.21252772v4.full-text.

Admassie, Assefa, Seid Nuru Ali, John F. May, et al. *The Demographic Dividend: An Opportunity for Ethiopia's Transformation*. Washington, DC: Population Reference Bureau and Ethiopian Economics Association, 2015.

Ahluwalia, Sanjan, and Daksha Parmar. "From Gandhi to Gandhi: Contraceptive Technologies and Sexual Politics in Postcolonial India, 1947-1977." In *Reproductive States: Global Perspectives on the Invention and Implementation of Population Policy*, edited by Rickie Solinger and Mie Nakachi, 124–55. New York: Oxford University Press, 2016.

Ahmad, Farida B., Jodi A. Cisewski, Arialdi Miniño, and Robert N. Anderson. "Provisional Mortality Data—United States, 2020." *Morbidity and Mortality Weekly Report*, 70, no. 14 (2021): 519–22.

Akwiri, Joseph, and Maggie Fick. "In Kenya, Covid-19's Rural Spread Strains Creaky Healthcare." *Reuters*, December 7, 2020, https://www.reuters.com/article/us-health-coronavirus-kenya/in-kenya-covid-19s-rural-spread-strains-creaky-healthcare-idUSKBN28H0J0.

Arias, Elizabeth, Betzaida Tejada-Vera, and Farida Ahmad. "Provisional Life Expectancy Estimates for January through June, 2020." NVSS Vital Statistics Rapid Release, US Department of Health and Human Services, Centers for Disease Control and Prevention, National Center for Health Statistics, National Vital Statistics System, 2021.

Arlosoroff, Meirav. "Haredim Are Leaving the Fold, but the Community Is Growing." *Haaretz*, November 13, 2019, https://www.haaretz.com/israel-news/.premium-haredim-are-leaving -the-fold-but-the-community-is-growing-1.8121764.

Arnold, Jens, and Alberto González Pandiella. "Towards a More Prosperous and Inclusive Bra-zil." OECD [blog], February 28, 2018, https://oecdecoscope.blog/2018/02/28/towards -a-more-prosperous-and-exclusive-brazil/.

Asad, Hina, and David O. Carpenter. "Effects of Climate Change on the Spread of Zika Virus: A Public Health Threat." *Reviews on Environmental Health* 33, no. 1 (2018): 31–42.

Auerswald, Philip, and Joon Yun. "As Population Growth Slows, Populism Surges." *New York Times*, May 22, 2018, https://mobile.nytimes.com/2018/05/22/opinion/populist-populism -fertility-rates.html.

Babiarz, Kimberly Singer, Karen Eggleston, Grant Miller, and Qiong Zhang. "An Exploration of China's Mortality Decline under Mao: A Provincial Analysis, 1950-80." *Population Studies* 69, no. 1 (2015): 39–56. doi: 10.1080/00324728.2014.972432.

Baklinski, Thaddeus. "Saudi Arabian King Asked to Consider Implementing Population Con-trol." *LifeSite*, January 12, 2015, https://www.lifesitenews.com/news/saudi-arabian-king -asked-to-consider-implementing-population-control.

Baranowski, Shelley. *Nazi Empire: German Colonialism and Imperialism from Bismarck to Hitler*. New York: Cambridge University Press, 2011.

Barclay, Marion S., and Frances Champion. *Teen Guide to Homemaking*, 2nd ed. St. Louis: McGraw-Hill, 1967.

"Barely Half of Population Born in Australia to Australian-Born Parents." *The Guardian*, June 26, 2017, https://www.theguardian.com/australia-news/2017/jun/27/australia-reaches -tipping-point-with-quarter-of-population-born-overseas.

Barry, John M. *The Great Influenza: The Story of the Deadliest Pandemic in History*. New York: Penguin Books, 2005. Kindle iOS version.

Barth, Fredrik. "Introduction." In *Ethnic Groups and Boundaries: The Social Organization of Cultural Difference*, edited by Fredrik Barth, 9–38. Long Grove, IL: Waveland Press, 1998.

Batalova, Jeanne, Mary Hanna, and Christopher Levesque. "Frequently Requested Statistics on Immigrants and Immigration in the United States." Migration Policy Institute, February 11, 2021, https://www.migrationpolicy.org/article/frequently-requested-statistics-immigrants -and-immigration-united-states-2020#refugees-asylum.

Bates, Karen Grigsby. "Nailing the American Dream, with Polish." NPR, June 14, 2012, https://www.npr.org/2012/06/14/154852394/with-polish-vietnamese-immigrant -community-strives.

Baum, L. Frank. *The Emerald City of Oz*. Champaign, IL: Project Gutenberg (n.d.).

Baum, Rob K. "Deconstruction of National Identity in the Third Reich: *Naziprache* and *Geopoli-tik*." *National Identities* 8, no. 2 (2006): 95–112.

Bearak, Jonathan, Anna Popinchalk, Leontine Alkema, and Gilda Sedgh. "Global, Regional, and Subregional Trends in Unintended Pregnancy and Its Outcomes from 1990 to 2014: Estimates from a Bayesian Hierarchical Model." *Lancet Global Health* 6, no. 4 (2018): E380–89.

Beaubien, Jason. "President Trump Announces That U.S. Will Leave WHO." NPR, May 29, 2020, https://www.npr.org/2020/05/29/865685798/president-trump-announces-that-us -will-leave-who.

Beissinger, Mark R. "A New Look at Ethnicity and Democratization." *Journal of Democracy* 19, no. 3 (2008): 85–97.

Berg, Ellen, and Douglas J. Besharov. "Patterns of Global Migration." In *Adjusting to a World in Motion: Trends in Global Migration and Migration Policy*, edited by Douglas J. Besharov and Mark H. Lopez, 58–80. New York: Oxford University Press, 2016.

Bernstein, Lenny. "U.S. Life Expectancy Declines Again, a Dismal Trend Not Seen since World War I." *Washington Post*, November 28, 2018, https://www.washingtonpost.com/national /health-science/us-life-expectancy-declines-again-a-dismal-trend-not-seen-since-world -war-i/2018/11/28/ae58bc8c-f28c-11e8-bc79-68604ed88993_story.html.

Biddlecom, Ann, Napaporn Chayovan, and Mary Beth Ofstedal. "Intergenerational Support and Transfers." In *The Well-Being of the Elderly in Asia: A Four-Country Comparative Study*, edited by Albert I. Hermalin, 185–230. Ann Arbor: University of Michigan Press, 2002.

Bloom, David E., David Canning, and Pia N. Malaney. *Demographic Change and Economic Growth in Asia*. Cambridge, MA: Center for International Development at Harvard University, 1999.

Bloom, David E., David Canning, and Jaypee Sevilla. *The Demographic Dividend: A New Perspective on the Economic Consequences of Population Change*. Population Matters. Santa Monica: RAND Corporation, 2003.

Bollyky, Thomas J. *Plagues and the Paradox of Progress: Why the World Is Getting Healthier in Worrisome Ways*. Cambridge, MA: MIT Press, 2018.

Bongaarts, John. "Africa's Unique Fertility Transition." *Population and Development Review* 43 (2017): 39–58.

———. "Can Family Planning Programs Reduce High Desired Family Size in Sub-Saharan Africa?" *International Perspectives on Sexual and Reproductive Health* 37, no. 4 (2011): 209–16.

Bricker, Noah Q., and Mark C. Foley. "The Effect of Youth Demographics on Violence: The Importance of the Labor Market." *International Journal of Conflict and Violence* 7, no. 1 (2013): 179–94.

Brinton, Mary C., and Dong-Ju Lee. "Gender-Role Ideology, Labor Market Institutions, and Post-Industrial Fertility." *Population & Development Review* 42, no. 3 (2016): 405–33.

Brown, Stephen. "The Impact of Covid-19 on Development Assistance." *Journal of Global Policy Analysis* (2021), https://journals.sagepub.com/doi/full/10.1177/0020702020986888.

Capps, R., J. Gelatt, A.G.R. Soto, and J. Van Hook. *Unauthorized Immigrants in the United States*. Migration Policy Institute, December 2020, https://www.migrationpolicy.org/sites/default/files /publications/mpi-unauthorized-immigrants-stablenumbers-changingorigins_final.pdf.

Castles, Stephen, Mark J. Miller, and Hein de Haas. *The Age of Migration*, 5th ed. New York: Guilford Press, 2014.

Catley-Carlson, Megan. "Foreword." In *Do Population Policies Matter? Fertility and Politics in Egypt, India, Kenya, and Mexico*, edited by Anrudh Jain. New York: Population Council, 1998.

Caute, David. *The Year of the Barricades: A Journey through 1968*. New York: Harper & Row, 1988.

"Census and Sensibility." *The Economist*, November 5, 2016, https://www.economist.com/middle -east-and-africa/2016/11/05/census-and-sensibility.

Centers for Disease Control and Prevention. "2009 H1N1 Pandemic (H1N1pdm09 Virus)." Centers for Disease Control and Prevention (n.d.), https://www.cdc.gov/flu/pandemic -resources/2009-h1n1-pandemic.html.

———. "Pandemic Influenza." Centers for Disease Control and Prevention (n.d.), https://www .cdc.gov/flu/pandemic-resources/index.htm.

Central Intelligence Agency. "Mother's Mean Age at First Birth." In *The World Factbook*. Langley, VA: Central Intelligence Agency, 2021.

Charlton, Emma. "Students in Milan Are Moving in with the Elderly to Fight Loneliness and Save Money." WeForum [blog], November 2018, https://www.weforum.org/agenda/2018/11/why-some-students-in-milan-are-moving-in-with-elderly-people?utm_source=Facebook%20Videos&utm_medium=Facebook%20Videos&utm_campaign=Facebook%20Video%20Blogs.

Chigwedere, Pride, George R. Seage, III, Sofia Gruskin, et al. "Estimating the Lost Benefits of Antiretroviral Drug Use in South Africa." *Journal of Acquired Immune Deficiency Syndrome* 49, no. 4 (2008): 410–15.

Chola, Lumbwe, Shelley McGee, Aviva Tugendhaft, and Ekhart Buchmann. "Scaling Up Family Planning to Reduce Maternal and Child Mortality: The Potential Costs and Benefits of Modern Contraceptive Use in South Africa." *PLoS ONE* 10, no. 6 (2015): e0130077.

"Cholera." World Health Organization, February 5, 2021, https://www.who.int/news-room/fact-sheets/detail/cholera.

"Cholera Count Reaches 500 000 in Yemen." WHO News Release, August 14, 2017, http://www.who.int/mediacentre/news/releases/2017/cholera-yemen-mark/en/.

Cincotta, Richard. "The Age-Structural Theory of State Behavior." *Oxford Research Encyclopedia of Politics*, August 2017, https://doi.org/10.1093/acrefore/9780190228637.013.327.

———. "Emulating Botswana's Approach to Reproductive Health Services Could Speed Development in the Sahel." New Security Beat, January 27, 2020, https://www.newsecuritybeat.org/2020/01/emulating-botswanas-approach-reproductive-health-services-speed-development-sahel/.

———. "Forecasting in Age-Structural Time." In *A Research Agenda for Political Demography*, edited by Jennifer D. Sciubba. Cheltenham, UK: Edward Elgar, 2021.

———. "Half a Chance: Youth Bulges and Transitions to Liberal Democracy." *Environmental Change and Security Program*, no. 13 (2009): 10–18.

———. "Iran's Chinese Future." *Foreign Policy*, June 25, 2009, https://foreignpolicy.com/2009/06/25/irans-chinese-future/.

Cincotta, Richard, and Elizabeth Leahy Madsen. "Bangladesh and Pakistan: Demographic Twins Grow Apart." New Security Beat, October 10, 2018, https://www.newsecuritybeat.org/2018/10/bangladesh-pakistan-demographic-twins-grow/.

Cincotta, Richard, and Karim Sadjadpour. *Iran in Transition: The Implications of the Islamic Republic's Changing Demographics.* Washington, DC: Carnegie Endowment for International Peace, 2017.

Cincotta, Richard P., and John Doces. "The Age-Structural Maturity Thesis: The Impact of the Youth Bulge on the Advent and Stability of Liberal Democracy." In *Political Demography: How Population Changes Are Reshaping International Security and National Politics*, edited by Jack A. Goldstone, Eric P. Kaufman, and Monica Duffy Toft, 98–116. Boulder: Paradigm Publishers, 2012.

Clemens, Michael. *The Emigration Life Cycle: How Development Shapes Emigration from Poor Countries.* Washington, DC: Center for Global Development, 2020, https://www.cgdev.org/publication/emigration-life-cycle-how-development-shapes-emigration-poor-countries.

Clemens, Michael A., and Hannah M. Postel. "Deterring Emigration with Foreign Aid: An Overview of Evidence from Low-Income Countries." *Population & Development Review* 44, no. 4 (2018): 667–93.

Clements, Benedict, Kamil Dybczak, Vitor Gaspar, et al. "The Fiscal Consequences of Shrinking Populations." In *Staff Discussion Notes.* Washington, DC: International Monetary Fund, 2015.

Cohen, Guillaume, and Michal Shinwell. "How Far are OECD Countries from Achieving SDG Targets for Women and Girls? Applying a Gender Lens to Measuring Distance to SDG Targets." OECD Statistics Working Papers, No. 2020/02, OECD Publishing, Paris, 2020.

Coleman, David. "A Demographic Rationale for Brexit." *Population & Development Review* 42, no. 4 (2016): 681–92.

Coleman, David, and Robert Rowthorn. "Who's Afraid of Population Decline? A Critical Examination of Its Consequences." *Population & Development Review* 37, Supplement (2011): 217–48.

Combs, Jerald A. *The History of American Foreign Policy*, Vol. II, 3rd ed. Armonk, NY: M.E. Sharpe, 2008.

Commonwealth of Australia. *Bringing Them Home*. Sydney: Commonwealth of Australia, 1997, https://bth.humanrights.gov.au/sites/default/files/documents/bringing_them_home _report.pdf.

Côté, Isabelle, and Matthew Mitchell. "Elections and "Sons of the Soil" Conflict Dynamics in Africa and Asia." *Democratization* 23, no. 4 (2015): 657–77.

Coughlin, Joseph F. *The Longevity Economy: Unlocking the World's Fastest-Growing, Most Misunderstood Market*. New York: PublicAffairs, 2017.

"Covid-19: Managing Supply Chain Risk and Disruption." Deloitte Canada (n.d.), https:// www2.deloitte.com/global/en/pages/risk/articles/covid-19-managing-supply-chain-risk -and-disruption.html.

Cramer, C. "Unemployment and Participation in Violence." World Development Report 2011 Background Paper. Washington, DC: World Bank, 2010.

Dalmia, Shikha. "How Foreign Aid Screwed up Liberia's Ability to Fight Ebola." *The Week*, October 24, 2014, https://theweek.com/articles/442800/how-foreign-aid-screwed -liberias-ability-fight-ebola.

Dauvergne, Peter. *Environmentalism of the Rich*. Cambridge, MA: MIT Press, 2018.

David, Patty, and Brittne Nelson-Kakulla. "Grandparents Embrace Changing Attitudes and Technology." *AARP Research*, April 2019, https://www.aarp.org/research/topics/life/info -2019/aarp-grandparenting-study.html.

Davis, Douglas. "Biological Warfare." *The Spectator*, September 6, 2003, https://www.spectator .co.uk/article/biological-warfare.

Davis, Kingsley. "The Urbanization of the Human Population." *Scientific American* 213, no. 3 (1965): 40–53.

Davis, Mike. *Planet of Slums*. New York: Verso, 2006.

"Democratic Republic of the Congo." International Displacement Monitoring Centre, 2019, https://www.internal-displacement.org/countries/democratic-republic-of-the-congo.

Denyer, Simon, and Annie Gowen. "Too Many Men." *The Washington Post*, April 18, 2018, https:// www.washingtonpost.com/graphics/2018/world/too-many-men/?noredirect=on&utm_ campaign=42d302f32e-newsletter_12_07_17&utm_medium=email&utm_source=Jocelyn %20K.%20Glei%27s%20newsletter&utm_term=.23aa9d7dc5a4.

DesRoches, Reginald, Mary Comerio, Marc Eberhard, et al. "Overview of the 2010 Haiti Earthquake." *Earthquake Spectra* 27, no. S1 (2011): S1–S21, https://escweb.wr.usgs.gov/share /mooney/142.pdf.

Diarrhea: Common Illness, Global Killer. US Department of Health and Human Services, Centers for Disease Control and Prevention, https://www.cdc.gov/healthywater/pdf/global/programs /Globaldiarrhea508c.pdf.

"Diarrhoea." UNICEF, 2021, https://data.unicef.org/topic/child-health/diarrhoeal-disease/.

Dimock, Michael. "Defining Generations: Where Millennials End and Post-Millennials Begin." Pew Research FactTank, March 1, 2018, http://www.pewresearch.org/fact-tank/2018/03 /01/defining-generations-where-millennials-end-and-post-millennials-begin/.

"Distribution of Population by Religion." Office of the Registrar General & Census Commissioner, India, Ministry of Home Affairs, Government of India, http://censusindia.gov.in/Census_And_You/religion.aspx.

Doerr, Sebastian, Stefan Gissler, Jose-Luis Peydro, and Hans-Joachim Voth, "From Finance to Fascism," SSRN, November 3, 2020, https://ssrn.com/abstract=3146746.

Dublin, Louis I. *Health and Wealth.* New York: Harper, 1928.

Duncan, Pamela. "Europeans Greatly Overestimate Muslim Population, Poll Shows." *The Guardian*, December 13, 2016, https://www.theguardian.com/society/datablog/2016/dec/13/europeans-massively-overestimate-muslim-population-poll-shows.

Eckstein, Susan, and Thanh-Nghi Nguyen. "The Making and Transnationalization of an Ethnic Niche: Vietnamese Manicurists." *International Migration Review* 45, no. 3 (2011): 639–74.

Economy, Elizabeth. *The River Runs Black.* Ithaca, NY: Cornell University Press, 2005.

El-Erian, Mohamad A., and Michael Spence. "The Great Unequalizer: The Pandemic Is Compounding Disparities in Income, Wealth, and Opportunity." *Foreign Affairs*, 2020, https://www.foreignaffairs.com/articles/united-states/2020-06-01/great-unequalizer.

Elizarov, Valeriy, and Victoria Levin. "Family Policies in Russia: Could Efforts to Raise Fertility Rates Slow Population Aging?" In *Russian Federation Aging Project*. Washington, DC: World Bank Group, 2015.

Elliott, Larry. "IMF Estimates Global Covid Cost at $28tn in Lost Output." *The Guardian*, October 13, 2020, https://www.theguardian.com/business/2020/oct/13/imf-covid-cost-world-economic-outlook.

Esipova, Neli, Rajesh Srinivasan, and Julie Ray. "Adjusting to a World in Motion." In *Adjusting to a World in Motion: Trends in Global Migration and Migration Policy*, edited by Douglas J. Besharov and Mark H. Lopez, 21–57. New York: Oxford University Press, 2016.

European Stability Initiative. *The Refugee Crisis through Statistics: A Compilation for Politicians, Journalists and Other Concerned Citizens.* Berlin, Brussels, and Istanbul: European Stability Initiative, 2017, https://www.esiweb.org/pdf/ESI%20-%20The%20refugee%20crisis%20through%20statistics%20-%2030%20Jan%202017.pdf.

Eurostat. "Asylum Statistics." Luxembourg: Eurostat, updated April 27, 2021, https://ec.europa.eu/eurostat/statistics-explained/index.php?title=Asylum_statistics#Age_and_gender_of_first-time_applicants.

———. "EU Population in 2020: Almost 448 Million." Eurostat News Release, July, 10, 2020, https://ec.europa.eu/eurostat/documents/2995521/11081093/3-10072020-AP-EN.pdf/d2f799bf-4412-05cc-a357-7b49b93615f1.

Ewing-Nelson, Claire. "All of the Jobs Lost in December Were Women's Jobs." National Women's Law Center, January 2021, https://nwlc.org/wp-content/uploads/2021/01/December-Jobs-Day.pdf.

Faour, Muhammad A. "Religion, Demography, and Politics in Lebanon." *Middle Eastern Studies* 43, no. 6 (2007): 909–21.

Farole, Thomas, Soraya Goga, and Marcel Ionescu-Heroiu. *Rethinking Lagging Regions: Using Cohesion Policy to Deliver on the Potential of Europe's Regions.* Washington, DC: World Bank, 2018.

Faulconbridge, Guy. "Russia Says Population up for First Year since 1995." *Reuters India*, January 19, 2010, http://in.reuters.com/article/idINTRE60I2KM20100119.

Federspiel, Frederik, and Mohammad Ali. "The Cholera Outbreak in Yemen: Lessons Learned and Way Forward." *BMC Public Health* 18, no. 1 (2018), 1338.

Fensom, Anthony. "Korea's Future Is Dying (Thanks to Demographics)." *National Interest*,

August 31, 2019, https://nationalinterest.org/blog/korea-watch/koreas-future-dying-thanks-demographics-77206.

Ferris-Rotman, Amie. "Putin's Next Target Is Russia's Abortion Culture." *Foreign Policy*, October 3, 2017, https://foreignpolicy.com/2017/10/03/putins-next-target-is-russias-abortion-culture/.

Filippi, V., D. Chou, C. Ronsmans, et al. "Levels and Causes of Maternal Mortality and Morbidity." In *Reproductive, Maternal, Newborn, and Child Health: Disease Control Priorities*, edited by R.E. Black, R. Laxminarayan, M. Temmerman, et al., Vol. 2, 3rd ed., chap. 3. Washington, DC: The International Bank for Reconstruction and Development / The World Bank, 2016, https://www.ncbi.nlm.nih.gov/books/NBK361917/doi: 10.1596/978-1-4648-0348-2_ch3.

FitzGerald, David Scott. *Refuge Beyond Reach: How Rich Democracies Repel Asylum Seekers*. New York: Oxford University Press, 2019.

Florida, Richard. *The New Urban Crisis: How Our Cities Are Increasing Inequality, Deepening Segregation, and Failing the Middle Class—and What We Can Do About It*. New York: Basic Books, 2017.

Focus on Geography Series, 2016 Census. Ottawa, Ontario: Statistics Canada, 2017, https://www12.statcan.gc.ca/census-recensement/2016/as-sa/fogs-spg/Facts-can-eng.cfm?Lang=Eng&GK=CAN&GC=01&TOPIC=7.

Freeman, Colin, and Matthew Holehouse. "Europe's Migrant Crisis Likely to Last for 20 Years, Says International Development Secretary." *Telegraph*, November 5, 2015, http://www.telegraph.co.uk/news/worldnews/europe/11977254/Warning-from-Justine-Greening-comes-as-new-EU-figures-say-three-million-migrants-could-arrive-in-next-two-years.html.

Frey, William H. *2018 Voter Turnout Rose Dramatically for Groups Favoring Democrats, Census Confirms*. Brookings Institution, 2019, https://www.brookings.edu/research/2018-voter-turnout-rose-dramatically-for-groups-favoring-democrats-census-confirms/.

Funaiole, M.P., B. Chan, and B. Hart. "Understanding China's 2021 Defense Budget." Critical Questions. CSIS, March 5, 2021, https://www.csis.org/analysis/understanding-chinas-2021-defense-budget.

Fund for Peace. "Fragile States Index: 2020." Washington, DC: The Fund for Peace, 2021, https://fragilestatesindex.org/data/.

Gates, Robert M. "A Balanced Strategy: Reprogramming the Pentagon for a New Age." *Foreign Affairs* 88, no. 1 (2009).

German, Erik, and Solana Pyne. "Dhaka: Fastest Growing Megacity in the World." *The World*, September 8, 2010, https://www.pri.org/stories/2010-09-08/dhaka-fastest-growing-megacity-world.

"German Army Floats Plan to Recruit Foreignters." *Reuters*, December 27, 2018, https://www.reuters.com/article/us-germany-military-foreigners/german-army-floats-plan-to-recruit-foreigners-idUSKCN1OQ14L.

"German Army Recruits More Minors Than Ever Before: Report." *TheLocal.de*, January 9, 2018, https://www.thelocal.de/20180109/german-army-recruits-more-minors-than-ever-before-report/.

"German MPs Are Younger Than French MPs." *L'Observatoire des Senioi*, April 12, 2017, https://observatoire-des-seniors.com/en/les-deputes-allemands-ont-en-moyenne-497-ans-et-les-francais-628-ans/.

"Global Health Bright Spots 2019." World Health Organization, 2019, https://www.who.int/news-room/feature-stories/detail/global-health-bright-spots-2019.

"Global Health Observatory Data." World Health Organization, 2021, https://www.who.int/data/gho.

Global Preparedness Monitoring Board. *A World at Risk: Annual Report on Global Preparedness for Health Emergencies.* Geneva: World Health Organization, 2019, https://apps.who.int/gpmb/assets/annual_report/GPMB_annualreport_2019.pdf.

Global Trends 2040: A More Contested World. Washington, DC: National Intelligence Council, 2021.

Goldstone, Jack A., and Larry Diamond. "Demography and the Future of Democracy." *Perspectives on Politics* 18, no. 3 (2020): 867–80.

Gollin, Douglas, Rémi Jedwab, and Dietrich Vollrath. "Urbanization with and without Industrialization." *Journal of Economic Growth* 21, no. 1 (2016): 35–70.

Gottesman, Evan. "Crossing the Threshold: Israel's Electoral Threshold Explained." *Israel Policy Forum,* February 19, 2019, https://israelpolicyforum.org/2019/02/19/crossing-the-threshold-israels-electoral-threshold-explained/.

Gray, Clark, "Climate Change and Migration." Presentation to the Climate Change and Population Dynamics webinar, 21 September 2021, https://iussp.org/sites/default/files/IUSSP-PERN_Webinar_Gray-Climate%20Change%20%26%20Population%20Dynamics_2021.pdf.

Grindle, Merilee. "Good Enough Governance Revisited." *Development Policy Review* 25, no. 5 (2007): 533–74.

Hackett, Conrad. "5 Facts About the Muslim Population in Europe." Pew Research FactTank, November 29, 2017, https://www.pewresearch.org/fact-tank/2017/11/29/5-facts-about-the-muslim-population-in-europe/.

Haddad, Yvonne Yazbeck, and Michael J. Balz. "The October Riots in France: A Failed Immigration Policy or the Empire Strikes Back?" *International Migration* 44, no. 2 (2006): 23–34.

Hajari, Nisid. *Midnight's Furies: The Deadly Legacy of India's Partition.* Gloucestershire: Amberley Publishing, 2015.

Hamilton, Brady E., Joyce A. Martin, and Michelle J.K. Osterman. *Births: Provisional Data for 2020.* US Department of Health and Human Services, Centers for Disease Control and Prevention, May 2021, https://www.cdc.gov/nchs/data/vsrr/vsrr012-508.pdf.

Hampshire, James. *The Politics of Immigration.* Cambridge, UK: Polity Press, 2013.

Handy, Bruce. *Wild Things: The Joy of Reading Children's Literature as an Adult.* New York: Simon & Schuster, 2017.

Harlan, Chico. "Strict Immigration Rules May Threaten Japan's Future." *Washington Post,* July 28, 2010, http://www.washingtonpost.com/wp-dyn/content/article/2010/07/27/AR2010072706053.html.

Harper, Sarah. "The Important Role of Migration for an Ageing Nation." *Population Ageing* 9 (2016): 183–89.

Haven, Bernard James, Nazmus Sadat Khan, Zahid Hussain, et al. *Bangladesh Development Update: Tertiary Education and Job Skills.* Washington, DC: World Bank Group, 2019.

Haver, Katherine. *Haiti Earthquake Response: Mapping and Analysis of Gaps and Duplications in Evaluations.* ALNAP-Active Learning Network for Accountability and Performance in Humanitarian Action, February 2011, https://www.oecd.org/countries/haiti/47501750.pdf.

Health, United States, 2017: With Special Feature on Mortality. Hyattsville, MD: National Center for Health Statistics, 2018.

Healthy Life Expectancy (Hale) - Data by Country. Edited by World Health Organization, Geneva, 2020.

Heilig, Gerhard, Thomas Büttner, and Wolfgang Lutz. "Germany's Population: Turbulent Past, Uncertain Future." *Population Bulletin* 45, no. 4 (1991): 1–46.

Henneman, John B., Jr. "France: A Fiscal and Constitutional Crisis." In *The Black Death: A Turning Point in History?*, edited by William M. Bowsky, 86–88. New York: Holt, Rinehart and Winston, 1971.

Herlihy, David. *The Black Death and the Transformation of the West*. Cambridge, MA: Harvard University Press, 1997.

———. "Malthus Denied." In *The Black Death: A Turning Point in History?*, edited by William M. Bowsky, 60–64. New York: Holt, Rinehart and Winston, 1971.

Hintjens, Helen M. "Explaining the 1994 Genocide in Rwanda." *Journal of Modern African Studies* 37, no. 2 (1999): 241–86.

"Historical Background and Development of Social Security." US Social Security Administration, accessed 4 November, 2020, https://www.ssa.gov/history/briefhistory3.html.

Hochschild, Arlie. *The Second Shift: Working Families and the Revolution at Home*. New York: Penguin, 2012.

Honigsbaum, Mark. *The Pandemic Century: One Hundred Years of Panic, Hysteria, and Hubris*. New York: Norton, 2019.

Hooglund, Eric. "Rural Participation in the Revolution." *MERIP Reports*, no. 87 (1980): 3–6.

"How a Slap Sparked Tunisia's Revolution." *60 Minutes*, 22 February 2011, https://www.cbsnews.com/news/how-a-slap-sparked-tunisias-revolution-22-02-2011/.

Huber, Daniela. "Youth as a New 'Foreign Policy Challenge' in Middle East and North Africa: A Critical Interrogation of European Union and US Youth Policies in Morocco and Tunisia." *European Foreign Affairs Review* 22, no. 1 (2017): 111–28.

Hudson, Valerie, and Andrea M. den Boer. "Patrilineality, Son Preference, and Sex Selection in South Korea and Vietnam." *Population & Development Review* 43, no. 1 (2017): 119–47.

Hudson, Valerie M., Donna Lee Bowen, and Perpetua Lynne Nielsen. *The First Political Order: How Sex Shapes Governance and National Security Worldwide*. New York: Columbia University Press, 2020.

Hudson, Valerie M. "Sex, Demographics, and National Security." In *A Research Agenda for Political Demography*, edited by Jennifer D. Sciubba. Cheltenham, UK: Edward Elgar, 2021.

Hudson, Valerie M., Andrea M. Den Boer, and Jenny Russell. "China's Mismatched Bookends: A Tale of Birth Sex Ratios in South Korea and Vietnam." Presented at the International Studies Association Annual Meeting, New Orleans, Louisiana, 2015.

Inkpen, Christopher. "7 Facts About World Migration." Pew Research FactTank, September 2, 2014, http://www.pewresearch.org/fact-tank/2014/09/02/7-facts-about-world-migration/.

Institute for Health Metrics and Evaluation. "Japan," 2020, http://www.healthdata.org/japan.

International Organization for Migration. *World Migration Report 2020*, edited by Marie McAuliffe and Binod Khadria. Geneva: IOM, 2019, https://publications.iom.int/books/world-migration-report-2020.

Israel Central Bureau of Statistics. "Jews, by Country of Origin and Age," 2020, https://www.cbs.gov.il/he/publications/doclib/2020/2.shnatonpopulation/st02_08x.pdf.

———. "Sources of Population Growth," 2020, https://www.cbs.gov.il/he/publications/doclib/2020/2.shnatonpopulation/st02_12.pdf.

———. *Statistical Abstract of Israel 2020*. Jerusalem: Israel Central Bureau of Statistics, 2020.

Jansen, Tiffany R., "The Nursing Home That's Also a Dorm." *CityLab. Bloomberg*, October

2, 2015, https://www.citylab.com/equity/2015/10/the-nursing-home-thats-also-a-dorm /408424/.

Jedwab, Rémi. "Urbanization without Structural Transformation: Evidence from Consumption Cities in Africa." Working paper, 2020, http://home.gwu.edu/~jedwab/JEDWAB _AfricanUrban_Feb2013.pdf.

Jerving, Sara. "Why Liberians Thought Ebola Was a Government Scam to Attract Western Aid." *The Nation*, September 16, 2014, https://www.thenation.com/article/archive/why-liberians -thought-ebola-was-government-scam-to-attract-western-aid/.

Jiang, Quanbao, Qun Yu, Shucai Yang, and Jesús J. Sánchez-Barricarte. "Changes in Sex Ratio at Birth in China: A Decomposition by Birth Order." *Journal of Biosocial Science* 49, no. 6 (2017): 826–41.

Jivraj, Stephen. "How Has Ethnic Diversity Grown 1991-2001-2011?" In *The Dynamic of Diversity: Evidence from the 2011 Census*. Manchester, UK: Center on Dynamics of Ethnicity, University of Manchester, 2012.

Jobs for Youth in Africa: Catalyzing Youth Opportunity across Africa. African Development Bank Group, March 2016, https://www.afdb.org/fileadmin/uploads/afdb/Images/high_5s/Job_youth _Africa_Job_youth_Africa.pdf.

Johnson, Steven. *The Ghost Map: The Story of London's Most Terrifying Epidemic—and How It Changed Science, Cities, and the Modern World*. New York: Riverhead Books, 2006. Kindle iOS version.

Kaneda, Toshiko, and Carl Haub. "How Many People Have Ever Lived on Earth?" *PRB*, March 9, 2018, https://www.prb.org/howmanypeoplehaveeverlivedonearth/.

Kanem, Natalia. "Statement on UK Government Funding Cuts." UNFPA News Release, April 28, 2021, https://www.unfpa.org/press/statement-uk-government-funding-cuts.

Karpov, Vyacheslav, and Kimmo Kääriäinen. "'Abortion Culture' in Russia: Its Origins, Scope, and Challenges to Social Development." *Journal of Applied Sociology* 22, no. 2 (2005): 13–33.

Kassam, Ashifa. "Ratio of Indigenous Children in Canada Welfare System Is 'Humanitarian Crisis'." *The Guardian*, November 4, 2017, https://www.theguardian.com/world/2017/nov/04 /indigenous-children-canada-welfare-system-humanitarian-crisis.

Kaufmann, Eric. *Whiteshift: Populism, Immigration and the Future of White Majorities*. London: Allen Lane, 2018.

———. "Why Culture Is More Important Than Skills: Understanding British Public Opinion on Immigration." LSE British Politics and Policy Blog, London School of Economics and Political Science, January 30, 2018, https://blogs.lse.ac.uk/politicsandpolicy/ why-culture-is-more-important-than-skills-understanding-british-public-opinion-on -immigration/.

Kaufmann, Eric P., and Vegard Skirbekk. "'Go Forth and Multiply'": The Politics of Religious Demography." In *Political Demography: How Population Changes Are Reshaping International Security and National Politics*, edited by J.A. Goldstone, E.P. Kaufmann, and M. Duffy Toft, 194–212. New York: Oxford University Press.

Keyfitz, Nathan. "The Limits of Population Forecasting." *Population & Development Review* 7, no. 4 (1981): 579–93.

Kim, Jaewon. "No Country for Old Koreans: Moon Faces Senior Poverty Crisis." *Nikkei Asian Review*, January 29, 2019, https://asia.nikkei.com/Spotlight/Asia-Insight/No-country-for -old-Koreans-Moon-faces-senior-poverty-crisis.

Kim, TongFi, and Jennifer Dabbs Sciubba. "The Effect of Age Structure on the Abrogation of Military Alliances." *International Interactions* 41, no. 2 (2015): 279–308.

Kluge, Hans Henri P., Zsuzsanna Jakab, Jozef Bartovic, et al. "Refugee and Migrant Health in the Covid-19 Response." *Lancet* 395, no. 10232 (2020): 1237–39.

Kuhn, Anthony. "As Japan Tries Out Immigration, Migrant Workers Complain of Exploitation." NPR, January 15, 2019, https://www.npr.org/2019/01/15/683224099/as-japan-tries -out-immigration-migrant-workers-complain-of-exploitation.

Kurlansky, Mark. *1968: The Year That Rocked the World.* New York: Ballentine Books, 2004.

Lall, Somik Vinay, J. Vernon Henderson, and Anthony J. Venables. *Overview—Africa's Cities: Opening Doors to the World.* Washington, DC: World Bank, 2017.

Lathrop, Eva, Denise J. Jamieson, and Isabella Danel. "HIV and Maternal Mortality." *International Journal of Gynaecology and Obstetrics* 127, no. 2 (2014): 213–15.

Lee, Everett S. "A Theory of Migration." *Demography* 3, no. 1 (1966): 47–57.

Lee, Ronald, and Andrew Mason. "What Is the Demographic Dividend?" *Finance and Development* 43, no. 3 (2006), http://www.imf.org/external/pubs/ft/fandd/2006/09/basics.htm.

Lemon, Edward. "Dependent on Remittances, Tajikistan's Long-Term Prospects for Economic Growth and Poverty Reduction Remain Dim." Migration Policy Institute, November 14, 2019, https://www.migrationpolicy.org/article/dependent-remittances-tajikistan-prospects -dim-economic-growth.

Léonard, Marie des Neiges. "The Effects of Political Rhetoric on the Rise of Legitimized Racism in France: The Case of the 2005 French Riots." *Critical Sociology* 42, no. 7–8 (2015): 1087–1107.

Levine, Phillipa. *Eugenics: A Very Short Introduction.* Very Short Introductions. New York: Oxford University Press, 2017.

Liulevicius, Vejas Gabriel. *War Land on the Eastern Front: Culture, National Identity, and German Occupation in World War I.* Cambridge, UK: Cambridge University Press, 2000.

Livi-Bacci, Massimo. *A Concise History of World Population*, 4th ed. Malden, MA: Blackwell, 2007.

Lopez, Gustavo, and Kristen Bialik. "Key Findings About U.S. Immigrants." Pew Research FactTank, May 3, 2017, http://www.pewresearch.org/fact-tank/2017/05/03/key-findings -about-u-s-immigrants/.

Loudenback, Tanza. "Here's How Much It Would Cost You to Live in the 10 Largest Megacities around the World." *BusinessInsider*, October 20, 2017, https://www.businessinsider.com /worlds-largest-cities-megacity-cost-of-living-2017-10.

"Louis Pasteur." Science History Institute, 2020, https://www.sciencehistory.org/historical -profile/louis-pasteur.

"Magufuli Advises against Birth Control." *The Citizen*, September 10, 2018, https://www.thecitizen .co.tz/News/Magufuli-advises-against-birth-control/1840340-4751990-4h8fqpz/index.html.

Malach, Gilad, and Lee Cahaner. *2019 Statistical Report on Ultra-Orthodox Society in Israel: Highlights.* Jerusalem: Israel Democracy Institute, 2019.

"Malaria Vaccine Pilot Launched in Malawi." WHO News Release, April 23, 2019, https://www .who.int/news-room/detail/23-04-2019-malaria-vaccine-pilot-launched-in-malawi.

Mapa, Claire Dennis S. "Total Number of OFWs Estimated at 2.2 Million." Philippine Statistics Authority, 2020, https://psa.gov.ph/content/total-number-ofws-estimated-22-million.

Martin, Nina, and Renee Montagne. "Nothing Protects Black Women from Dying in Pregnancy and Childbirth." *ProPublica*, December 7, 2017, https://www.propublica.org/article /nothing-protects-black-women-from-dying-if-pregnancy-and-childbirth.

Maternal Mortality: Levels and Trends 2000 to 2017. WHO, UNICEF, UNFPA, World Bank Group, & UN Population Division, 2019, https://www.who.int/reproductivehealth/publications /maternal-mortality-2000-2017/en/.

May, John F. "The Politics of Family Planning Policies and Programs in Sub-Saharan Africa." *Population & Development Review* 47 (2017): 308–29.

McCurry, Justin. "The Changing Face of Japan: Labour Shortage Opens Doors to Immigrant Workers." *The Guardian*, November 8, 2018. https://www.theguardian.com/world/2018/nov/09/the-changing-face-of-japan-labour-shortage-opens-doors-to-immigrant-workers.

———. "Japanese Centenarian Population Edges Towards 70,000." *The Guardian*, September 14, 2018, https://www.theguardian.com/world/2018/sep/14/japanese-centenarian-population-edges-towards-70000.

McFarlane, Deborah R. "Population and Reproductive Health." In *Global Population and Reproductive Health*, edited by Deborah R. McFarlane, 1–26. Burlington, MA: Jones & Bartlett, 2015.

McFarlane, Deborah R., and Richard Grossman. "Contraceptive History and Practice." In *Global Population and Reproductive Health*, edited by Deborah R. McFarlane, 143–70. Burlington, MA: Jones & Bartlett, 2015.

McKay, Fiona H., Samantha L. Thomas, and Susan Kneebone. "'It Would Be Okay if They Came through the Proper Channels': Community Perceptions and Attitudes Towards Asylum Seekers in Australia." *Journal of Refugee Studies* 25, no. 1 (2012): 113–33.

McKeever, Amy. "We Still Don't Know the Origins of the Coronavirus. Here Are 4 Scenarios." *National Geographic*, April 2, 2021, https://www.nationalgeographic.com/science/article/we-still-dont-know-the-origins-of-the-coronavirus-here-are-four-scenarios.

Meagher, Kate. "The Scramble for Africans: Demography, Globalisation and Africa's Informal Labour Markets." *Journal of Development Studies* 52, no. 4 (2016): 483–97.

"Measles Cases and Outbreaks." Centers for Disease Control and Prevention, updated May 3, 2021, https://www.cdc.gov/measles/cases-outbreaks.html.

Medhora, Shalailah. "'Nope, Nope, Nope': Tony Abbott Says Australia Will Take No Rohingya Refugees." *The Guardian*, May 20, 2015, http://www.theguardian.com/world/2015/may/21/nope-nope-nope-tony-abbott-says-australia-will-take-no-rohingya-refugees.

"Median Age at First Marriage of Grooms and Brides by Educational Qualification, Annual." Government of Singapore, 2019, https://data.gov.sg/dataset/median-age-at-first-marriage-of-grooms-and-brides-by-educational-qualification-annual.

Meek, Ronald L., ed. *Marx and Engels on the Population Bomb: Selections from the Writings of Marx and Engels Dealing with the Theories of Thomas Robert Malthus.* London: Ramparts Press, 1953.

Merkle, Christoph, Philipp Schreiber, and Martin Weber. "Framing and Retirement Age: The Gap between Willingness-to-Accept and Willingness-to-Pay." *Economic Policy* 32 (2017): 757–809.

Michelena, Liliana. "Protests against President Disrupt Brazil's Major Cities." *Associated Press*, June 30, 2017, https://apnews.com/article/michel-temer-brazil-rio-de-janeiro-caribbean-strikes-b35d78ac7c4645a895adfc4eff7851f9.

Miller, Claire Cain. "Women's Gains in the Work Force Conceal a Problem." *New York Times*, January 21, 2021, https://www.nytimes.com/2020/01/21/upshot/womens-gains-in-the-work-force-conceal-a-problem.html.

Mills, Greg. "Strategic Dilemmas: Rewiring Africa for a Teeming, Urban Future." *PRISM* 6, no. 4 (2017): 46–63.

Mineo, Liz. "Forcing the UN to Do Right by Haitian Cholera Victims." *Harvard Gazette*, 2020, https://news.harvard.edu/gazette/story/2020/10/a-decade-of-seeking-justice-for-haitian-cholera-victims/.

Moller, Herbert. "Youth as a Force in the Modern World." *Comparative Studies in Society and History* 10, no. 3 (1968): 237–60.

Moorehead, Caroline. *Human Cargo: A Journey among Refugees.* New York: Picador, 2006.

Morin, Rebecca, and Matthew Brown. "Migrant Encounters up 71% in March as Biden Administration Grapples with Border." *USA Today*, April 8, 2021, https://www.usatoday .com/story/news/politics/2021/04/08/migrants-border-were-up-march-biden-grapples -immigration/7130399002/.

Morland, Paul. *Demographic Engineering: Population Strategies in Ethnic Conflict.* International Population Studies, edited by Philip Rees. London: Routledge, 2014.

Mubarak, Hosni. "President Hosni Mubarak on Egypt's Population." *Population & Development Review* 34, no. 3 (2008): 583–86.

Müller, Christopher, and Nina Kutzbach. "World Robotics 2020." Frankfurt am Main, Germany: Industrial Robots, IFR Statistical Department, VDMA Services GmbH, 2020.

Murphy, Caryle. "Saudi Arabia's Youth and the Kingdom's Future." Occasional Paper Series. Washington, DC: Middle East Program, Woodrow Wilson International Center for Scholars, 2011.

Murray, Christopher J.L. "The State of US Health, 1990-2016: Burden of Diseases, Injuries, and Risk Factors among US States." *Journal of the American Medical Association* 319, no. 14 (2018): 1444–72.

Neuman, Scott. "Why No One Wants the Rohingyas." NPR, May 15, 2015, http://www.npr.org /sections/thetwo-way/2015/05/15/407048785/why-no-one-wants-the-rohingyas.

Newman, David. "Population as Security: The Arab-Israeli Struggle for Demographic Hegemony." In *Redefining Security: Population Movements and National Security*, edited by Nana Poku and David T. Graham, 163–86. Westport, CT: Praeger, 1998.

"Nigeria Lowers Minimum Ages for Office in Victory for Youth Campaign." *Reuters*, June 1, 2018, https://www.reuters.com/article/ozatp-uk-nigeria-politics-youth-idAFKCN1IX410 -OZATP.

Nikolayenko, Olena. "The Revolt of the Post-Soviet Generation: Youth Movements in Serbia, Georgia, and Ukraine." *Comparative Politics* 39, no. 2 (2007): 169–88.

Noakes, Jeremy. "Hitler and 'Lebensraum' in the East." *BBC*, March 30, 2011, http://www.bbc .co.uk/history/worldwars/wwtwo/hitler_lebensraum_01.shtml.

Nunn, N. "The Long-Term Effects of Africa's Slave Trades." *Quarterly Journal of Economics* 123, no. 1 (2008): 139–76, https://doi.org/10.1162/qjec.2008.123.1.139

OECD. *Ageing and Employment Policies—Statistics on Average Effective Age of Retirement.* OECD, 2018, https://www.oecd.org/els/emp/average-effective-age-of-retirement.htm.

———. "Average Effective Age of Retirement Versus the Normal Age in 2018 in OECD Countries." Paris: OECD, 2019.

———. *Investing in Youth: Korea.* Paris: OECD, 2019. https://doi.org/10.1787/4bf4a6d2-en.

———. "OECD Databases on Migration." Paris: OECD (n.d.).

———. "OECD Family Database." Paris, OECD, 2020. https://www.oecd.org/els/family /database.htm.

———. *Pensions at a Glance 2017: OECD and G20 Indicators.* Paris, OECD Publishing, 2017, https://dx.doi.org/10.1787/pension_glance-2017-en.

———. *Pensions at a Glance 2019: OECD and G20 Indicators.* Paris: OECD Publishing, 2019, https://doi.org/10.1787/b6d3dcfc-en.

———. "Sf2.3: Age of Mothers at Childbirth and Age-Specific Fertility." Paris: OECD, 2017.

———. "Sf2.4: Share of Births Outside of Marriage." Paris: OECD, 2016.

Oeppen, Jim, and James W. Vaupel. "Broken Limits to Life Expectancy." *Science* 296, no. 5570 (2002): 1029–31.

Osterholm, Michael T., and Mark Olshaker. "Chronicle of a Pandemic Foretold: Learning from the Covid-19 Failure—Before the Next Outbreak Arrives." *Foreign Affairs*, May/June, 2020, https://www.foreignaffairs.com/articles/united-states/2020-05-21/coronavirus-chronicle -pandemic-foretold.

Pew Research Center. *Europe's Growing Muslim Population*. Washington, DC: Pew Research Center, 2017.

———. *The Whys and Hows of Generations Research*. Washington, DC: Pew Research Center, 2015, http://www.people-press.org/2015/09/03/the-whys-and-hows-of-generations-research/.

Pham, Kimberly. "The Vietnamese-American Nail Industry: 40 Years of Legacy." *Nails Magazine*, December 29, 2015, https://www.nailsmag.com/vsarticle/117757/the-vietnamese-american -nail-industry-40-years-of-legacy.

Philippine Statistics Authority. "2017 Survey on Overseas Filipinos (Results from the 2017 Survey on Overseas Filipinos)." Philippine Statistics Authority, updated May, 18, 2018, https:// psa.gov.ph/content/2017-survey-overseas-filipinos-results-2017-survey-overseas-filipinos.

Phillips, Janet. *Boat Arrivals and Boat 'Turnbacks' in Australia since 1976: A Quick Guide to the Statistics*. Sydney: Commonwealth of Australia, 2017, https://www.aph.gov.au/About_Parliament/ Parliamentary_Departments/Parliamentary_Library/pubs/rp/rp1617/Quick_Guides/ BoatTurnbacks.

Pickles, Dorothy. "France in 1968: Retrospect and Prospect." *World Today* 24, no. 9 (1968): 393–402.

"Population by Migration Status." Federal Statistical Office, Switzerland, https://www.bfs .admin.ch/bfs/en/home/statistics/population/migration-integration/by-migration-status .html.

"Population by Religious Community." Office of the Registrar General & Census Commissioner, India, Ministry of Home Affairs, Government of India, http://censusindia.gov .in/2011census/C-01.html.

"Population of Israel on the Eve of 2021." Israel Central Bureau of Statistics, News Release, December 31, 2020, https://www.cbs.gov.il/en/mediarelease/pages/2020/population-of -israel-on-the-eve-of-2021.aspx.

"Population Projections for Japan (2016-2065): Summary." National Institute of Population and Social Security Research, accessed May 3, 2021, http://www.ipss.go.jp/pp-zenkoku/e/ zenkoku_e2017/pp_zenkoku2017e_gaiyou.html.

Population Reference Bureau. "2019 World Population Data Sheet." Washington, DC: Population Reference Bureau, 2019.

———. "2020 World Population Data Sheet." Washington, DC: Population Reference Bureau, 2020, https://www.prb.org/wp-content/uploads/2020/07/letter-booklet-2020 -world-population.pdf.

———. "Family Planning Data." Washington, DC: Population Reference Bureau (n.d.), https:// www.prb.org/fpdata.

———. "U.S. Indicators." Washington, DC: Population Reference Bureau, 2021, https://www .prb.org/usdata/indicator/fertility/snapshot.

"Population Statistics." Statistics Sweden, Population and Economic Welfare Statistics Unit, 2021, https://www.scb.se/en/finding-statistics/statistics-by-subject-area/population/population -composition/population-statistics/.

Putin, Vladimir. "Vladimir Putin on Raising Russia's Birth Rate." *Population & Development Review* 32, no. 2 (2006): 385–88.

"Putin's Trust Rating Falls to New Low Amid Far East Protests." *Moscow Times*, July 29, 2020, https://www.themoscowtimes.com/2020/07/29/putins-trust-rating-falls-to-new-low -amid-far-east-protests-a71012.

Rao, Mohan. "Love Jihad and Demographic Fears." *Indian Journal of Gender Studies* 18, no. 3 (2011): 425–30.

"Remittances to Somalia." Oxfam (n.d.), https://policy-practice.oxfamamerica.org/work/ in-action/remittances-to-somalia/.

Riddle, John M., ed. *Contraception and Abortion from the Ancient World to the Renaissance*. Cambridge, MA: Harvard University Press, 1992.

Riley, Nancy E. *Population in China*. Cambridge, UK: Polity Press, 2017.

Risley, Amy. *The Youngest Citizens: Children's Rights in Latin America*. Latin American Tópicos, edited by Michael LaRosa. New York: Routledge, 2019.

"Robert Koch 1843-1910." Science Museum Group, 2020, http://broughttolife.sciencemuseum .org.uk/broughttolife/people/robertkoch.

Robertson, Graeme B. *The Politics of Protest in Hybrid Regimes: Managing Dissent in Post-Communist Russia*. Cambridge, UK: Cambridge University Press, 2011.

Robinson, James A. "Botswana as a Role Model for Country Success." In *Achieving Development Success: Strategies and Lessons from the Developing World*, edited by Augustin K. Fosu, 187–203. Oxford: Oxford University Press, 2013.

Rodrick, Dani. *Premature Deindustrialization*. Cambridge, MA: National Bureau of Economic Research, 2015, https://www.nber.org/system/files/working_papers/w20935/w20935.pdf.

Ross, Kaz. "An 'Army of Bachelors'? China's Male Population as a World Threat." *Journal of Asia Pacific Studies* 1, no. 2 (2010): 338–63.

Rydell, Anders. *The Book Thieves: The Nazi Looting of Europe's Libraries and the Race to Return a Literary Inheritance*. Translated by Henning Koch. New York: Viking, 2017.

Sadot, Uri. "Israel's 'Demographic Time Bomb' Is a Dud." *Foreign Policy*, December 18, 2013, http://foreignpolicy.com/2013/12/18/israels-demographic-time-bomb-is-a-dud/.

Sambira, Jocelyne. "Africa's Mobile Youth Drive Change." *Africa Renewal* (May 2013), https:// www.un.org/africarenewal/magazine/may-2013/africa's-mobile-youth-drive-change.

Schwab, Klaus. *The Fourth Industrial Revolution*. New York: Crown Business, 2016.

Sciubba, Jennifer Dabbs. "Coffins Versus Cradles: Russian Population, Foreign Policy, and Power Transition Theory." *International Area Studies Review* 7, no. 2 (2014): 205–21.

———. "Rhetoric and Action on Aging in Germany, Italy, and Japan: Party Platforms and Labor Policies in the World's Oldest Democracies." In *Ageing Population in Postindustrial Democracies*, edited by Pieter Vanhuysse and Achim Goerres, 54–78. Abingdon, UK: Routledge, 2011.

———. *The Future Faces of War: Population and National Security*. Santa Barbara: Praeger Security International/ABC-CLIO, 2011.

Sciubba, Jennifer Dabbs, and Chien-Kai Chen. "The Politics of Aging in Singapore and Taiwan." *Asian Survey* 57, no. 4 (2017): 642–64.

"Secretary-General Calls Vaccine Equity Biggest Moral Test for Global Community, as Security Council Considers Equitable Availability of Doses." United Nations News Release, February 14, 2021, https://www.un.org/press/en/2021/sc14438.doc.htm.

Sellström, Tor, and Lennart Wohlgemuth. *Historical Perspective: Some Explanatory Factors*. Joint

Evaluation of Emergency Assistance to Rwanda, 1996, https://www.oecd.org/derec/united states/50189653.pdf.

Semple, Kirk. "Mexico Once Saw Migration as a U.S. Problem. Now It Needs Answers of Its Own." *New York Times*, December 5, 2018, https://www.nytimes.com/2018/12/05/world /americas/mexico-migrants.html.

Shapiro, Judith. *Mao's War against Nature: Politics and the Environment in Revolutionary China*. Cambridge, UK: Cambridge University Press, 2001.

"Share of Youth Not in Employment, Education or Training (Neet) by Sex—ILO Modelled Estimates, Nov. 2019: Annual." Edited by International Labour Organization. ILOSTAT database, 2020.

Skodo, Admir. "Sweden: By Turns Welcoming and Restrictive in Its Immigration Policy." Migration Policy Institute, December 6, 2018, https://www.migrationpolicy.org/article /sweden-turns-welcoming-and-restrictive-its-immigration-policy.

Smith, Kate. "Asylum Denials Hit Record-High in 2018 as Trump Administration Tightens Immigration Policy." *CBS News*, December 4, 2018, https://www.cbsnews.com/news/ asylum-seekers-asylum-denials-hit-record-high-in-2018-as-trump-administration-tightens -immigration-policy-as-the-caravan-arrives/.

Sobotka, Tomáš. "Fertility in Central and Eastern Europe after 1989: Collapse and Gradual Recovery." *Historical Social Research* 36, no. 2 (2011): 246–96.

———. "Post-Transitional Fertility: The Role of Childbearing Postponement in Fueling the Shift to Low and Unstable Fertility Levels." *Journal of Biosocial Science* 49, no. S1 (2017): S20–S45.

"Speech: President Museveni's National Address." Uganda Media Centre Blog, updated September 9, 2018, https://ugandamediacentreblog.wordpress.com/2018/09/09/speech-president -musevenis-national-address/.

Squires, D., and C. Anderson. "U.S. Health Care from a Global Perspective: Spending, Use of Services, Prices, and Health in 13 Countries." *Issue Brief (Commonwealth Fund)* 15 (2015): 1–15.

Srinivasan, Sharada, and Shuzhuo Li. "Unifying Perspectives on Scarce Women and Surplus Men." In *Scarce Women and Surplus Men in China and India: Macro Demographics Versus Local Dynamics*, edited by Sharada Srinivasan and Shuzhuo Li, 1–23. New York: Springer, 2018.

Starodubov, Vladimir, Laurie B. Marczak, Elena Varavikova, et al. [GBD 2016 Russia Collaborators]. "The Burden of Disease in Russia from 1980 to 2016: A Systematic Analysis for the Global Burden of Disease Study 2016." *Lancet* 392, no. 10153 (2018): 1138–46.

Statistics Canada. "Immigrant Population in Canada, 2016 Census of Population." Statistics Canada, October 25, 2017, https://www150.statcan.gc.ca/n1/pub/11-627-m/11-527-m2017028 -eng.htm.

Statistics Korea. *Population Projections for Korea (2017~2067)*. Statistics Korea, March 28, 2019, http://kostat.go.kr/portal/eng/pressReleases/8/8/index.board?bmode=read&bSeq=&a Seq=375684&pageNo=1&rowNum=10&navCount=10&currPg=&searchInfo=&sTarget =title&sTxt=.

SteelFisher, Gillian K., Robert J. Blendon, Mark M. Bekheit, and Keri Lubell. "The Public's Response to the 2009 H1N1 Influenza Pandemic." *New England Journal of Medicine* 310, no. 3 (2010): e65.

Stone, Lyman. "African Fertility Is Right Where It Should Be." Institute for Family Studies, October 29, 2018, https://ifstudies.org/blog/african-fertility-is-right-where-it-should-be.

Strand, Håvard, Henrik Urdal, and Isabelle Côté. "Ethnic Census Taking, Instability, and Armed Conflict." In *People Changing Places: New Perspectives on Demography, Migration, Conflict, and the*

State, edited by Isabelle Côté, Matthew I. Mitchell, and Monica Duffy Toft, 66–85. London: Routledge, 2019.

Suzuki, Sotaro. "South Korean Population on Cusp of Steep Decline." *Nikkei Asian Review*, March 29, 2019, https://asia.nikkei.com/Economy/South-Korean-population-on-cusp-of-steep -decline.

Szreter, Simon. "Marx on Population: A Bicentenary Celebration." *Population & Development Review* 44, no. 4 (2018): 745–69.

Teitelbaum, Michael S., and Jay Winter. *A Question of Numbers: High Migration, Low Fertility, and the Politics of National Identity.* New York: Hill and Wang, 1998.

Tetlock, Philip, and Dan Gardner. *Superforecasting: The Art and Science of Prediction.* New York: Crown Publishers, 2016.

"The Number of International Migrants Reaches 272 Million, Continuing an Upward Trend in All World Regions, Says UN." United Nations News Release, September 17, 2019, https:// www.un.org/development/desa/en/news/population/international-migrant-stock-2019 .html.

"The Stolen Generations." Australians Together (n.d.), https://australianstogether.org.au /discover/australian-history/stolen-generations/.

Thompson, Gavin, Oliver Hawkins, Aliyah Dar, and Mark Taylor. "Olympic Britain: Social and Economic Change since the 1908 and 1948 London Games." London: House of Commons Library, 2012.

Tikkanen, Roosa, and Melinda K. Abrams. "U.S. Health Care from a Global Perspective, 2019: Higher Spending, Worse Outcomes?" Commonwealth Fund, https://www .commonwealthfund.org/publications/issue-briefs/2020/jan/us-health-care-global -perspective-2019.

Toft, Monica Duffy. *The Geography of Ethnic Violence.* Princeton, NJ: Princeton University Press, 2003.

———. "Wombfare: Religious and Political Dimensions of Fertility and Demographic Change." In *Political Demography: Interests, Conflict and Institutions*, edited by Jack A. Goldstone, Monica Duffy Toft, and Eric Kaufmann, 213–25. Basingstoke, UK: Palgrave Macmillan, 2011.

Traister, Rebecca. *All the Single Ladies: Unmarried Women and the Rise of an Independent Nation.* New York: Simon & Schuster, 2016.

Truth and Reconciliation Commission of Canada. "Honouring the Truth, Reconciling for the Future: Summary of the Final Report of the Truth and Reconciliation Commission of Canada," 2015, https://publications.gc.ca/site/eng/9.800288/publication.html.

Tsuya, Noriko O. *Low Fertility in Japan—No End in Sight.* Honolulu: East-West Center, June 2017.

Twigg, Judy. "Vaccine Dreams and Russian Reality." ThinkGlobalHealth.org, August 12, 2020, https://www.thinkglobalhealth.org/article/vaccine-dreams-and-russian-reality.

"Unemployment Rate by Sex and Age—ILO Modelled Estimates Nov. 2019 (%): Annual." Edited by International Labour Organization. ILOSTAT database, 2020.

UN General Assembly. "Draft Convention Relating to the Status of Refugees." New York: UN General Assembly, 1950.

UN-HABITAT. *State of the World's Cities 2010/2011: Bridging the Urban Divide.* London: Earthscan for UN-HABITAT, 2010.

UNHCR. "Africa: African Union." UNHCR (n.d.), https://www.unhcr.org/en-us/africa.html.

———. "Figures at a Glance." UNHCR (n.d.), https://www.unhcr.org/en-us/figures-at-a-glance .html.

———. "Internally Displaced People." UNHCR (n.d.), https://www.unhcr.org/en-us/internally -displaced-people.html.

———. "Syrian Regional Refugee Response: Inter-Agency Information Sharing Portal." UNHCR, updated April 30, 2021, https://data2.unhcr.org/en/situations/syria.

UNICEF. *Ending Child Marriage: A Profile of Progress in Ethiopia*. New York: UNICEF, 2018, https://www.unicef.org/ethiopia/sites/unicef.org.ethiopia/files/2018-10/Child%20 Marriage%20Ethiopia-%20online-%20version_0.pdf.

———. "UNICEF Data." New York: UNICEF, May 5, 2020, https://data.unicef.org/country/hti/.

United Nations. "The United Nations in Yemen." United Nations, 2021, https://yemen.un.org /en/about/about-the-un.

United Nations, Department of Economic and Social Affairs. *Government Response to Low Fertility in Japan*. New York: UN DESA, Population Division and East-West Center, 2015.

———. *International Migration Report 2017: Highlights*. New York: United Nations, 2017.

———. *The World's Cities in 2018*. New York: United Nations, 2018.

United Nations, Department of Economic and Social Affairs, Population Division. *International Migration Report 2013*. New York: United Nations, 2013, https://www.un.org/en /development/desa/population/publications/pdf/migration/migrationreport2013/Full _Document_final.pdf.

———. "Key Facts: World Urbanization Prospects: The 2018 Revision." New York: United Nations, 2018, https://population.un.org/wup/Publications/Files/WUP2018-KeyFacts.pdf.

———. "The Speed of Urbanization around the World." In *POPFACTS*. New York: United Nations, 2018.

———. *United Nations Demographic Yearbook 2018*. New York: United Nations, 2019.

———. *United Nations: World Population Prospects: The 2004 Revision*. New York: United Nations, 2005, http://pratclif.com/demography/unitednations-world-population%20rev%202004.htm.

———. *World Population Prospects: The 2019 Revision*. New York: United Nations, 2019.

———. *World Population Prospects 2019 Highlights*. New York: United Nations, 2019.

———. *World Urbanization Prospects: The 2018 Revision*. New York: United Nations, 2019.

United Nations, Office for the Coordination of Humanitarian Affairs. "Under-Secretary-General for Humanitarian Affairs/Emergency Relief Coordinator Stephen O'Brien: Statement to the Security Council on Missions to Yemen, South Sudan, Somalia and Kenya and an Update on the Oslo Conference on Nigeria and the Lake Chad Region." ReliefWeb, March 10, 2017, https://reliefweb.int/report/yemen/under-secretary-general-humanitarian-affairs emergency-relief-coordinator-stephen-o

United Nations Office on Drugs and Crime. *Global Report on Trafficking in Persons*. New York: United Nations, 2016.

———. *Global Report on Trafficking in Persons 2020*. Vienna: United Nations Office on Drugs and Crime, 2020.

———. "Human Trafficking and Migrant Smuggling." UN Office on Drugs and Crime (n.d.), https://www.unodc.org/unodc/human-trafficking/.

United Nations Population Fund. "United Kingdom of Great Britain and Northern Ireland" (n.d.), https://www.unfpa.org/data/donor-contributions/united-kingdom.

United Nations Relief and Works Agency for Palestine Refugees in the Near East. "Who We Are," 2021, https://www.unrwa.org/who-we-are 2021.

Urdal, Henrik. "The Demographics of Political Violence: Youth Bulges, Insecurity, and Conflict." In *Too Poor for Peace? Global Poverty, Conflict, and Security in the 21st Century*, edited by Lael Brainard and Derek Chollet, 90–100. Washington, DC: Brookings Institution Press, 2007.

US Census Bureau. "Historical Marital Status Tables." US Census Bureau, December 2020, https://www.census.gov/data/tables/time-series/demo/families/marital.html.

———. "International Data Base." US Census Bureau, 2021, https://www.census.gov/data -tools/demo/idb/.

US Customs and Border Protection. "Southwest Border Unaccompanied Alien Children Fy2014." US Customs and Border Protection, updated November 24, 2015, http://www.cbp .gov/newsroom/stats/southwest-border-unaccompanied-children/fy-2014.

"Venezuela Situation." UNHCR, https://www.unhcr.org/en-us/venezuela-emergency.html.

Villarosa, Linda. "Why America's Black Mothers and Babies Are in a Life-or-Death Crisis." *New York Times Magazine*, April 11, 2018, https://www.nytimes.com/2018/04/11/magazine /black-mothers-babies-death-maternal-mortality.html.

"Vital Statistics of the United States, 2003, Volume I, Natality." Centers for Disease Control and Prevention, 2005, https://www.cdc.gov/nchs/products/vsus/vsus_1980_2003.htm.

Vogl, Anthea. "Over the Borderline: A Critical Inquiry into the Geography of Territorial Excision and the Securitisation of the Australian Border." *UNSW Law Journal* 38, no. 1 (2015): 114.

Vonnegut, Kurt. "Tomorrow and Tomorrow and Tomorrow." In *Welcome to the Monkey House*, 315–31. New York: Dial Press, 2006.

Wang, Hansi Lo. "How the 2020 Census Citizenship Question Ended up in Court." NPR, November 4, 2018, https://www.npr.org/2018/11/04/661932989/how-the-2020-census -citizenship-question-ended-up-in-court.

Waugh, Colin M. *Paul Kagame and Rwanda: Power, Genocide and the Rwandan Patriotic Front*. Jefferson, NC: McFarland & Company, 2004.

Weiner, Myron, and Michael S. Teitelbaum. *Political Demography, Demographic Engineering*. New York: Berghahn Books, 2001.

"What's Behind Saudi Arabia's Pivot Away from Foreign Workers." *World Politics Review*, August 16, 2019, https://www.worldpoliticsreview.com/insights/28129/pushing-for-a-saudization -of-its-workforce-saudi-arabia-pivots-away-from-foreign-workers.

"What Effect Does Social Security Have on Poverty?" Fiscal Blog, Peter G. Peterson Foundation, September, 10, 2018, https://www.pgpf.org/blog/2018/09/what-effect-does-social -security-have-on-poverty.

"What Is the Economic Cost of Covid-19?" *The Economist*, January 7, 2021, https://www.economist .com/finance-and-economics/2021/01/09/what-is-the-economic-cost-of-covid-19.

White, Roger. *Immigration Policy and the Shaping of U.S. Culture: Becoming America*. Cheltenham, UK: Edward Elgar, 2018.

White, Tyrene. "China's Population Policy in Historical Context." In *Reproductive States: Global Perspectives on the Invention and Implementation of Population Policy*, edited by Rickie Solinger and Mie Nakachi, 329–68. New York: Oxford University Press, 2016.

Williams, Rebecca Jane. "Storming the Citadels of Poverty: Family Planning under the Emergency in India, 1975–1977." *Journal of Asian Studies* 73, no. 2 (2014): 471–92.

Winter, Jay, and Michael Teitelbaum. *The Global Spread of Fertility Decline: Population, Fear, and Uncertainty*. New Haven, CT: Yale University Press, 2013.

Woetzel, Jonathan. "Tackling the World's Affordable Housing Challenge." McKinsey & Company, 2014.

Woolf, Steven H., and Laudan Aron. "Failing Health of the United States." *British Medical Journal* 360 (2018): k496.

World Bank. "World Development Indicators." World Bank (n.d.), https://data.worldbank.org.

World Health Organization. *Alcohol Policy Impact Case Study. The Effects of Alcohol Control Measures on Mortality and Life Expectancy in the Russian Federation*. Copenhagen: WHO Regional Office for Europe, 2019.

———. *Bugs, Drugs & Smoke: Stories from Public Health.* Geneva: World Health Organization, 2011.

———. *Cholera Situation in Yemen.* Cairo, Egypt: World Health Organization, Regional Office for the Eastern Mediterranean, December 2020.

———. "Drones Take Rwanda's National Blood Service to New Heights." World Health Organization, https://www.who.int/news-room/feature-stories/detail/drones-take-rwandas-national-blood-service-to-new-heights.

———. "Family Planning/Contraception Methods." World Health Organization, https://www.who.int/news-room/fact-sheets/detail/family-planning-contraception.

———. *HIV/AIDS Key Facts.* Geneva: World Health Organization, November 30, 2020, https://www.who.int/news-room/fact-sheets/detail/hiv-aids.

———. *Polio Endgame Strategy 2019-2023: Eradication, Integration, Certification and Containment.* Geneva: World Health Organization, 2019, https://polioeradication.org/wp-content/uploads/2019/06/english-polio-endgame-strategy.pdf.

———. "Statue Commemorates Smallpox Eradication." WHO News Release, May 17, 2010, https://www.who.int/mediacentre/news/notes/2010/smallpox_20100517/en/.

———. "Trends in Maternal Mortality: 1990 to 2015: Estimates by WHO, UNICEF, UNFPA, World Bank Group and the United Nations Population Division." Geneva: World Health Organization, 2015.

———. "WHO Declares End of Ebola Outbreak in Nigeria." WHO News Release, October 29, 2014, https://www.who.int/mediacentre/news/statements/2014/nigeria-ends-ebola/en/.

———. "World Health Statistics Overview 2019: Monitoring Health for the SGDs, Sustainable Development Goals." Geneva: World Health Organization, 2019.

———. "World Health Statistics 2020: Monitoring Health for the SDGs." Geneva: World Health Organization, 2020.

World Health Organization Africa. "The Ebola Outbreak in Liberia." World Health Organization Africa, https://www.afro.who.int/news/ebola-outbreak-liberia-over.

"Year-on-Year Increase of 4.4% in the Population with a Migrant Background in 2017." Statistisches Bundesamt News Release, August 1, 2018, https://www.destatis.de/EN/PressServices/Press/pr/2018/08/PE18_282_12511.html.

Yglesias, Matthew. *One Billion Americans: The Case for Thinking Bigger.* New York: Portfolio/Penguin, 2020.

Yigit, Metin, Aslinur Ozkaya-Parlakay, and Emrah Senel. "Evaluation of Covid-19 Vaccine Refusal in Parents." *Pediatric Infectious Disease Journal* 40, no. 4 (2021): e134–136. doi: 10.1097/INF.0000000000003042.

Yoon, Young-sil. "S. Korea's Total Fertility Rate Falls Below 1." *BusinessKorea*, August 29, 2019, http://www.businesskorea.co.kr/news/articleView.html?idxno=35471.

"Youth, Women's Rights, and Political Change in Iran." Population Reference Bureau, 2009, http://www.prb.org/Articles/2009/iranyouth.aspx.

Zhong, Raymond. "For Poor Countries, Well-Worn Path to Development Turns Rocky." *Wall Street Journal*, November 24, 2015, http://www.wsj.com/articles/for-poor-countries-well-worn-path-to-development-turns-rocky-1448374298?tesla=y.

Ziegler, Philip. "Germany: The Flagellants and the Persecution of the Jews." In *The Black Death: A Turning Point in History?*, edited by William M. Bowsky, 65–79. New York: Holt, Rinehart and Winston, 1971.

IMAGE CREDITS

Figure 1:   United Nations, Department of Economic and Social Affairs, Population Division, *World Population Prospects: The 2019 Revision*. New York: United Nations (2019).

Figure 2:   United Nations, Department of Economic and Social Affairs, Population Division, *World Population Prospects: The 2019 Revision*. New York: United Nations (2019).

Figure 3:   United Nations, Department of Economic and Social Affairs, Population Division, *World Population Prospects: The 2019 Revision*. New York: United Nations (2019).

Figure 4:   United Nations, Department of Economic and Social Affairs, Population Division, *World Population Prospects: The 2019 Revision*. New York: United Nations (2019).

Figure 5:   US Census Bureau, "International Data Base." US Census Bureau (2021). https://www.census.gov/data-tools/demo/idb/#/country?YR_ANIM=2021&dashPages=DASH.

Figure 6:   United Nations, Department of Economic and Social Affairs, Population Division, *World Population Prospects: The 2019 Revision*. New York: United Nations (2019).

Figure 7:   US Census Bureau, "International Data Base." US Census Bureau (2021). https://www.census.gov/data-tools/demo/idb/#/country?YR_ANIM=2021&dashPages=DASH.

Figure 8:   US Census Bureau, "International Data Base." US Census Bureau (2021). https://www.census.gov/data-tools/demo/idb/#/country?YR_ANIM=2021&dashPages=DASH.

Figure 9:   United Nations, Department of Economic and Social Affairs, Population Division, *World Population Prospects: The 2019 Revision*. New York: United Nations (2019).

Figure 10: The Fund for Peace, "Fragile States Index: 2020." Washington, DC: The Fund for Peace (2021). https://fragilestatesindex.org/data/.

Figure 11: US Census Bureau, "International Data Base." US Census Bureau (2021). https://www.census.gov/data-tools/demo/idb/#/country?YR_ANIM=2021&dashPages=DASH.

Figure 12: Gerhard Heilig, Thomas Biittner, and Wolfgang Lutz, "Germany's Population: Turbulent Past, Uncertain Future." *Population Bulletin* 45, no. 4 (1990). Washington, DC: Population Reference Bureau, Inc.

Figure 13: US Census Bureau, "International Data Base." US Census Bureau (2021). https://www.census.gov/data-tools/demo/idb/#/country?YR_ANIM=2021&dashPages=DASH.

Figure 14: OECD, "Average Effective Age of Retirement Versus the Normal Age in 2018 in OECD Countries." Paris: OECD (2019).

Figure 15: Israel Central Bureau of Statistics, *Statistical Abstract of Israel 2020*. Israel Central Bureau of Statistics (2020).

Figure 16: US Census Bureau, "International Data Base." US Census Bureau (2021). https://www.census.gov/data-tools/demo/idb/#/country?YR_ANIM=2021&dashPages=DASH.

Figure 17: United Nations, Department of Economic and Social Affairs, Population Division, *World Population Prospects: The 2019 Revision*. New York: United Nations (2019); and United Nations, Department of Economic and Social Affairs, Population Division, *World Urbanization Prospects: The 2018 Revision*. New York: United Nations (2018).

Figure 18: United Nations, Department of Economic and Social Affairs, Population Division, *World Population Prospects: The 2019 Revision*. New York: United Nations (2019).

Figure 19: United Nations, Department of Economic and Social Affairs, Population Division, *World Population Prospects: The 2019 Revision*. New York: United Nations (2019).

Figure 20: United Nations, Department of Economic and Social Affairs, Population Division, *World Population Prospects: The 2019 Revision*. New York: United Nations (2019).

Figure 21: United Nations, Department of Economic and Social Affairs, Population Division, *World Population Prospects: The 2019 Revision*. New York: United Nations (2019); and Brady E. Hamilton, Joyce A. Martin, and Michelle J.K. Osterman, *Births: Provisional Data for 2020*. US Department of Health and Human Services, Centers for Disease Control and Prevention (May 2021).

INDEX

A page number followed by *f* refers to a figure, and a page number followed by *n* indicates a footnote.

industrialization and, 182, 183, 187, 203
before jobs or infrastructure, 182
market-based solutions and, 183
quality of life and, 180
in "superstar" cities vs. slums, 204
variable pace of, 180–82, 181*f*
Urdal, Henrik, 48

vaccines, 92–94
against COVID-19, 92–93, 95, 112
against influenza, 113–14
public trust and, 113–14
role of Soviet Union, 111, 112
against smallpox, 110, 111
variolation, 92
Vaupel, James, 11–12
vector-borne diseases, 117
Venezuela, 20, 128
Vietnam
devaluation of women in, 45
manicurists from, 119–20, 123
Vietnamese American community, 123
Vietnam War, 52, 55
violence
exploitative employment of youth and, 191
fueled by inequality, 209
fueled by young populations, 3, 4–5
against women, 44–45
Voltaire, 139
Vonnegut, Kurt, 59, 61, 71
voting age in United States, 52–53, 54
voting rights of expatriates, 159

wealthy countries. *See* developed countries
Weiner, Myron, 149, 156
White Australia policy, 153–54
Williams, Serena, 101
window of opportunity, 171–73, 175–76, 190, 192, 206
Wizard of Oz series, 135–36
wombfare, 157–58, 160

women
age at first birth, 62–65
caring for aging parents, 88
devaluation of, 44–45, 101–2
economic shocks of epidemics and, 109
with final years in poor health, 104
in Japanese workforce, 135
labor force participation, 190, 205
politics of health and, 101–2
pressures of work and family, 66–68, 87
reproductive ages, 34
strategies for lowering fertility and, 34–36
violence against, 44–45
women's education
delaying first births and, 63, 64–65
encouraged in Iran, 40
preference for fewer children and, 36
World War I, 50, 52, 155
World War II, 156, 159

Yemen, 5, 20, 94, 96, 209
youth bulge age structure
African unemployment and, 191
chance of democracy and, 56–57
failing economic policies and, 58
of Germany in 1920s, 50, 51*f*
political protest and, 53
of Tunisia in 2011, 49, 49*f*
unrealistic positive reframing of, 58
youth cohorts. *See also* unemployment of youth
educating and training, 206
lacking opportunity in high-fertility countries, 37
opportunities for men in, 57–58
societal consequences if large, 46
transition to adulthood, 54, 58
youthful age structures
aging out of, 56
Arab Spring and, 48–49
chances of democracy and, 56